TEACHING
SOCIAL STUDIES

TEACHING
SOCIAL STUDIES

Handbook of Trends, Issues, and Implications for the Future

Edited by Virginia S. Wilson, James A. Litle, and Gerald Lee Wilson

Greenwood Press
Westport, Connecticut • London

Library of Congress Cataloging-in-Publication Data

Teaching social studies : handbook of trends, issues,
  and implications for the future / edited by Virginia S. Wilson,
  James A. Litle, and Gerald Lee Wilson.
      p. cm.
  Includes bibliographical references and index.
  ISBN 0–313–27881–4 (alk. paper)
  1. History—Study and teaching—United States.   2. Social
sciences—Study and teaching—United States.   I. Wilson, Virginia
S.   II. Litle, James A.   III. Wilson, Gerald L. (Gerald Lee)
D16.3.T35   1993
907'.1273—dc20   92–17837

British Library Cataloguing in Publication Data is available.

Library of Congress Catalog Card Number: 92–17837
ISBN: 0–313–27881–4

First published in 1993

Greenwood Press, 88 Post Road West, Westport, CT 06881
An imprint of Greenwood Publishing Group, Inc.

Printed in the United States of America

∞

The paper used in this book complies with the
Permanent Paper Standard issued by the National
Information Standards Organization (Z39.48–1984).

10 9 8 7 6 5 4 3 2

Copyright Acknowledgments

The publisher and editors thank the National Commission for the
Social Studies for permission to extract from: Stanley P. Wronski and
Donald H. Bragaw, *Social Studies and the Social Sciences: A Fifty-
Year Perspective*; National Commission on Social Studies in the
Schools, *Charting a Course: Social Studies for the 21st Century*; and
National Council for the Social Studies, ''Report of the Task Force on
Scope and Sequence,'' *Social Education*. Copyright © National
Council for the Social Studies, used with permission.

To our teacher-colleague-friend, William H. Cartwright

CONTENTS

PREFACE

The chapters of this volume are intended to serve as a set of reference sources for at least three categories of readers. First, social studies educators at all levels who want and need to understand the total scope of the field, as well as specific insights into individual subjects within the field, will find in this volume both a panoramic view and a microscopic examination of the social studies. It is a fact—sometimes a blessing, sometimes a bane—that social studies teachers both at the secondary level and at smaller colleges may be pushed or pulled into teaching courses in a field for which they have had no specific preparation. Ironically, those outside the field, especially budget-minded administrators, often see the discipline as far more of a unity than insiders do. Perhaps distance gives a perspective that practitioners in the field have missed. These chapters can serve as a starting point for preparing, "retooling," as it were, such teachers.

Second, this volume can serve as a ready reference for social studies teachers who are competent in their specific subjects but who may wish, in view of changing times and changing demands, to approach those subjects in a more interdisciplinary manner, with infusions of material and insights from other subjects in the discipline.

Third, teachers of teachers may find this reference work to be of particular value in methods courses since it provides an overview of the discipline as a whole, discussing both its substance and its pedagogical questions and controversies as well as defining enduring issues for the social studies.

This volume is organized not only to be "user friendly" for reference purposes, but also to encourage the reader to examine it as a whole. The introduction places the discipline in context and connects it with the society and the world that it explains, a society and a world which in turn largely determine its substance and methodology. Stanley Wronski's lead chapter, "Persistent Issues in the Social Studies," defines the nature and purpose of the social studies and discusses the place of values in the discipline. In an attempt at definition, he addresses the anomaly of the social studies being "defined holistically and taught separately" and the influence this anomaly has had on the discipline's development. Both the questions of purpose and of the place of values in the social studies have at their core the prior question of responsibility. That is, is the primary purpose of the field solely a search for truth or does it have a mission to educate for and to influence societal decisions, ivory tower or cutting-edge philosophy?

Following Wronski's discussions of "Persistent Issues," two chapters, Beverly Armento's "Reform Revisited: The Story of Elementary Social Studies at the Crest of the 21st Century" and Donald Bragaw's "A Century of Secondary Social Studies: Looking Backward and Forward," survey the course of social studies education during the twentieth century. The key descriptive words for both the elementary and the secondary levels seem to be "relevance," "revisitation," "reform," and "resistance." Both chapters explore the overall direction of social studies programs and the total social studies curriculum.

A subsequent series of chapters are all by specialists—practitioners who examine individual subjects within the discipline. The discipline-specific chapters, as well as the survey chapters by Beverly Armento and Don Bragaw, are organized according to a common systematic structure. Each chapter begins with "Reflections," an overview of the subject's historical development. Some subjects, such as history, have an ancient lineage, while others, such as psychology, are relative newcomers, reflecting new areas of research and knowledge. Still others, such as international studies, are often viewed as "spin-offs" from core courses and are now seeking their rightful places in the curriculum. Following "Reflections," each chapter moves on to "Current Issues and Trends," a section covering the present state of the particular subject and the influence of reform movements on its scope and sequence. Each chapter's concluding section, "Projections," points to future directions anticipated for the subject as a result of technological and societal changes that may influence, perhaps even intrude on and protrude from, the subject.

The last two chapters, Baird Shuman's "Writing in the Social Studies" and Barbara Parramore's "The Social Studies Curriculum and Teacher

Preparation,'' like the first three chapters, examine matters common to all subjects in the discipline. As Shuman points out, the current Writing-Across-the-Curriculum (WAC) movement presents a new challenge and a new opportunity for the social studies. Parramore's concluding chapter on "Teacher Preparation" discusses the all-important issue of how best to prepare those who are the vital element in education's delivery system. She recognizes the need for genuine reform in teacher education, but also notes that those responsible for teacher education will be expected, as in the past, to meet the often conflicting expectations of competing groups.

Although initially and primarily conceived as a reference source, this volume may well have an additional value. As the authors researched and prepared their material, they became engaged in the process of synthesis and analysis, a process which led them into the realms of speculation and subjectivity. As a result, this volume has acquired the characteristics of both a useful tool and a practical cogitator, not only providing information but evoking further thought and, perhaps, provoking further controversy.

The authors of the chapters in this volume come from different backgrounds and pursue different approaches with a variety of styles, yet they all have one thing in common: they were all students-colleagues-friends of William H. Cartwright. The use of the compound noun is quite deliberate, for to know Will Cartwright was to be a student of his, either informally or formally. To be his student in either sense was to be considered by Will a colleague and a friend. Will Cartwright was a rare breed, in his dealings both with individuals and with groups of professionals. In the latter case he was a prophet, honored in his own time and in his own house. As any participant in the meetings of the Undergraduate Faculty Council at Duke University no doubt remembers, whenever Will posed a question or made a comment, he was awarded the ultimate gesture of respect in that body—absolute silence while he spoke. For his faculty colleagues knew that what he said would not only be of great value, but would also determine the course of the discussion and, more often than not, the fate of the matter under consideration.

This scholar and leader in the field of education, through his numerous books and articles, his service as president of the National Council for the Social Studies (1957), and his tenure as chairman of the Department of Education at Duke, has been both a muse for us all and, to make a positive out of a negative metaphor, something of a "shadow on the ballroom floor." For in our professional lives we are always keenly aware of his presence as an inspiration and, very probably, as a standard against which we continue to measure our accomplishments.

TEACHING
SOCIAL STUDIES

INTRODUCTION

In a democracy such as ours, every person is an "expert" on politics, religion, and, increasingly, education. In the latter instance, the "experts" know both what should be taught (content) and how it should be taught (method). This is especially true of the social studies for reasons which are evident. First, social studies deal with matters which, although presented in grand scope, are basically personal (for example, each individual is a part of history, has a psychological makeup, and is an economic being). Second, because the social studies are personal, they become controversial at the societal level (that is, individual and group preferences and prejudices often prevail when issues raised by the social studies come to the fore). Third, it appears that anyone can approach the social studies de novo, with no previous training in the field, and make himself or herself an "expert." (One is reminded of a commercial for a phonics reading course in which some facts of American history are used to teach people to read—the commercial's tag line is "learn to read and at the same time become an expert in American history.")

This "everyone-is-expert" factor has influenced the past and the present, as it will undoubtedly influence the future, of the disciplines constituting the social studies. This shows up in the content of each discipline, for the social studies are, more than any other area of study, responsive to public attitudes and opinions. It is also worth noting that when various professional organizations within the social studies periodically appoint study commissions which issue reports, interestingly enough, quotations and summaries from these reports lend themselves to a "guess when it was written" game because the reports of the 1890s, 1930s, and 1990s all inevitably say similar things, including the obligatory clarion call for (vaguely defined) reform.

In addition, political, social, economic, scientific, and technological changes have led to the demand for corresponding educational changes. Looking toward the future of the social studies is to envision a discipline which is always expected both to reflect the current times and to project into the future. It is a matter of perpetually searching for a usable past that can lead to an understandable present and a meaningful future. The chapters in this volume sketch the process of these changes in each discipline, for all of the fields within the social studies truly lend themselves to a "shifting sands" metaphor.

If the social studies of the future are, to coin a phrase, to be useful rather than just ornamental, what factors need to be taken into account? First, there is the knowledge explosion, with all of its ramifications, including the fact that this explosion has led to a corresponding implosion in each separate field of the social studies. This implosion, in turn, has led to an increased emphasis on specialization at a time when both specialization and greater comprehension of the whole are necessary. Such a concurrent explosion and implosion of knowledge will place greater demands both on the field as a whole and on each individual subject. In short, the cry is at once for a total interdisciplinary approach and for each discipline of the social studies to incorporate more aspects of other fields. Individual teachers are being asked both to specialize in one field and to be more knowledgeable in a number of fields.

The second factor, and an obvious one, is that of the presence of technology. Increasingly, technology will determine the way in which we teach, and, if "the medium is the message," then technology will also have an impact on content. According to educational lore, the lecture style of teaching arose in the Middle Ages when there were no books for students. However, once books became available, although the lecture style did not die out, there was not only another way of learning, but also an expanded content. Given the technological advances of the twenty-first century, books as we know them now may well become obsolete relics enshrined in museums. What will be the impact of this development on the methodology and content of education in general and the social studies in particular?

For technology not only organizes information and makes it rapidly available in a more usable form allowing for practice and drill and simulation, it can also afford the individual an opportunity to observe events as they unfold to gain "first-hand" knowledge and a sense of "participation." Beginning with Vietnam, "the living room war," we have come increasingly to live in what David Halberstam in *The Next Century* (21) calls a "wired world." Both teachers and students will have access to this information, but how will they fit it meaningfully into classroom instruction? For that matter, where in a "wired world" will social studies teachers fit into the classroom? Some years ago a national publication ran a cartoon showing a classroom in which a voice from a tape player addressed a roomful of, you guessed it, tape recorders. Yet, experience seems to indicate that the more technical and impersonal teaching becomes, the more students want contact and interaction with a living, breathing human being. The question is, what will be the nature of this interaction? Given the availability of interactive computer programs, neither Henry Adams's ideal education, with Mark Hopkins on one end of a log and himself on the other, nor Socrates' systematic questioning now seems to be appropriate. What will a teacher do in the twenty-first century?

Third, the social studies of the twenty-first century will be increasingly called on to "teach" decision-making skills. The growing complexity of both the decisions to be made and the process of making them will cause people to turn to the social studies for information and for process. Decisions in the modern world have to be made in a context of multiple causation and complex consequences. Logic, perhaps once a solid tool for intelligent decision making, now must be supplemented by the content of the social studies if decision making is to be effective, as the author of each chapter here acknowledges.

Fourth, in the twenty-first century, the social studies may take on a more significant role in values clarification. It is not too much to say that in the past the establishment of value systems and the clarification of values have been the province of religion and philosophy. Although these two may well remain the primary fields for these purposes, it is clear that input from the social studies is both appropriate and necessary. Values will be viewed by many not as something to be "handed down" or, for that matter, "reasoned out," but rather as something to be hammered out on the anvil of the total experience of humankind. This, of course, is the province of the social studies.

Finally, the authors of the various chapters in this volume acknowledge that the goals of social studies must be re-examined in light of the current questioning of the basic assumptions that have historically defined these goals. Implicit in the teaching of the subjects within the discipline has been the idea of conveying a common heritage and body of knowledge for the purpose of preparing students to exercise the rights and responsibilities of citizenship, to live meaningful lives, and to take advantage of the opportunities this nation offers. However, several new factors have emerged that call for a re-evaluation of these traditional goals.

First, the acceptance of cultural pluralism as a desirable reality, with the corresponding potential abandonment of assimilation as a societal goal, has, needless to say, profound implications for both the content and the teaching of the social studies. As "heritage" becomes plural, the traditional bonding agents of various groups in our society no longer serve that purpose. The American Dream has provided a common focus; if the dream ceases to be shared by all, the unifying element is lost.

Second, the social studies have always insisted that ideas are more important than individual or cultural heritage. Yet, at least in the initial stages of seeking a cultural identity, as is now the case, heritage often takes priority. The issue facing the social studies is one of both adjustment and boundary setting.

Third, the concept of responsible citizenship has included the assumption that there *is* a commonly accepted definition of "responsible citizenship" which overrides individual or specific group definitions. Current trends are turning this given into an open question as both individuals and groups seek definitions more relevant to themselves.

Fourth, another bonding agent of society, and hence of social studies, has been the assumption that our nation is one of unlimited opportunity. In popular culture this translates into such slogans as "more is better," "rags to riches," and "anyone can become President." As we approach the twenty-first century, our society and the social studies based on it may well have to deal with rising expectations in a time of increasingly limited opportunities."

Finally, when the Italian philosopher and historian Benedetto Croce wrote, "Every true history is contemporary history," he might well have included the entire range of the social studies. For the social studies have always sought to speak to the contemporary mind, to be "relevant" as we say. Thus, the social studies have had built-in mechanisms to take into account and deal with change. Change gives us new questions to answer and forces us to re-examine old answers from a new perspective. A casual examination of the various editions of a history textbook, for example, will reveal that each new edition is revised not only to bring it up to date chronologically, but also to incorporate the new questions being asked. Change is a constant, but in the twenty-first century the accelerated speed of change will present new challenges to the social studies that affect both content and method.

These themes run throughout this volume as leitmotifs upon which all of the authors play their variations. Their purpose is not so much to lay down paths to be followed as to provoke discussion and thought and, above all, to prepare us as teachers, scholars, and citizens for the challenges of the twenty-first century.

Virginia S. Wilson
James A. Litle
Gerald Lee Wilson

1

PERSISTENT ISSUES IN THE SOCIAL STUDIES

Stanley P. Wronski

"The social studies invite controversy." So wrote the members of the Commission on the Social Studies in the 1930s. And so it is in the 1990s. The Commission members, being mostly historians and social scientists, had mainly in mind such pressing social controversies of the time as how to deal with unemployment, how to revive a depressed economy, and how to strike a just balance between governmental intervention and the maintenance of a free enterprise economic system. In the 1990s a litany of similar controversies would also include such issues as how best to avoid the dangers of nuclear proliferation and how to resolve the abortion question.

In addition to these societal problems, the social studies are also involved in their own internal pedagogical controversies. The list is almost endless, but it would include such issues as the proper balance between subject matter and method as well as the roles of inquiry, discovery, concept formation, performance-based objectives, and computer-assisted instruction. In the late 1960s and early 1970s, for example, the annual meetings of the National Council for the Social Studies were replete with speakers' presentations, section meetings, and special sessions devoted to the inquiry approach to social studies instruction. Methods textbooks with an inquiry emphasis abounded, and inquiry-oriented lesson plans and units proliferated. As we enter the 1990s, no such single overwhelming concern is evident in professional meetings, professional literature, or teachers' lounge debates.

The history of social studies teaching includes numerous other "burning issues" that, like some kind of pedagogical comet, briefly lit up the educational skies and then faded into the oblivion of outer space. What is your stand on fusion? No, not the nuclear type, but the curricular principle that involves joining (fusing) two or more subjects (e.g., history and geography) into one. For the 1920s and 1930s this was such a hot topic that one author (Bye 1933) was impelled to write an article entitled "Fusion or Confusion?" to set the educational community straight. And what about the Life Adjustment Curriculum of the 1950s? This was viewed as the savior of the educational enterprise by its proponents and as a prostitution of the profession by its critics.

What is proposed in this chapter is *not* to denigrate past efforts to identify and grapple with issues of relevance to social studies educators, however ephemeral they may seem now, but rather to deal with a few *significant, persistent issues*. These are the kind of deep-seated issues that were endemic when the social studies were first conceptualized, are unresolved to this day, and will undoubtedly be a source of controversy for the foreseeable future. The opening chapter of the recently published *Handbook of Research on Social Studies Teaching and Learning* stresses the importance of this kind of historical perspective.

The knowledge that men and women more than 70 years ago struggled with questions of social education remarkably similar to those encountered today, and arrived at answers much like modern ones, should help us to understand our tendency to overvalue the importance of *our* thoughts and activities. That understanding is history's unique contribution to education. (Lybarger 1991: 13 [emphasis added])

The topics chosen for treatment in this chapter have relevance for the entire range of the social studies curriculum, K–12. Three such topics are (1) the nature of the social studies, (2) the purpose of the social studies, and (3) the place of values in the social studies. The chapter concludes with a brief consideration of three *current* issues which have the potential of becoming persistent: (1) how to deal with cultural diversity in both society and schools, (2) the impact of new educational technology, such as computer-assisted instruction, and (3) the significance of increasing demands for teacher and student accountability.

THE NATURE OF THE SOCIAL STUDIES

The social studies are defined holistically and taught separately. Consider the following typical definitions:

In contrast with the social sciences, the social studies are designed primarily for instructional purposes. They include those substantive portions of human behavior as well as those procedural modes of inquiry that have been selected and adapted for use in the schools or other instructional situations. (Wesley and Wronski 1973: 5)

The social studies is an integration of experience and knowledge concerning human relations for the purpose of citizenship education. (Barr, Barth, and Shermis 1977: 69)

We believe that social studies includes history, geography, government and civics, economics, anthropology, sociology and psychology as well as subject matter drawn from the humanities—religion, literature and the arts—and that social studies combines those fields and uses them in a direct way to develop a *systematic* and *interrelated* study of people in societies, past and present. (National Commission 1989: ix)

In classroom practice the prevailing pattern at the secondary school level is to teach separate subjects. On the front cover of the May 1980 issue of *Social Education*, a typical scope and sequence for American schools appeared, with the following subjects listed for the secondary schools: Grade 9—Civics, Grade 10—World History, Grade 11—American History, Grade 12—Government. Although there is some variation among local school districts, most states typically follow this same "rock of tradition" pattern (Joyce, Little, and Wronski 1991: 325).

This dichotomy between theoretical curricular constructs and classroom practice is a significant, persistent, and unresolved problem in social studies. What are the consequences of having a curricular area defined as one holistic field but taught as separate subjects? Besides the field's becoming "a schizophrenic bastard child" (Barr et al. 1977: 1), there are these potential outcomes:

—The practice of teaching exclusively separate subjects deprives the social studies of its raison d'etre. Some may (and have) argued, Why maintain the fiction of a holistic field? Let's either redefine or abolish the concept of social studies.

—If only separate subjects are taught, there are course-scheduling limitations on how many different subjects can be offered in a typical secondary school. Such traditional subjects as history and geography appear to have a secure place in the curriculum, but how much opportunity will there be to introduce courses in less frequently taught subjects, such as anthropology, sociology, and psychology?

—Fewer opportunities will exist for experimental offerings, such as interdisciplinary courses in global education, environmental education, futuristics, and science-related social problems.

—Although not a necessary concomitant of separate subject teaching, such compartmentalized courses *tend* to emphasize subject matter over process, such as those of reflective thinking, inquiry, problem solving, and decision making.

But all is not lost in the continued effort to bridge the gap between theory and practice in the social studies. The recent recommendations of the National Commission on Social Studies in the Schools (1989) are a step in this direction—even though the emphasis still falls heavily on history and geography. Proposed courses for grades 9 through 11 *combine* world history, American history, and geography. Similarly, the board of directors of the National Council for the Social Studies has endorsed *three* significantly different scope-and-sequence models, all of which entail breaking away from traditional separate subject teaching.

Perhaps the ultimate resolution of the holistic-versus-separate subject dichotomy will be formulated by classroom teachers. In increasing numbers they are demonstrating a willingness to strike out on new curricular paths involving experimental and interdisciplinary studies. The forging of a new synthesis is in their hands.

THE PURPOSE OF SOCIAL STUDIES

In Wagner's opera *Siegfried,* the god Wotan invites the gnome Mime to ask him three questions. The gnome responds by asking, "What race of people lives under the earth? What race lives on the face of the earth? What race lives on the cloudy height?" After correctly answering Mime's questions, Wotan chides the gnome, "Why did you ask these questions? Why didn't you ask about something that is of more immediate need and interest to you?"

This exchange illustrates a persistent question in education as a whole and the social studies in particular: Education for what? If it is assumed that attaining knowledge is one of education's major purposes (attitudes and skill development being significant others), then the responses to this question can range along a continuum from "knowledge for the sake of knowledge" to "knowledge for a utilitarian purpose."

The proponents of knowledge for knowledge's sake argue that the social studies, especially history, need no more justification than poetry, music, and art need. Each is an end in itself. Although few classroom teachers, if pushed to this extreme position, would overtly subscribe to it, they frequently teach as if they need not justify the import of their subject. Many are hard-pressed to give a rational, coherent response to their students' most frequent question (whether stated or unstated), "Why do we have to learn this stuff in the first place?" One answer was provided by William Cartwright in 1950:

Many reasons are advanced for the study of history. . . . The inclusive objectives most strongly asserted for teaching history are that it should lead to an understanding of society, that it should train in the use of the historical method, and that it should make loyal and efficient citizens. (Cartwright and Bining 1950: 7)

In the 1960s and 1970s the "new" social studies ushered in the age of relevance. The litmus test for many of the new curricula and instructional materials was their utility for understanding the present. This obsession with relevance was not a new phenomenon. As Henry Johnson (1943), a student of the history of history teaching, observed, "It was certainly an old idea in the 5th century B.C. when the Father of History [Herodotus] discovered it, and he simply took it for granted." Johnson went on to ask,

How can any idea so old be regarded as new? An explanation is not far to seek. The conditions which educational reformers strive to meet are actually new. There is always an old education to attack. There is always a new education implying a break with the past, inviting us to begin at the beginning as if nothing had ever been begun before, and leaving an impression that any principle called into play by new conditions must be as new as the conditions themselves. With here and there an unnoticed exception, the second generation of history teachers, and their critics and advisors, thus forgot the first, the third generation forgot the second, and the process of forgetting continued down to the present. (241)

But the criticism of traditional history courses has not subsided. Many critics have refined their arguments to point out that they are not opposed to history per se. History can have utility. It can have relevance. It can be helpful in the same way that an encyclopedia or a dictionary is helpful. But history should be looked upon as a readily available storehouse of data and interpretations that should be used to understand contemporary society. This was the position taken by Edgar Wesley (1967) in his iconoclastic article "Let's Abolish History Courses." Supporters of this position currently point to the increased use of computers, with their enormous data bases, to justify the idea that history should be *used* and not necessarily taught as a course. After all, they argue, this would be like teaching a course on the dictionary or the encyclopedia.

History has always occupied a central position in the social studies curriculum—although some see its position as having shifted "from monopoly to dominance" (Robinson and Kirman 1986: 15). But what about the other subjects? What is their purpose within the social studies curriculum? What follows is a brief summary of how each subject is viewed by leading social studies educators. It must be stressed that listing these subjects individually should in no way be construed as an endorsement of a separate subject curriculum in preference to a holistic social studies curriculum. The subjects are listed for ease of treatment and in recognition of the reality that, at the secondary school level, the social studies curriculum is still predominantly organized around separate subjects.

Geography

Barbara Winston (1986) is concerned about the status of geography in the schools as well as the geographic illiteracy prevalent among students, one of the reasons for which is a "confusion about the nature and purpose of geography" (55) in the social studies curriculum. She approvingly cites recent efforts by geographers and teachers to improve teaching standards. If these are successfully implemented, they should greatly assist in achieving the following major goals of geographic education:

—formulate enlightened opinions on complex global issues related to peace, hunger, trade, environment, refugees, development, or overpopulation, to name a few;
—cast informed votes for government leaders with stands on the above issues, and evaluate whether records of leaders' actions reflect that they know and take account of geographic realities surrounding the issues;
—make informed decisions about personal foreign policies, and evaluate related individual and group behaviors;
—gain perspectives about similarities and differences in ways people in other societies live and interact with each other and their environments—a preliminary step to reduce ethnocentric and stereotypic thinking;
—understand, and find creative solutions to, problems such as those in community or urban planning;
—deal with regional issues such as open space or transportation problems;
—see ways in which apparently local, regional or national issues are linked inextricably to global issues;
—gain skills to select and use maps with understanding because comprehension of so many issues depends on one's ability to use media that answer questions about "where?" "how far?" or "in what direction?" (43)

Civics and Government

To James Shaver and Richard Knight (1986),

The most persistent issue in the teaching of civics and government . . . can be posed in terms of whether the curriculum for elementary and secondary school students is to reflect essentially the scholarly interests of those in the field of political science and government or whether there is some broader, more encompassing civic purpose for K–12 social studies. (71)

Although they point out that a proper response to this issue involves many complexities, they stress that the overriding purpose is to promote a citizenship education grounded in the study of societal problems which require the student to analyze and make value judgments. An important dimension of such a citizenship education is to use the school itself as an environment worthy of careful study.

Economics

After pointing out that there have been various disagreements during the past fifty years over why economic education should be included in the schools, Beverly Armento (1986) concludes, "The primarily social science, analytical approach tends to dominate current economic education curriculum development" (103). The motivating force behind this "rational approach" to economic education was the 1961 report of the National Task Force on Economic Education, which proposed that students need to

acquire a modest amount of factual information about the economic world, but the primary obligation of schools is to help (students) develop the capacity to think clearly, objectively and with a reasonable degree of sophistication about economic problems. Mere description of economic institutions is not what we mean by economic education. (*National Task Force* 1961: 13)

The "structure of the discipline" approach emphasized in this report has its drawbacks. It tends to ignore such issues as the extent to which personal economics should be included in the curriculum, the relevance of the social-scientific approach for minority students, and the role of value judgments in economic education.

Sociology

The teacher of sociology is faced with an intriguing (and some would say impossible) dilemma. S/he is obligated to assist youthful students in becoming functional parts of the social order while also helping them to get "outside of themselves," as it were, in order to take a detached, objective view of the social mechanism of which they are a part. To complicate matters further, students are often asked to analyze complex societal problems and come up with plausible responses. They are both part of the problem and part of the solution. Thomas Switzer (1986) has identified this social problems approach as "the dominant theme in precollegiate sociology" (128).

Since the late 1960s there has been an attempt to modify this social problems approach by placing more emphasis on learning by inquiry. Students would not only read sociology; they would *do* sociology. The recurring instructional pattern was (1) to raise a question about some aspect of society, (2) to gather data on the topic, (3) to make an analysis of the data, frequently employing elementary statistical and probability principles, and (4) to arrive at a tentative answer.

Robert Angell (1981), who directed the production of many inquiry-oriented instructional materials, concluded, "Though qualified judges pronounced the materials to be of high quality, their ultimate impact seems likely to be less than originally hoped. This would be unfortunate, since high school students would be missing the challenge of inquiry learning" (42). Unfortunate, but true.

Anthropology

Nearly a hundred years ago Franz Boas (1990) wrote:

Modern anthropology has discovered the fact that human society has grown and developed everywhere in such a manner that its forms, opinions and actions have many fundamental traits in common. This momentous discovery implies that laws exist that govern the development of society; that they apply to our society as well as to those of past times and distant lands; that their knowledge will be a means to understand the causes furthering and retarding civilization; and that, guided by this knowledge, we may hope to govern our actions so that the greatest benefit to mankind will accrue from them. (270)

Modern anthropologist Roger Owen (1986) feels that this rationale still provides a valid justification for teaching anthropology at both the pre-collegiate and collegiate levels. Recent research on the status of anthropology in the schools (Dynesson 1986) reveals that anthropology began to have an impact on the social studies curriculum with the advent of the new social studies during the years 1965–1975. "It is viewed by most educators as an integrated part of the social studies. It might be taught as an elective, but its main role would be to supplement ongoing subjects that dominate the curriculum" (162).

Psychology

The usual rationale given for including psychology in the school curriculum is that society demands it (Bare 1986). Expressions of this need for psychology can be found as early as the nineteenth century, in the writings of Horace Mann, in the 1916 report of the Commission on the Reorganization of Secondary Education, in the 1938 report of the Educational Policies Commission, and in the writings of those seeking to sustain the morale of the American people during World War II. Influential members of society perceived psychology as a source of worthwhile knowledge about the individual and assumed that teaching the subject in the schools would meet individual and societal needs. These perceptions "were limited, if not erroneous, and the assumption was only partially true" (Bare 1986: 181).

The purposes of teaching psychology in the secondary schools can best be deduced by examining various textbooks, instructional materials, and curriculum development efforts. One high school psychology course focuses on three stages in individual human development: early childhood, adolescence, and adulthood. Throughout the course students are asked to "personalize" their learning. Another course, developed by the American Psychological Association, the *Human Behavior Curriculum Project,* emphasizes the principles of behavior (Bare 1986). Modules in other courses deal with classical conditioning, operant conditioning, observational learning, and avoidance behavior, among other topics.

J. K. Bare summarizes curriculum development efforts in psychology to date with the observation that they "have not produced a general course in psychology that is widely taught in high schools. . . . Instead, teachers with varying amounts of formal preparation will, with considerable ingenuity and no less effort, continue to teach a variety of courses that range from attempts to produce self-understanding to attempts to produce an understanding of one another in terms of principles of psychology" (186–87).

THE PLACE OF VALUES

Despite being labeled the "hidden curriculum," values education has been anything but ignored or unrecognized in the educational literature. Numerous lesson plans dealing with values in the classroom have been developed, several social studies textbooks incorporate the word in their titles, and the National Council for the Social Studies has issued a yearbook (Metcalf 1971) devoted entirely to the teaching of values. So the question of whether the social studies should deal with values has been answered overwhelmingly in the affirmative. However, the persistent, unresolved questions are "What values?" and "How should they be handled in the classroom?"

One plausible position that may be taken with respect to values is to adopt—or at least attempt to adopt—a stance of neutrality. In the classroom, this would be manifested by avoiding issues that are value laden, such as current political controversies, abortion, religion, international relations, and so on. If these topics did come up in class, the teacher's response would be one of "just the facts, please," thus avoiding any discussion of value implications. It is not surprising that such a position has been, and still is, maintained by many social studies teachers, paralleling the positivist position taken by a substantial number of social scientists, or at least their *perceived* position. It does not seem to matter to these social studies teachers that the vast majority of contemporary social scientists reject the rigid positivism of their predecessors (Gunnell 1986). There are even some teachers, for example, who refuse to teach *about* religion because they think it is either too controversial to discuss (itself a value judgment) or intrinsically too value laden.

Positions other than one of complete neutrality are possible when it comes to dealing with values in the classroom. An illustration of the range of these positions can be found in considering the place of global education in the schools. Because global education deals with highly controversial and value-laden issues, it is not surprising that the whole area frequently comes under attack. Critics charge that it is not in keeping with American values because it promotes moral relativism and moral equivalency. Moral relativism, say the critics, supports the idea that students cannot and should not make judgments about actions taken by a nation or society whose values differ from our own. Moral equivalency takes this argument one step further by teaching students that, because one society cannot be judged in terms of the values of another, all societies have an equal status and thus are morally equivalent.

In order to meet such criticism, it is necessary to introduce a third and prior concept, that of cultural relativism. As it is formulated in most introductory college-level sociology or anthropology courses, cultural relativism simply means that it is inappropriate for society A to judge society B in terms of the values of society A, and vice versa. Problems arise, however, when the concept of *cultural* relativism is confused with that of *moral* relativism. This distinction is addressed at quite some length in the report of the Ad Hoc Committee on Global Education (1987) of the National Council for the Social Studies:

Moral relativism tells us not to pass judgment on another society or culture. Suppose, however, that that society or culture is itself aggressively intolerant and disrespectful of others. If we refuse to condemn intolerance and disrespect in it, why do we have reason to condemn it in ourselves? How can we believe tolerance and respect are centrally important values without believing they are important for others too? Indifference to the intolerance of others cannot effectively motivate concern about tolerance in ourselves.

The chauvinist disparages all differences because he fails to see that basic moral values can be advanced in social forms not familiar to himself. The antidote to chauvinism is not an indiscriminate nonjudgmentalism. By refusing to pass judgment on any customs not his own, even when they badly serve or actually violate basic moral values, the relativist signals no confidence in the reasonableness of his own moral convictions, including convictions about tolerance and respect. This is not an effective way to recommend them to others. (246–47)

As for the criticism of moral equivalency, it is essentially a straw-man argument, since the data (i.e., global education lessons, learning activities, and readings) do not support the allegation. But this entire treatment of relativism applies just as much to the social studies as a whole as it does to global education in particular.

It is not difficult to get agreement in American society on what over-arching values the schools should promote. At the personal level these would include honesty and integrity, and at the societal level respect for the individual and equality before the law. The difficulty arises when these principles are applied to specific situations, especially those situations where the choice is not between a good and a bad but between two or more competing goods. Here the contributions of Maurice Hunt and Lawrence E. Metcalf (1968) have been of great significance to social studies. They have not only identified important substantive issues, but have also provided a method of analysis that requires students to make value judgments. Among the substantive issues, which Hunt and Metcalf term "closed areas," they include the following: race relations, social class, sex, and religion.

Another major contributor to values education has been Lawrence Kohlberg (1981). His emphasis is on the *reasons* that students give for making a moral judgment. These reasons indicate what level of moral reasoning a learner has achieved. Kohlberg's original analysis posited three *levels* of reasoning, each subdivided into two *stages*. At the first stage, for example, a child may give as a reason for not stealing the fact that he or she would probably be punished. As the child matures, the reasoning becomes more complex so that at stage five a young person would support welfare for the needy on the grounds of its being in harmony with the principle of a social compact. The means by which teachers develop moral reasoning in their students are to confront them with actual or hypothetical moral dilemmas. For example, one hypothetical dilemma involves the case of a man (named Hans) who has a sick wife. She will probably die if she does not obtain a certain kind of medication, but Hans does not have the money to buy the medicine. Should he steal it from a druggist?

The key to the Kohlberg analysis of this and similar dilemmas is found in the reasons the students give for their answer. These can range from fear of punishment (stage 1) as the reason for a negative answer to acknowledging the existence of universal codes of justice which transcend any temporal, man-made laws (stage 6) as the reason for a positive answer. Kohlberg's contributions to this kind of value analysis in the classroom have undoubtedly enhanced the status of values education in the schools. In a similar way, Hunt and Metcalf's reflective-thinking approach has added an intellectual and philosophical dimension that was noticeably absent from earlier "value-free" efforts in values clarification. Both approaches, however, have drawbacks. In Kohlberg's case, he has himself acknowledged that probably only fifteen percent of the total population

Figure 1
The Decision-Making Process

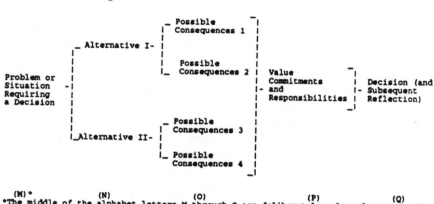

*The middle of the alphabet letters M through Q are deliberately selected to emphasize
the point that the "steps" in this model really have no beginning or end. Decision
making is a continuously reflective process. (Wesley and Wronski)

(including teachers) normally operate at stage 5 or above. (Some wags have opined that only three persons on earth ever achieved stage 6— Jesus Christ, Mohandas Gandhi, and Lawrence Kohlberg.) If most teachers operate at stage 4 or below, it is unlikely that they can pull themselves or their students above that level. Similarly, the Hunt and Metcalf method frequently bogs down both teachers and students in tendentious definitions and formal logic procedures.

A somewhat more modest, but still practical, approach to values education involves incorporating it within a more broadly conceived process of decision making. One generic model for this process was developed by Carl Gross, Stanley Wronski, and John Hanson (1962) and modified specifically for the social studies (Wesley and Wronski 1973). The model is depicted in Figure 1. The issue selected to illustrate the model in Figure 1 was that of environmental pollution. For example, Alternative I was to impose several financial penalties on all convicted polluters. Alternative II was to rely mainly on voluntary efforts by individuals and businesses to minimize pollution. After taking the reader step by step through the model, Wesley and Wronski had this to say:

In our example involving pollution control the students may subscribe to several values—some of which may be conflicting. These may include such literally mundane ones as valuing the conservation of natural resources and the replenishment of replaceable ones to the more cosmic one of valuing worldwide collective responsibility for the preservation of homo sapiens as a species. What should be the role of the teacher in dealing with the idea of commitment on the part of students? One important function is to widen the range of value choices open to students. For example, individual gratification and self-satisfaction may be perfectly understandable initial commitments by some students. But a decision always to act from such premises may create problems that eventually will deny this option—and maybe even deny life itself to succeeding generations. Only the most obtuse will fail to see the need for at least considering other commitments. (117–18)

The persistent controversy relating to the place of values in the social studies curriculum is exemplified by a series of unanswered questions posed by Robert Fullinwider (1991) in a paper entitled "Philosophical Inquiry and Social Studies."

Social studies curricula often deal with personal and social values. What understanding of values and valuing underlies them? What distinctions, if any, are drawn between facts and values, emotion and cognition, thinking and acting? Is the social studies classroom the proper arena for inculcating values? Which values? How are value-charged controversies to be dealt with in the school? How can teachers distinguish between indoctrinating and teaching, manipulating and correcting, proselytizing and clarifying? Do social studies approaches encourage or discourage moral relativism? (18–19)

EMERGENT ISSUES: EPHEMERAL OR PERSISTENT?

Literally scores of topics and issues dot the current social studies landscape. The following are listed as samples:

Classroom organization and management;

Cognitive versus affective learning;

Subject matter versus methodology;

The social content of education;

Divergent versus convergent thinking;

Philosophy *and* social studies;

Philosophy *of* social studies;

The role of social criticism;

Heterogeneous versus homogeneous grouping;

The local school community as an object of study;

Measurement and evaluation in social studies;

Scope and sequence;

Goals and objectives.

Without belittling the significance of any of these topics, three issues will be given further consideration here because they are currently receiving heightened attention in the educational literature and because they reflect concerns that may have a considerable element of persistence.

Cultural Diversity in Student Clientele

The 1990 census revealed significant increases in the population of certain ethnic groups in American society, mainly Hispanic, Asian-American, and Native American. African-Americans, while representing a larger proportion, increased only moderately in terms of percentage of the total population. Corresponding increases also occurred in school enrollment figures. At issue for the social studies teacher is how best to deal with this cultural diversity in the classroom.

Geneva Gay (1991) has summarized the research findings on the class-room-participation patterns of different ethnic groups. With regard to the social studies, she observes,

The participation structures of many culturally different students raise interesting questions about how they may affect students' response patterns to some of the instructional techniques frequently used in social studies education. It might be hypothesized that because of their cultural socialization and preferred partici-pation structures (a) most Asian-American students will be reluctant to participate in open-ended discussions, values analysis, and inquiry teaching; (b) informal social contexts in social studies classrooms will improve the participation and performance of Hispanics, African-Americans, and American Indians; (c) as teachers use more cooperative learning strategies the involvement, time on task, and academic achievement of African-American, Hispanic, and Indian students will increase; and (d) divergent questioning and indirect teaching strategies are more suited to the participation structures of some culturally different students than others. (147)

Gay is careful to point out that all these hypotheses need to be empirically tested, but she does suggest that "some culturally different students prefer more kinetic and tactile stimulation, active involvement, and cooperative social environments" (ibid.). This is in contrast to the prevailing pattern in which students are the passive recipients of knowledge dispensed by an authority figure.

Differences in learning styles exhibited by African-Americans also seem to be confirmed by Barbara Shade (1982), who found that these students tend to use relational, holistic, and functional criteria for processing in-formational data, whereas Anglocentric teachers encourage analytical, specific, taxonomic, and descriptive strategies in learning.

One type of teaching and learning strategy has met with almost universal approval and endorsement by teachers and researchers. Falling under the category of cooperative learning, this strategy employs such procedures as group tasks, instruction by peers, team efforts, class projects, one-on-one tutoring, and incorporating aesthetic expression into social studies. Such learning tends to engender better intercultural race relations, more cross-ethnic friendships, improved self-esteem, and the development of peer norms in assessing academic performance. Cooperative learning enables students to develop a core of shared values and social relationships.

Educational Technology

If the social studies curriculum were producing automobiles rather than citizens, most of us would be driving Model Ts. For the most part, we have yet to avail ourselves of the technology required for modern-day democratic citizenship. Stated in educational terms, most of our technology is geared to achieving the lowest levels of those objectives exemplified by the *Taxonomy of Educational Objectives* (Bloom 1956). In the cognitive domain such objectives range from the simple to the complex—from isolated knowledge, through comprehension, application, analysis, and synthesis, to evaluation, that is, making value judgments about social issues.

The problem is not in the hardware; it is mainly in the software. For most computer-assisted instruction, the programs contain a vast array of data to be "processed," and it is in this processing that the problem lies. Typically, the programs call for elementary sorting, categorizing, and grouping of data. Few require the students to formulate applications, create syntheses, or make value judgments based on the data. Fortunately, there have been indications in recent years that some social studies programmers have upgraded their software. Three developments show particular promise: (1) the construction of computer software by teachers *in cooperation with* their students, (2) programs that have data bases *compiled by students,* and (3) programs that not only permit but *require* students to engage in decision making, which involves higher mental processes.

One example of student collaboration in constructing a computer program has been provided by Mike Roessler (1987), a middle school teacher. His eighth grade class designed a computer-assisted simulation of the Great Depression. A few years later his eighth-graders designed a program dealing with acid rain. In an evaluation questionnaire, Roessler's students responded to five open-ended questions. Two of the questions and selected responses to them follow:

Q. What parts of making the simulation were most rewarding to you?

A. I think it really was just the thinking you had to do in order to write and type the program.
   I think the thing I like is when it's over. I say that because you can play it and look at the hard work you put in.

Q. How could this simulation assignment be improved to make it a better learning experience?

A. I don't know of a way it could be improved because you gave the responsibility to us and we had to handle that, which was its own learning experience.

It helped me see more about life itself. (51)

Timothy Little (1991) gives an example of a program in which the students provide the data base and generate their own conclusions and generalizations based on their processing of the data. A program that can be adapted for courses in either history or sociology, it requires students to establish a data base consisting of demographic information on actual immigrants to a small North Dakota town (with the pseudonym "Elm-ville"). These immigrants came from a variety of countries during the second half of the nineteenth and early twentieth centuries. The data, which are derived from family histories, old photos, early newspapers, personal papers, and books on local history, enable students to answer such questions as

• Did the early settlers consist of nuclear families or did the first wave consist primarily of males (the Dodge City/*Gunsmoke* stereotype)?
• What were the countries of origin of the immigrants in descending order of frequency?
• In terms of social class, did Elmville tend to be heterogeneous or homogeneous in composition for the first generation? The second? The third?

Even this brief description suggests the range of possible investigations that a creative teacher and class can pursue.

The *Newsweek* Social Studies Program provides a third example of a program requiring students to engage in higher mental processes. Its *Policy Maker* (Little and Goldsmith 1990) is a decision-making software program that requires students to select from among various policy options for resolving social issues. A unique feature of this program is that the *students* select and define the problems to which they will address themselves. The steps in the decision-making process are as follows:

1. Identification of the problem (e.g., illicit drug abuse in the United States).
2. Creation of a broad goal.
3. Identification of policy options.
4. Identification of specific objectives.
5. Assigning weights to objectives.
6. Rating (on a scale of 1–4) of policy options.
7. (Optional) probability of implementation of the policy options.

The reader may wish to compare this computer-assisted decision-making model with that depicted in Figure 1, noting especially that although value commitments are implied in the *Policy Maker* model, they are not explicitly incorporated. Despite this limitation, *Policy Maker* clearly has the potential to provide secondary school students with an interactive technology that can significantly enhance learning in the social studies.

Accountability for What?

The topic of teacher accountability has evoked a great deal of meaningless response from professionals and the public alike. It is literally meaningless in that "accountability" in an educational context has been either ill defined or misconstrued, or both.

As applied to education in general, the concept of accountability implies that teachers should be held accountable for the progress, or lack thereof, of their students. Progress is usually defined in terms of students' performance on achievement tests. In order to meet the presumed standards of objectivity and fairness, these tests usually consist of quantifiable— that is, "objective"—test items. Examples of such test items in the social studies are completion, true-false, and multiple-choice questions. These are easily scored because they are free of subjectivity, unambiguous, and quantifiable. And therein lies the rub.

The essence of the social studies consists of content and processes (1) that are frequently subjective (e.g., the making of value judgments); (2) whose purposes are not always agreed on by all (e.g., to promote critical thinking or indoctrination); and (3) whose very nature (e.g., concern with *human* relationships) is not always amenable to quantification. Not surprisingly, these are the very issues that comprise the focus of this chapter precisely because they persist and remain unresolved.

In order for any discussion of accountability in social studies to be meaningful, it must address in some depth the issues of the nature and purpose of the social studies, as well as the place of values in the total enterprise. Very few of the pronouncements made on accountability are informed by such a necessary pre-condition.

So the beat goes on.

REFERENCES

Ad Hoc Committee on Global Education. "Report." *Social Education* 50 (April/ May 1987): 246–47.

Angell, R. C. "Reflections on the Project: Sociological Resources for the Social Studies." *The American Sociologist* 16 (1981): 41–43.

Armento, B. J. "Promoting Economic Literacy." In S. P. Wronski and D. H. Bragaw, eds., *Social Studies and the Social Sciences: A Fifty Year Perspective*. Bulletin No. 78. Washington, DC: National Council for the Social Studies, 1986.

Bare, John K. "Teaching Psychology in Schools." In S. P. Wronski and D. H.

Bragaw, eds., *Social Studies and the Social Sciences: A Fifty Year Perspective.* Bulletin No. 78. Washington, DC: National Council for the Social Studies, 1986.

Barr, R. D., J. L. Barth, and S. S. Shermis. *Defining the Social Studies.* Bulletin No. 51. Washington, DC: National Council for the Social Studies, 1977.

Bloom, B. S. *Taxonomy of Educational Objectives: Cognitive Domain.* New York: David McKay, 1956.

Boas, F. "The Limitations of the Comparative Method of Anthropology" (1896). In Frank Boas, ed., *Race, Language and Culture.* New York: Macmillan, 1990.

Bye, Edgar C. "Fusion or Confusion?" *Historical Outlook* 24 (1933): 264–67.

Cartwright, W. H., and A. C. Bining. *The Teaching of History in the United States.* México, D. F.: Instituto Panamericano de Geografía e Historia, Comisión de Historia, 1950.

Dynesson, T. L. "Trends in Precollegiate Anthropology." In S. P. Wronski and D. H. Bragaw, eds., *Social Studies and the Social Sciences: A Fifty Year Perspective.* Bulletin No. 78. Washington DC: National Council for the Social Studies, 1986.

Fullinwider, Robert K. "Philosophical Inquiry and Social Studies." In James P. Shaver, ed., *Handbook of Research on Social Studies Teaching and Learning.* New York: Macmillan, 1991.

Gay, G. "Culturally Diverse Students and Social Studies." In James P. Shaver, ed., *Handbook of Research on Social Studies Teaching and Learning.* New York: Macmillan, 1991.

Gross, C. H., S. P. Wronski, and J. W. Hanson. *School and Society.* Boston: Heath, 1962.

Gunnell, J. G. *Between Philosophy and Politics: The Alienation of Political Theory.* Amherst, MA: University of Massachusetts Press, 1986.

Hunt, M. P., and L. E. Metcalf. *Teaching High School Social Studies: Problems in Reflective Thinking and Social Understanding.* 2d ed. New York: Harper & Row, 1968.

Johnson, H. *The Other Side of Main Street.* New York: Columbia University Press, 1943.

Joyce, W. W., T. H. Little, and S. P. Wronski. "Scope and Sequence, Goals, and Objectives: Effects on Social Studies." In James P. Shaver, ed., *Handbook of Research on Social Studies Teaching and Learning.* New York: Macmillan, 1991.

Kohlberg, L. *The Philosophy of Moral Development: Moral Stages and the Idea of Justice.* San Francisco: Harper & Row, 1981.

Little, T. H. "In Search of the Promised Land: Immigration to North Dakota." *Michigan Association for Computer Users in Learning Newsletter* 11 (1991): 22–23.

Little, T. H., and W. B. Goldsmith, Jr. *"Policy Maker:* A Decision-Making Model for Selecting Policy Options to Resolve Social Issues" (software disk and users' manual). *Newsweek* Social Studies Program, 1990.

Lybarger, M. B. "The Historiography of Social Studies: Retrospect, Circumspect, and Prospect." In James P. Shaver, ed., *Handbook of Research on Social Studies Teaching and Learning.* New York: Macmillan, 1991.

Metcalf, L. E., ed. *Values Education: Rationale, Strategies, and Procedures.* 41st Yearbook. Washington, DC: National Council for the Social Studies, 1971.

National Commission on Social Studies in the Schools. *Charting a Course: Social Studies for the 21st Century.* Washington, DC: National Commission on Social Studies in the Schools, 1989.

National Task Force on Economic Education. *Economic Education in the Schools.* New York: Committee for Economic Development, 1961.

Owen, R. "Coming of Age in Anthropology." In S. P. Wronski and D. H. Bragaw, eds., *Social Studies and the Social Sciences: A Fifty Year Perspective.* Bulletin No. 78. Washington, DC: National Council for the Social Studies, 1986.

Robinson, P., and J. M. Kirman. "From Monopoly to Dominance." In S. P. Wronski and D. H. Bragaw, eds., *Social Studies and the Social Sciences: A Fifty Year Perspective.* Bulletin No. 78. Washington, DC: National Council for the Social Studies, 1986.

Roessler, M. "Students Design a Depression Simulation." *Social Education* 51 (1987): 48–51.

Shade, B. J. "Afro-American Cognitive Style: A Variable in School Success." *Review of Educational Research* 52 (1982): 219–44.

Shaver, J. P., and R. S. Knight. "Civics and Government in Citizenship Education." In S. P. Wronski and D. H. Bragaw, eds., *Social Studies and the Social Sciences: A Fifty Year Perspective.* Bulletin No. 78. Washington, DC: National Council for the Social Studies, 1986.

Switzer, T. J. "Teaching Sociology in K–12 Classrooms." In S. P. Wronski and D. H. Bragaw eds., *Social Studies and the Social Sciences: A Fifty Year Perspective.* Bulletin No. 78. Washington, DC: National Council for the Social Studies, 1986.

Wesley, E. B. "Let's Abolish History Courses." *Phi Delta Kappan* 49 (1967): 3–8.

Wesley, E. B., and S. P. Wronski. *Teaching Secondary Social Studies in a World Society.* 6th ed. Lexington, MA: Heath, 1973.

Winston, B. J. "Teaching and Learning in Geography." In S. P. Wronski and D. H. Bragaw, eds., *Social Studies and the Social Sciences: A Fifty Year Perspective.* Bulletin No. 78. Washington, DC: National Council for the Social Studies, 1986.

2

REFORM REVISITED: THE STORY OF ELEMENTARY SOCIAL STUDIES AT THE CREST OF THE 21ST CENTURY

Beverly J. Armento

The life of social studies education during the twentieth century has been punctuated by reform efforts, committee recommendations, and ongoing controversies. Many of the issues and proposals for classroom practice have been revisited anew by each generation of social studies educators. Many of the ideas proposed over the years as fresh and provocative by reformers sound surprisingly similar when viewed in juxtaposition. Take, for example, the following two recommendations for reform in social studies; see if you can identify the source and the date of each proposal.

Recommendation 1: History and the allied subjects should be taught by "new methods." These methods include inquiry, extensive use of comparison, field trips, debates, individual work, and audio-visual aids; recitation, extensive lecturing, and stress on the facts should be minimized. Schools need better texts, containing social as well as political history. When taught using such methods, these subjects "serve to broaden and cultivate the mind; they help to counteract a narrow and provincial spirit."

Recommendation 2: Schools need new and inspiring textbooks that focus on social history and emphasize broad, significant themes and questions rather than the short-lived memorization of facts presented without context. When taught using new methods, history "helps students develop a shared humanity; understand themselves and otherness; . . . and develop a sense of judgment."

Almost 100 years separate these two quite similar recommendations for reform in social studies. The first was made in 1893 by the "Committee of Ten," the group appointed by the National Education Association (1893) to study the social studies curriculum. The second was made in 1988 by the Bradley Commission on History in Schools (1988; see also Gagnon 1988). National reports on the status of social studies have opened and will no doubt close the twentieth century. In reflecting on 100 years of elementary social studies education, one might ask what progress we have made with this important curricular component dedicated to citizenship education. Where is the field today, and where might we be tomorrow?

This chapter is devoted to an exploration of these questions as they relate to the elementary school social studies curriculum. In the first section, "Reflections," the focus is on the past, namely, on the approaches, methods, and issues in elementary social studies during the twentieth century. The second section, "Current Issues and Trends," emphasizes today's issues and reform recommendations for elementary school social studies. And, finally, in the third section, "Projections," the focus shifts to looking at how the world is changing and how those changes could or should affect the elementary social studies curriculum.

REFLECTIONS

The reform efforts in social studies education during the twentieth century have been haunted by questions that seem to defy answering. The dominant issues of the 1900s were the same as those of the 1960s, and they remain in the forefront of contemporary discussions today, reflected in such questions as

- How should the education of citizens be defined?
- What should be the basis of the social studies curriculum?
- What relationship should social studies have to the realities of the social world and to the realities of schools and students?
- What methodologies and materials will best achieve the goals?

Over the last 100 years, educators have grappled with these issues, and creative "solutions" have been proposed. In some cases, these have resulted in actual change in elementary school classrooms; in other cases, reformers have been essentially talking only to themselves. And, as Hazel Whitman Hertzberg (1981) pointed out in her insightful history of the field, in many instances, the reformers operated in historical and contextual vacuums, ignoring prior reports and neglecting to account for either the realities in the lives of teachers and students or those operating in schools.

Thus, according to Hertzberg, there has continued to be a gap between "reform advocated" and "reform accomplished" (xi).

While many of the reform efforts of the twentieth century have been directed at the high school, recommendations have also been made for the elementary school. And, in some ways, these recommendations have had such enduring power that many contemporary educators believe there is a "national curriculum" for elementary school social studies. In the same way that the reform proposals of the late 1800s set the tone for change in the 1900s, perhaps the reform movement of the late 1900s will set the direction for change in the twenty-first century. Let us briefly survey some of the more significant reform efforts that have influenced elementary school social studies in the twentieth century.

The First Fifty Years

The emergence of professional associations late in the nineteenth century strongly influenced the direction of the social studies curriculum. History led, with the establishment of the American Historical Association in 1884, followed by the creation of the American Economic Association in 1885. By the time other social science associations were formed two decades later, history had already established itself as the curricular leader. The report of the NEA's Committee of Ten in 1893 proposed four years of history study at both the high school and upper elementary levels. For the elementary school, the committee recommended the study of "biography, mythology, American History, and government, and Greek/ Roman History with Oriental connections" (National Education Association 1893).

On the heels of the report of the Committee of Ten, the American Historical Association formed the "Committee of Seven" to make recommendations for college entrance requirements. However, this committee's report (American Historical Association 1899) went beyond that charge to propose a high school program of world and American history, complete with ideas for pedagogy and teacher education. History was viewed by the committee as a unifying and synthesizing subject, and one that was "dynamic, open-minded, concerned with critical thinking, active and inspirational" (Hertzberg 1981: 14).

In 1905, the American Historical Association appointed the "Committee of Eight" to make recommendations for the elementary school social studies curriculum. A scope and sequence was proposed: for grades 1 and 2, the committee recommended "Indian life, historical aspects of Thanksgiving, the story of Washington, and local events"; for grade 3, "heroes of other times, Columbus, the Indians, and historical aspects of July 4th"; for grades 4 and 5, "a biographical approach to American history"; for grade 6, a course in "Old World or European backgrounds of American history''; and for grades 7 and 8, parallel programs in a chronological approach to American history along with a course in elementary civics that emphasized state and national governments'' (16).

This *heroes-holidays-history* elementary school social studies curriculum is known to teachers and students alike, for this is the scope and sequence with which many of us grew up and which continues to be followed in some cases, especially in the primary grades. By 1916, another highly influential report was published, that of the NEA's Commission on the Reorganization of Secondary Education (National Education Association 1916). The report proposed courses for junior and senior high school. For grades 7 and 8, courses in geography, European history, American history, and civics were recommended. All social science courses, said the Commission, should strive for the "cultivation of good citizenship" (Hertzberg 1981: 26).

By the time the National Council for the Social Studies was founded in 1921, other professional associations related to the social studies curriculum had made proposals for the precollege course of study. Each, of course, placed its own social science discipline at the center of the curriculum, claiming that it best served citizenship goals. By the mid 1920s, the "ambiguity and rivalry" (Lybarger 1991) that continue to plague the field today had become more evident. Ambiguity existed then and now over the meaning of citizenship education and what sort of curriculum would best promote effective citizenship. Rivalry existed then and now over the relative roles of history and the various social sciences in the curriculum: What knowledge should serve as the intellectual basis of the curriculum, and was that knowledge to be taught in separate courses or in some sort of fused or integrated manner? Furthermore, should the knowledge base be organized around topics or social issues? While many reformers favored an integrated or fused knowledge base, few have had any practical ideas about how to do this. For example, in 1934, the American Historical Association's Commission on the Social Studies recommended that the elementary school curriculum should revolve around the theme of "the community and the nation," but offered few examples of what this theme would look like in practice, (American Historical Association 1934).

Efforts to promote "learning citizenship by doing it" and the "human relations" curriculum characterized some of the literature on social studies during the 1940s and 1950s. However, there was also a strong effort to promote a "learning the facts of history approach" following World War II and a *New York Times* article about the inadequacy of Americans' historical knowledge (Nevins 1942).

The Second Fifty Years

Major efforts to reform the total school curriculum during the 1950s and the resultant "New Social Studies" led to a very different emphasis in elementary schools during the last half of the century. Several factors influenced the character of reform for the subsequent three decades. First of all, social science departments at universities had gained in strength and had also become more interested in precollege curricula. In addition, the general perception that the curriculum should be more "academic" to meet new international challenges was strengthened by the ideas of people like Jerome Bruner (1960). Bruner's basic premise, that any child could learn any idea provided it was presented appropriately, gave fuel to the "structure of the disciplines" approach that was to follow in social studies.

At the heart of the "structure of the disciplines" approach was the idea that the fundamental concepts and inquiry processes of history and the social science fields held powerful analytic abilities. That is, conceptual knowledge could be applied to numerous examples, not merely to single bits of information. Thus, if students understood the major analytic ideas of a social science discipline, they could better comprehend various aspects of the social world, not merely the examples they learned in school instruction. Moreover, the inquiry processes associated with history and the social sciences should generalize to problems in the learner's world, thus promoting decision-making and problem-solving skills (Price 1958).

While the "New Social Studies" had (and continues to have) a major influence on elementary programs, perhaps the most powerful ideas and certainly some of the most enduring and persistent were those of Paul Hanna (1963). Hanna's scope-and-sequence design used a concentric circles metaphor known as "Expanding Environments" or "Expanding Horizons." The focus was the study of humans living in societies, with the societies expanding in scope as children matured. The youngest students would study families, then neighborhoods, communities, and so on, studying regions and the national community by grade 7.

At each grade level, proposed Hanna, the study of life in societies would be organized around themes, such as communicating, educating, organizing, and governing. Hanna's "expanding horizons" approach was blended, especially by textbook developers, with the "structure of the disciplines" approach. Thus, the study of the family, for example, often emphasized the sociological concepts of group and role, the anthropological concepts of culture and tradition, and the historical concept of change. This approach to elementary school social studies has been popular for almost three decades and remains the dominant tradition today, in spite of its critics.

The curriculum resulting from this "marriage" of the "expanding horizons" and "structure of the disciplines" approaches has been criticized for its "trivial and noninformative" nature (Larkins, Hawkins, and Gilmore 1987) and its lack of substance and meaning for children (Akenson 1989; Ravitch 1987). Much of the justification for the "expanding horizons" framework lies in the perception that young children's limited cognitive capacity precludes their comprehending much more than what this sort of curriculum offers. However, current theories of cognition and research with elementary school students suggest otherwise (see Alleman and Rosaen 1991; Atwater 1986; and Cornbleth 1985). Constructivist views of learning and teaching (see Armento 1991; Vygotsky 1978; and Wittrock 1974, 1978) offer powerful insights into the processes of learning. Applications of constructivist theory to the social studies curriculum will occur during the 1990s, as more educators realize the import of this body of work.

In addition to the "expanding horizons" and "structures of the disciplines" approaches of the 1960s, there were other movements and activities that influenced the elementary school social studies curriculum: namely, specially developed social studies projects, multicultural curricula, and curricula on current topics of interest.

Many special curriculur projects were developed during the 1960s, primarily by university faculty, and many were funded by private foundations or by government grants. *Our Working World,* developed by Lawrence Senesh, was an elementary school curriculum based on economics and very much part of the "structure of the disciplines" approach. Thus, the emphasis was on the basic concepts and generalizations of economics, presented in narrative format. Similarly, *Man: A Course of Study (MACOS)* featured the essential ideas of anthropology, set in provocative case studies and presented in multimedia format. Many of these projects were immediately popular in some classrooms, although it has generally been reported that the implementation was neither widespread nor did teachers use these materials very much during the second and third years after purchase (Hertzberg 1981).

Some critics, like William H. Cartwright, wondered if the "new social studies" was an improvement over the old, and how educators "could prevent adoption of the worst in the new, in the face of pressures to be up to date." Further, he asked, "How can we keep the best of what we now have? Are any of the projects working to help teachers become increasingly competent?" (ibid.: 114). In addition, the 1960s was a time of social crisis, social activism, and change. Where in the "new social studies," asked other critics, did students learn about poverty, discrimination, cultural diversity, and equality? How was the social studies curriculum relevant to minority students and to females? (Banks 1969; Gibson 1969; Harlan 1969).

Such critiques led to the development of instructional add-ons; these included curriculum projects on various ethnic groups and women as well as on such topics as career awareness, economic education, peace education, drug education, consumer education, and so on. While many of these projects had considerable intrinsic value, they added to the fragmentation of the social studies curriculum. In addition, and perhaps more importantly, these efforts had little influence on textbook development during the 1970s and 1980s.

If you were to look into elementary school social studies classrooms today, which of the reform recommendations would you see? Which of the specially developed curriculum materials would students be using? Research on social studies classrooms conducted in the late 1970s and the 1980s indicated that few of the "new" materials were in use. Teachers primarily depended on their textbooks to define the curriculum. The dominant mode of instruction combined lectures with readings from the text, and social studies was generally not liked by either students or teachers (Fancett and Hawke 1982; Gross 1976; Patrick 1982; and Shaver, Davis, and Helburn 1979). However, some recent ethnographic studies of elementary social studies classrooms present a more positive image. For example, Stodolsky (1988) observed thirty-nine fifth-grade social studies classrooms and found a wide range of instructional diversity. In addition to the typical reading and answering questions, students were also engaged in peer work groups, simulations, and projects. High-level thinking was stressed, as were social skills and problem-solving skills. Students were conducting research and using a range of resource materials.

Summary

Up to the present, there have been two primary scope-and-sequence proposals for elementary school social studies. The first proposal came in 1905 when the American Historical Association's "Committee of Eight" recommended the "heroes-holidays-history" curriculum. Then, in 1963, Paul Hanna proposed the "expanding environments" model. Interestingly, both of these approaches can still be found in elementary school social studies curricula and in social studies textbooks. In spite of the many reform efforts over the last 100 years, it appears that few fundamental changes have occurred in the social studies curriculum used by most elementary school teachers and students. However, these two scope-and-sequence proposals have both had the power to endure, and in many ways, the "Committee of Eight" and Paul Hanna defined between them what we today know as elementary social studies education.

CURRENT ISSUES AND TRENDS

During the 1980s and the early 1990s, talk of school reform, school restructuring, and curriculum reconstruction reached new levels of intensity. Today, there are many voices in the social studies reform movement and, needless to say, many controversies. Some of today's issues are the unresolved issues of the past, cloaked in modern garb. Some issues are new, however, a function of the changing society or of new ways of thinking about children and schooling. Many of the ideas being proposed now have been heard before; some have even been heard many times before.

Speaking to the issue of elementary school social studies are national reports, state frameworks, and numerous independent voices representing a range of perspectives about the "best" ideas for the field. In this section of the chapter, we will begin with a discussion of the national dialogue on elementary social studies; in particular, the discussion will focus on the reports of two national commissions, the Bradley Commission on History in Schools and the National Commission on Social Studies in the Schools. In addition, the pivotal state frameworks and other voices of reform will be highlighted. Finally, the discussion will turn to identifying the major issues facing elementary school social studies today. Alternative perspectives on these issues will be presented.

National Reform Reports

The two major national reform reports, that of the Bradley Commission on History in Schools (1988) and that of the National Commission on Social Studies in the Schools (1989), were responses to widespread concern over the inadequacy of student knowledge and skill in social studies. For example, student performance on the history and geography items of the 1988 National Assessment of Educational Progress (NAEP) indicated only superficial understanding of important ideas and skills. Fourth graders, for instance, appeared to know basic historical facts of the type that could be learned from everyday experience, such as the names of certain key figures in United States history, but they showed few signs of any in-depth understanding of the issues associated with these persons. Eighth graders also demonstrated less than in-depth understanding of topics and issues; for example, eighty-four percent appeared to know how Abraham Lincoln died, but only one-fourth knew what Lincoln's objective was in the Civil War (Educational Testing Service 1990: 8).

The Bradley Commission on History in Schools was created in 1987, bringing together seventeen scholars and classroom teachers for a twofold purpose: (1) to explore the conditions that contribute to or impede the effective teaching of history in American schools, kindergarten through grade 12; and (2) to make recommendations on the curricular role of history and on how all of those concerned—teachers, students, parents, school administrators, university professors, publishers, and boards of education—might improve the teaching of history as the core of social studies in schools (Bradley Commission 1988: 2).

The commission's expressed rationale for the study of history is grounded in the need, in a democracy, for all citizens to "reach an understanding of ourselves and of our society, in relation to the human

condition over time, and of how some things change and others continue"
(5). "An historical grasp of our common political vision is essential to
liberty, equality, and justice in our multicultural society" (6).

The Bradley Commission made nine recommendations, each fully developed not only by a rationale, but also by specific implementation proposals. The commission recommended that the study of history should
focus on broad, significant themes and questions rather than on the short-
lived memorization of facts; the curricular time given to historical study
should be increased at all levels of schooling; the K–6 social studies
program should be history-centered; every student should have an understanding of the world that encompasses the historical experiences of
peoples of Africa, the Americas, Asia, and Europe; and, because history
can best be understood when the roles of all constituent parts of society
are included, that the experiences of women, racial and ethnic minorities,
and people of all classes and conditions should be represented (7–8).

Criticizing current elementary school social studies programs, the commission proposed three curricular patterns that would fulfill its recommendations and would result in imaginative and meaningful programs for
children. It also strongly recommended the use of literature and biography
to add interest and enrichment to the elementary school program.

Finally, the Bradley Commission tried to clarify its conception of history, that is, as interdisciplinary and complex, not merely a litany of
names, dates, and heroes. History, declared the Commission, is interpretation, and there are often several different viewpoints on any given
event or issue. In order to truly understand a particular event or issue,
one must look at it from the perspectives of the various participants.

The report of the National Commission on Social Studies in the Schools
(1989), *Charting a Course: Social Studies for the 21st Century,* was a
joint project of the American Historical Association, the Carnegie Foundation for the Advancement of Teaching, the National Council for the
Social Studies, and the Organization of American Historians. The goal of
the commission was to rally these forces into a coalition that would formulate and enunciate a coherent vision of the social studies' role in the
general education of young people. Such a vision needed to clarify what
it was that students should know and value in order to become responsible
citizens in a society characterized by increasing complexity, diversity,
and worldwide interdependence.

The Curriculum Task Force of the commission defined "social studies
as including history, geography, government and civics, economics, anthropology, sociology, psychology, as well as subject matter drawn from
the humanities (religion, literature and the arts)." According to the task
force, "social studies combines those fields and uses them in a direct way
to develop a systematic and interrelated study of people in societies, past
and present" (ix). The commission proposed five goals for social studies

and identified ten desirable characteristics of the social studies curriculum for the twenty-first century. A social studies program should enable students to develop "civic responsibility and active civic participation; perspectives on their own lives; a critical understanding of history and geography, and of the economic, political, and social institutions of the United States; an understanding of other peoples; and critical attitudes and analytical perspectives appropriate to the analysis of the human condition" (6).

For grades K–3, the commission described the characteristics of an improved social studies program, especially one with an enriched curriculum that could excite the interest and natural curiosity of young children. Citing problems with the superficiality of contemporary instruction, the commission urged that new curricula be well defined and relevant; use local, national, and global examples; develop multicultural perspectives in an authentic and culturally sensitive manner; frame all examples in temporal and spatial terms; balance examples drawn from the U.S. context with those of other countries; and integrate literature, art, and documents from primary sources into social studies programs (7–9).

The specific way in which these recommendations would lead to changes in the K–3 program, however, were left somewhat vague. The National Commission suggested that kindergarten children could study their own environment through neighborhood walks, and more remote environments through films and pictures. Student engagement and understanding could be enhanced by means of "songs, stories, pictures, artifacts, role-play, map-making, model-building, and similar classroom experiences" (8).

First graders, in their study of communities, "can understand that communities, past and present, local and worldwide, were developed to meet human needs for love and affection, for protection from natural and human dangers and for the production and dissemination of goods and services" (ibid.). It was suggested that "heroes and heroines" as well as "common people" be studied to provide role models for "emulation and admiration" (ibid.). Overall, the commission urged that the K–3 program have "coherence and balance" and that it be "sound and imaginative" (9). However, little detail about how this might be done was provided, and the specific examples given sound strikingly similar to the proposals made in 1905 by the "Committee of Eight" and in 1963 by Paul Hanna.

For grades 4–6, the commission proposed a more systematic exploration of historical time and place through three courses: United States history, world history, and geography. A broad sweep of United States history should occur in fourth grade, the commission proposed, "covering the entire range of national history in a captivating narrative approach, strongly aimed toward students' identification with signal figures and an appreciation of the symbolic, as well as historical, importance of key events" (26). A two-year sequence of world history and geography was proposed for grades 5 and 6, with courses that provided a "rich exposure to political, historical evolutions, to religious and cultural trends, and to the geographic factors in human life" (10–11, 26). In general, the commission felt that the aim at these grade levels should be to develop systematic global knowledge.

A two-year sequence was also proposed for grades 7 and 8: for grade 7 a course in local history, and for grade 8 a course in United States history. The United States history course would be organized chronologically, but it would be analytical in its emphasis, drawing on concepts from the various social sciences (11–14).

State Frameworks and Other Reform Voices

Leading the states in curricular reform, the California State Board of Education (1988) adopted its *History-Social Science Framework* in 1987. Today, several other states, including Michigan, Florida, New York, and Texas, are developing new guidelines for the total K–12 social studies curriculum. The California framework is organized around three broad goals: (1) democratic understanding and civic values, (2) knowledge and cultural understanding, and (3) skills attainment and social participation (11). "We want our students to understand the value, the importance, and the fragility of democratic institutions . . . to develop a keen sense of ethics and citizenship, and to care deeply about the quality of life in their community, their nation, and their world," declared the framework authors (2).

The California framework is built around seventeen distinguishing characteristics, but is centered in the chronological study of history. It proposes an integrated, correlated approach to the teaching of history-social sciences, emphasizing the importance of using literature and primary sources. Introducing a new, enriched program for the primary grades, the framework emphasizes the in-depth study of events and issues rather than the superficial skimming of survey data and incorporates a multicultural perspective, stressing the experiences and viewpoints of all peoples. The time spent on world history is extended to three years, in grades 6, 7, and 10. The framework urges the frequent study and discussion of the fundamental principles embodied in the United States Constitution and the Bill of Rights, and it encourages teachers to present controversial issues honestly and accurately within their historical or contemporary context. The importance of religion in human history is acknowledged by the framework's authors. Finally, a variety of content-appropriate teaching methods that engage students actively in the learning process is endorsed (4–8).

The California framework also goes into considerable detail about its proposals for the course of study at each grade level. Besides this state framework and the two national commission reports, however, several individuals have published their own detailed blueprints for elementary school social studies in the twenty-first century. Among those who have made proposals and recommendations are R. Freeman Butts (1988), Shirley Engle and Anna Ochoa (1988), John Goodlad (1984), Greene (1988), and D. E. Purpel (1989).

The Engle and Ochoa (1988) critique and proposal for change is embodied in their book, *Education for Democratic Citizenship*. They believe that the "best hope for democracy lies . . . with the cultivation of citizens who, with open eyes and awareness of democratic values, have the facility to make intelligent political judgments related to controversial issues in our society" (5). A social studies curriculum that could achieve such a goal would be grounded in ideas similar to those of John Dewey (1922), namely, that in a democracy, learning has to do with the active involvement of students in problem solving, not merely their passive reception of information.

The Engle/Ochoa framework proposes an open-ended and problem-centered approach to social studies and specifies seven guidelines for an effective program: the curriculum would be highly selective, with a small number of topics or episodes to be studied in depth; these topics would be those with the greatest potential to encourage thinking; students would be continually urged to make judgments about the problematic situations; geography, history, and the social sciences would be treated as alternative sources of information; the curriculum would utilize a large fund of information from other disciplines, such as literature, art, and music; and the first-hand experiences of students and teachers would serve as sources of data (128–29).

When it comes to the application of their social studies approach to elementary school students, however, Engle and Ochoa seem to compromise their proposal by suggesting that elementary school "children are not sufficiently experienced to study in great depth comprehensive social problems . . . they should receive straight narrative history as told by knowledgeable elders or even as it is presented in textbooks. We hope, however, that the textbooks will be rich in detail . . . and that the emphasis on remembering a few facts . . . will be abandoned in favor of the sheer pleasure of hearing the story, as told by the historian, biographer, or historical novelist, in all of its vivid detail" (157–58). However, the authors also suggest that these students do indeed have cognitive powers, and they recommend the use of questioning and the analysis of alternative perspectives.

Up to this point, the discussion has focused on the primary reform proposals that address elementary school social studies. Now, we will turn to the fundamental issues facing the field today.

Major Contemporary Issues in Elementary Social Studies

Reformers tend to agree that social studies is the curricular area dedicated to the education of citizens in a democratic society. Beyond that, people often disagree about exactly what this education entails and about how to develop a curriculum that would achieve the goal of good citizenship. Interestingly, most of the debate over the last 100 years has not been about goals, but about the actual instructional means, the classroom practice, and above all, the content core of the social studies. Today, heated debate is occurring over *what* is being taught, *how* it is being taught, and how instruction is being *evaluated*. The following related issues will be briefly discussed:

- *What knowledge?* What should be the content core of elementary school social studies?
- *Whose knowledge?* Whose interpretation of the past and present should be included in elementary school social studies?
- *What form?* How should students interact with ideas and data?
- *What K–3 curriculum?* What is developmentally appropriate for primary school students?
- *What skills?* What should be the skill component of elementary school social studies?
- *How evaluated?* How should student learning and teacher performance be evaluated?

What knowledge? What should be the knowledge core of the elementary school social studies curriculum? Most social studies educators acknowledge that the field draws on material from history, the social sciences (anthropology, sociology, psychology, economics, geography, political science), and the humanities. The question that arises as a consequence of such interdisciplinarity is how to organize so much material into a coherent, meaningful sequence that can produce useful ideas about the social world for children.

There are three general answers to this question: (1) teach each "subject" as a separate course, (2) create a fused or integrated body of knowledge, or (3) create a core of topics or issues that determines the relevant knowledge to be taught. Each of these "solutions" has been tried in some form during the past century. The "structure of the disciplines" approach used from the 1960s to the 1980s treated each of the social sciences as a separate course, emphasizing the central concepts and inquiry processes of the academician. Engle and Ochoa (1988) favor structuring the curriculum around themes or issues (such as the environment, culture, or social problems), and then drawing on material from history and the social sciences that illuminates the theme.

The report of the National Commission on Social Studies in the Schools (1989) appears to recommend both separate and integrated courses. The proposal for the K–3 curriculum is vague, but it would seem to necessitate an integrated approach. However, three separate courses are proposed for grades 4–6: United States history, world history, and geography. Integrated courses are then proposed for the seventh and eighth grades, which would study the local community and the nation, respectively. There is little discussion in this report of the specific means by which this integration might be achieved.

The Bradley Commission report and the California framework, on the other hand, clearly state that the core of the social studies should be history. This is not the "old" history of facts, leaders, and wars but, rather, a social history, a history of all the people. Both reports build on the assumption that history is not only interdisciplinary by nature, but that it is also interpretive. In addition, these reports offer examples of how knowledge from the humanities and the social sciences can be integrated with the story of the past and present.

The issue of "what knowledge" also has to do with whether the emphasis is on factual or conceptual knowledge. Elementary school social studies has been criticized for stressing low-level facts in isolation from any meaningful context. This has been a particular problem in the upper elementary grades, where the dates and leaders of battles in United States history are often the focus. All contemporary reform efforts decry such practices, and all emphasize the need to develop knowledge meaningfully.

Whose knowledge? The social studies curriculum has long been criticized for being unidimensional, Eurocentric, and unrepresentative of the cultural diversity in this country and in the world. Today, perhaps the most serious issues facing the social studies field are those relating to the multicultural nature of society and to the curriculum's necessary provision of a full, accurate, and honest portrayal of the past and the present. If one believes that history is interpretive, then one must believe, as the Bradley Commission's report suggests, that the roles and perspectives of all constituent parts of society should be included in history/social studies instruction: namely, women as well as men, people of all ethnic/cultural/ religious groups, and people of all social classes.

In a democratic society, it is imperative that all citizens find themselves and their ancestors in the pages of history/social studies textbooks. Furthermore, most events and issues throughout history can be examined in multiple ways; these various perspectives can be explored by elementary students as they study any culture or time period. Students should also realize that as people interact with one another conflicts can and do arise. The story of the past or the present, as well as any topic associated with it, should be presented, even in the elementary school, with openness.

Students can better understand the viewpoints of participants in events through exposure to their actual voices (such as are found in the literature, music, art, and primary source documents of a given time period).

The importance of multicultural perspectives was almost totally ignored in the *National Commission's* report, and this was a serious oversight. We know that young children can easily develop stereotypical ideas about people who are different from themselves unless they are positively exposed to others and can interact with them. The social studies curriculum, committed to developing a sense of human dignity for all persons (according to the NCSS curriculum guidelines of 1979), must address the issues associated with cultural diversity. Today, those groups who were ignored, underrepresented, or misrepresented in the social studies curriculum of the past are demanding that changes be made, but only some of the reformers are listening.

What form? Traditionally, fifth-grade students have studied the history of many centuries in only a single year. That is, their social studies program typically begins with early life on the North American continent and continues up to the present day. Teachers using this survey approach can hardly expect students to learn more than superficial facts, and the national test data indicate that many students don't even learn those.

Each of the contemporary reform-oriented reports highlighted in this chapter has recommended in-depth study over the "broad sweep" approach. If students had a chance to spend some time exploring the multiple dimensions of an event, analyzing primary source documents, reading literature and/or singing the songs of a period, and ultimately assessing the relevant issues, perhaps they would actually retain what they had "learned." In addition, such an approach would promote critical thinking and problem solving (Newmann 1988).

What K–3 curriculum? Research on cognition, comprehension, and learning holds much promise for social studies educators who think that the time has come to improve the primary grades curriculum. Young children today have many direct and vicarious social experiences; their natural curiosity prompts them to want to "know more." And, today we know more about these experiences and processes; we also know more about the reading process, thanks to extensive research on reading and comprehension. Many educators believe that it is time to go beyond the mindless social studies curriculum of the past and create challenging learning experiences for young children.

What skills? The skills of reflective thinking, judgment, critical analysis, distinguishing fact from opinion, and decision making are promoted by all contemporary reformers. Again, the research literature (see Voss 1986) on such skills is mature enough to provide insights to social studies curriculum developers. For example, we know that such high-level skills are best developed in the context of meaningful knowledge, not of isolated facts. In addition, high-level thinking skills demand practice to ensure their transfer to other contexts.

How evaluated? There is a current movement to reform the traditional methods of evaluation, too. The old tests, measuring the retention of low-level factual data, do not meet the anticipated demands of the twenty-first century, when the workplace and the sociopolitical world will expect workers and citizens to think, to solve problems, and to express reasoned judgments. Major efforts are under way in both student and teacher assessment to bring the test instruments more in line with contemporary views of teaching and learning.

The space of a single chapter does not permit further exploration of the six questions discussed above, nor of other controversial issues. For example, how should the historical topic of religion be treated in elementary school social studies? What is meant by common societal and political values, and how should these be treated in the elementary school curriculum?

PROJECTIONS

Today, the peoples and nations of the world are interdependent in many ways: through trade of goods and services, through travel and cultural exchanges, through shared ideas and technologies, and through living with one another. The United States is, without a doubt, a culturally diverse nation; in many communities the idea of "minority groups" has little meaning, for yesterday's minorities are today's majorities. Many groups fought for political power, then for economic power; now, many are fighting for the power of their voices to be heard in the curriculum used to educate their children. Each of these battles is far from over; the ways the issues are addressed will influence the content and form of the elementary school social studies curriculum in the twenty-first century.

In a democracy, every citizen plays a part in the essential decision making of society. Today, there are complex issues that demand not only creative solutions, but also the commitment to be involved. A sound social studies program in the elementary school can do much to involve students in real-life decision-making dilemmas, including those faced by people in the past as well as more contemporary ones. In addition, young students can begin to understand how truly complex many issues are by identifying the alternative perspectives that can or could be taken on any issue. The elementary school is the place where children can learn that, in a democracy, people collaborate on problem resolution. We know from the research on cooperative learning that such collaboration is apt to foster both learning and a positive regard for other students (Sharan 1980; Slavin 1980).

The world of work is continuing to change; most students no longer go from school to jobs in factories; many will work with information and with people in jobs requiring not only thinking and judgment skills, but also respect for others, including people who are different from themselves. During the elementary years, there are many, many opportunities for the social studies curriculum to enhance the development of these skills and attitudes. Tomorrow's adults will need information-processing skills in order to sift through the data that bombard people daily.

In large part, it is because of technological advances that the world community has become so interdependent. Satellites and computer networks can give us the news in the Commonwealth of Independent States instantaneously. Most children today have had some experience with computers; however, the full impact of computers and other technological advances has yet to be felt in the elementary school social studies curriculum. Computers could bring a wealth of resources to the fingertips of students. For example, primary source texts and other reference materials can be stored in computers for easy retrieval, cross-referencing, and analysis. Computers already enable some students to prepare "new age" reports and documents, complete with visuals and graphics. The video-camcorder, now available in many schools, can be a valuable tool in the social studies classroom. Students can videotape interviews with community resource persons; they can tape and edit their field trips as well as one another's preparations for a play or panel discussion. Interactive videodisks open up new possibilities for student learning and for changing the ways in which students and teachers typically interact with one another. The possibilities are endless.

In this chapter, we have taken a brief journey through the past century of elementary school social studies. In many ways, it has been a time of "reform revisited." There have been many efforts to propose change but few to affect change. The elementary school social studies curriculum has essentially changed little since the mid–1960s. However, the societal world has certainly changed considerably since then, and the world of children has changed, too. Today, something else is also different: We know better. We know more about what children can do and what they like to do. The research base on teaching and learning is mature and useful. We now have more data on what children know and on how that has changed over the years. We also know more about the culture of schools and about educational leadership and change in schools.

We now know more about the past; historians and social scientists have provided us with more accurate and complete data on the full story of the past. We also know more about the views and activities of women and members of various socioeconomic and ethnic groups. We know enough to create a more honest and comprehensive social studies curriculum.

What better time than now to develop alternative curricular models for the elementary school that would more closely align the realities of the social studies classroom with the lofty goals the field professes?

REFERENCES

Akenson, James E. "The Expanding Environments and Elementary Education: A Critical Perspective." *Theory and Research in Social Education* 17 (1989): 33–52.

Alleman, Janet, and Cheryl Rosaen. "The Cognitive, Social-Emotional, and Moral Development Characteristics of Students: Basis for Elementary and Middle School Social Studies." In James P. Shaver, ed., *Handbook of Research on Social Studies Teaching and Learning*. New York: Macmillan, 1991.

American Historical Association. *The Study of History in Schools*. New York: Macmillan, 1899.

American Historical Association's Commission on the Social Studies. *Conclusions and Recommendations of the Commission*. New York: Charles Scribner's Sons, 1934.

Armento, Beverly. "Changing Conceptions of Research on the Teaching of Social Studies." In James P. Shaver, ed., *Handbook of Research on Social Studies Teaching and Learning*. New York: Macmillan, 1991.

Atwater, Virginia A., ed. *Elementary School Social Studies: Research as a Guide to Practice*. Washington, DC: National Council for the Social Studies, 1986.

Banks, James A. "Relevant Social Studies for Black Pupils." *Social Education* 33 (Jan. 1969): 66–69.

———. "Multicultural Education: Its Effect on Students' Racial and Gender Role Attitudes." In James P. Shaver, ed., *Handbook of Research on Social Studies Teaching and Learning*. New York: Macmillan, 1991.

Bradley Commission on History in Schools. *Building a History Curriculum: Guidelines for Teaching History in Schools*. Westlake, OH: National Council for History Education, 1988.

Bruner, Jerome. *The Process of Education*. Cambridge, MA: Harvard University Press, 1960.

Butts, R. Freeman. *The Morality of Democratic Citizenship: Goals for Civic Education in the Republic's Third Century*. Calabasas, CA: Center for Civic Education, 1988.

California State Board of Education. *History/Social Science Framework for California Public Schools: Kindergarten through Twelfth Grade*. Sacramento: California State Board of Education, 1988.

Cornbleth, Cathy. "Critical Thinking and Cognitive Processes." In W. Stanley, ed., *Review of Research in Social Studies Education: 1976–1983*. Washington, DC: National Council for the Social Studies, 1985, 11–63.

Dewey, John. *Democracy and Education*. New York: Macmillan, 1922.

Educational Testing Service. *The U.S. History Report Card*. Washington, DC: U.S. Department of Education, Office of Educational Research and Improvement, 1990.

Engle, Shirley H., and Anna S. Ochoa. *Education for Democratic Citizenship: Decision Making in the Social Studies*. New York: College Press, 1988.

Fancett, V. S., and Sheryl Hawke. "Instructional Practices in Social Studies." In *The Current State of Social Studies: A Report of Project SPAN*. Boulder, CO: Social Science Education Consortium, 1982.

Gagnon, Paul. "Why Study History?" *The Atlantic Monthly* (Nov. 1988): 43–80.

Gibson, Emily Fuller. "The Three D's: Distortion, Deletion, Denial." *Social Education* 33 (April 1969): 405–9.

Goodlad, John I. *A Place Called School: Prospects for the Future*. New York: McGraw-Hill, 1984.

Greene, Maxine. *The Dialectic of Freedom*. New York: Teachers College Press, 1988.

Gross, Richard. "The Status of the Social Studies in the Public Schools of the United States: Facts and Impressions of a National Survey." *Social Education* 40 (1976): 194–96.

Hanna, Paul R. "Revising the Social Studies: What is Needed?" *Social Education* 27 (April 1963): 190–96.

Harlan, Louis R. "Tell It Like It Was: Suggestions on Black History." *Social Education* 33 (April 1969): 390–95.

Hertzberg, Hazel Whitman. *Social Studies Reform: 1880–1980*. Boulder, CO: Social Science Education Consortium, 1981.

Larkins, A. G., M. Hawkins, and A. Gilmore. "Trivial and Noninformative Content of Elementary Social Studies: A Review of Primary Texts in Four Grades." *Theory and Research in Social Education* 15 (1987): 299–311.

Lybarger, Michael Bruce. "The Historiography of Social Studies: Retrospect, Circumspect, and Prospect." in James P. Shaver, ed., *Handbook of Research on Social Studies Teaching and Learning*. New York: Macmillan, 1991.

National Commission on Social Studies in the Schools. *Charting a Course: Social Studies for the 21st Century*. Joint Project of the American Historical Association, Carnegie Foundation for the Advancement of Teaching, National Council for the Social Studies, and the Organization of American Historians, Washington, DC: National Commission on Social Studies in the Schools, 1989.

National Education Association. *Report of the Committee of Ten on Secondary Social Studies*. Washington, DC: Government Printing Office, 1893.

National Education Association. *The Social Studies in Secondary Education*. Bulletin 28. Washington, DC: Government Printing Office, 1916.

Nevins, Allan. "American History for Americans." *New York Times Magazine* (May 3, 1942): 23–4.

Newmann, Fred M. *Higher Order Thinking in High School Social Studies: Analysis of Classrooms, Teachers, Students, and Leadership*. Madison: University of Wisconsin-Madison, National Center on Effective Secondary Schools, 1988.

Patrick, John J. *Social Studies Curriculum Materials: A Report of Project SPAN*. Boulder, CO: Social Science Education Consortium, 1982.

Price, Ray A., ed. *New Viewpoints in the Social Sciences*. Washington, DC: National Council for the Social Studies, 1958.

Purpel, D. E. *The Moral and Spiritual Crisis in Education: A Curriculum for Justice and Compassion in Education.* Westport, CT: Bergin and Garvey, 1989.

Ravitch, Diane. "Tot Sociology: What Happened to History in the Grade Schools?" *The Key Reporter* 53 (1987): 1–4.

Sharan, S. "Cooperative Learning in Small Groups: Recent Methods and Effects on Achievement, Attitudes, and Ethnic Relations." *Reviews of Educational Research* 50 (1980): 241–72.

Shaver, James P., O. L. Davis, and Suzanne W. Melburn. "The Status of Social Studies Education: Impressions from Three NSF Studies." *Social Education* 43 (1979): 150–53.

Slavin, R. E. "Cooperative Learning." *Review of Educational Research* 50 (1980): 315–42.

Stake, R. E., and J. A. Easley. *Case Studies in Science Education.* Washington, DC: National Science Foundation, 1978.

Stodolsky, Susan. *The Subject Matters: Classroom Activity in Math and Social Studies.* Chicago: University of Chicago Press, 1988.

The Social Studies in General Education: A Report of the Committee on General Education for the Commission on Secondary School Curriculum. New York: Appleton-Century, 1940.

Voss, James F. "Social Studies." In R. F. Dillan and R. J. Sternberg, eds., *Cognition and Instruction.* New York: Academic Press, 1986.

Vygotsky, Lev C. *Mind in Society: The Development of Higher Psychological Processes.* Cambridge, MA: Harvard University Press, 1978.

White, Jane. "Searching for Substantial Knowledge in Social Studies Texts." *Theory and Research in Social Education* 16 (1988): 115–40.

Wittrock, M. C. "Learning as a Generative Process." *Educational Psychologist* 11 (1974): 87–95.

―――. "The Cognitive Movement in Education." *Educational Psychologist* 13 (1978): 15–29.

3

A CENTURY OF SECONDARY SOCIAL STUDIES: LOOKING BACKWARD AND FORWARD

Don Bragaw

In 1932, Charles Beard defined an "ideologue" as one who "praised a perfection which he believes to exist here and now," and a "utopian" as one who "praises a perfection which is to exist." But in Beard's view, the one best able to understand civic instruction was to be identified as a "progressive": one who "combines elements of both." The progressive's "mental picture of the social order is only a partial mosaic, not a fixed and copper-riveted status quo, or utopia; and in that partial mosaic are elements of the existing arrangements of things, elements of things already in the process of formation, and elements of things deemed desirable and hoped for." Beard suggests that civic instruction (the key to social studies education) "is founded on the assumption that what we actually have to deal with in reality is a process, a changing order of things" (Beard 1932: 54–5). In at least two respects, social studies is best understood as a process. It is the subject in our schools that best helps students to understand what the "process" is that enables us both to be what we are and to become what we want to be, as individuals, as a nation, and as a member of the global community. But more to the point of this book is the very real idea that social studies, as a field of professional study and as a school subject, is constantly in the "process" of development.

This chapter will be concerned with that development, especially with the evolution of secondary school social studies programs over the twen-

tieth century. Current efforts to reform the field of social studies will also
be addressed, and finally, areas where greater emphasis may occur in the
future will be suggested.

REFLECTIONS

While not called "social studies" at the time of its birth, the social
studies program that exists in our secondary schools today was formally
instituted in 1893. The history of secondary social studies since that time
has tended to be one of uniformity and consistency; where there has been
change, it has tended to be sporadic and fleeting. What seems to be shown
by several research studies on social studies classrooms across the nation
is that they all look and act pretty much alike, a uniformity that has been
sustained over the past 100 years (Morrissett and Stevens 1971; Goodlad
1984; Shaver, Davis, and Helburn 1978).

There have been only a few major adjustments made to the secondary
social studies curriculum—the most significant one was probably the
change from requiring ancient and French/English history to modern European history initially and then to world history, which is still not always
required by state education agencies. Others would suggest that the most
major change, occurring sometime in the period 1920–1950, was the shift
of emphasis from history to the social sciences (Ravitch 1987). Social
studies at the ninth and twelfth grade levels have also been somewhat
modified over the years—these seem to be the most flexible grade levels—
but in the case of the twelfth grade, social studies are seldom required,
so change at that level is not a significant indicator. But all of these changes
are relative to the requirements (or mandates) for educational programs
instituted at the state level and to actual classroom practice. Both of these
factors are primary influences on the kinds of social studies programs that
exist.

A recent survey of state departments of education has revealed the
basic configuration of secondary social studies programs to be pretty much
the same as it has been since 1916 (*National Survey* 1991). The majority
of secondary school programs (i.e., seventh to twelfth grade) begin at the
middle school, or junior high school, level in grades seven to nine (some
middle grade programs start as early as the fifth and go only through the
eighth grade). Traditionally, these grades have a year of American history,
some geography or culture studies, and, at the ninth grade, civics (or
some other course in government, or a combined political science/eco-
nomics course), state studies, or culture studies. High school social studies (i.e., grades ten to twelve) follow the pattern initially established in
1893 and modified in 1899. Tenth graders most often study European or
world history (similar to college-level western civilization courses). American (*sic*) history became fairly well entrenched at the eleventh grade in

1916 and has remained at that level ever since. While the eighth grade United States history course was intended to "Americanize" (especially those not continuing on in school), the second exposure to United States history was a college preparatory course. In many states with a three-year social studies requirement, a fourth year (required by only two states) is encouraged and may be offered at the twelfth grade (or selected by students earlier, if their program allows). The fourth year of social studies frequently consists of a course in government, advanced-placement American or European history, a selection of social science courses, or an experimental program of some type.

Secondary schools throughout the nineteenth century were standardized for those students fortunate enough even to attend. If any "social studies" program existed in this century, it was a highly nationalistic and moralistic one, with history and civics emphasized in all schools and textbooks (Belok 1981; Elson 1964). In 1893, the first "social studies" goals-setting meeting was called by the National Education Association to determine what courses in history, civics, and economics would be needed by students for college admission. The rhetoric stressed citizenship, and citizenship meant the strict transmission of patriotic history and civics. A committee was appointed "to consider the teaching of History, Civil Government, and Political Economy in the schools" (Committee of Ten 1893). "Social studies" was not the term used at that time. The committee determined that civil government (except as it was interwoven with history) and political economy courses were probably best left to the colleges and universities. But the committee, which included both James Harvey Robinson (a leading revisionist historian of his day) and Woodrow Wilson (then a political scientist at Princeton), drew up the following secondary school program:

Grade   7: American History and Government
Grade   8: Greek and Roman History
Grade   9: French History
Grade 10: English History
Grade 11: American History
Grade 12: optional historical studies in depth.

This first major scope-and-sequence arrangement had enormous influence on the course of social studies education throughout this century, as it will probably continue to have in the next. Because the history profession was the first to organize itself (in 1884), it became the dominant force on these early committees concerned with secondary education. The historians, as was to be expected, designed a history program, which, while occasionally changing titles and grade levels, has remained the constant in, or core of, social studies programs up to today. The one-year sequences devoted to Greek, Roman, French, and English history have disappeared, their essence remaining in the present world history courses. (One recent set of reform recommendations has restored ancient history to a place of prominence in the California framework for history and the social sciences [*History-Social Science Framework* 1988]). The "Committee of Ten's" program was a professional educators' curriculum. Public opinion had a negligible impact on education at that point, and despite the fact that it was the National Education Association who had called the meeting, neither university academics nor primary and secondary school educators played a significant role. The 1893 recommendations in many ways reaffirmed what was already going on in the schools, which reflected the college and university sequence of studies.

In 1899, the American Historical Association appointed a committee both to investigate the status of history in the schools (this was the first task force actually to survey the schools) and to recommend a program of studies. As might be expected, the "Committee of Seven," like their 1893 colleagues, came up with a comprehensive history program, although French history (which had largely disappeared from the schools) was incorporated into a more general medieval and modern European history course to be taught at the tenth grade level. This was to be preceded by a year of ancient history and followed by a year each of English (*sic*) and American (*sic*) history. This particular report is notable for the amount of space that its authors devoted to the issues of methodology (primary sources, Socratic teaching, and a heavy emphasis on cause and effect) and of teacher preparation (through good, solid, liberal arts history courses [Committee of Seven 1899]).

It is interesting that the secondary (and elementary) school recommendations now being advanced (particularly in California) bear a striking resemblance to those made in the two earlier reports. One of the major debates raging today, which was not an issue at the earlier time, is over whether the curriculum should continue to reflect the Eurocentric emphasis (clearly evident in the 1890s and not too different in 1990) or should reflect a more multicultural perspective. The immigrants of the 1890s were to be assimilated into the culture, and that culture was white, Protestant, and Anglo-Saxon: those circumstances have had a powerful impact on American education throughout the entire twentieth century and may be the most sensitive and serious issue of our schools' social studies programs today. But it is important to recognize that the historical base for social studies, whatever its nature, was built before "social studies" came into being; with its power rooted in patriotism and nationalism, history, as the "queen" of the curriculum, remains firmly in control. Few in the social studies profession would dispute the importance of history; the critical debate today concerns how much of it is to be included in the total program and in what form.

The present secondary social studies curriculum has been around almost intact since 1916, when the National Education Association (NEA) tried again to bring about agreement on what schools should teach and children should learn. To this end, the NEA appointed a Commission on the Reorganization of the Secondary Curriculum, which became best known for producing the "Cardinal Principles"—a set of educational goals which were a reflection of the progressive movement and its recognition of the radically changed demographic, social, and economic nature of American society. Clearly enunciated as one of these cardinal principles was citizenship—not history or any other subject in the social sciences or humanities—and how students would be educated for their roles in a democratic society. While the previous commission reports had all singled out citizenship as a key goal of history instruction, it was not foremost; academic history was the focus, with citizenship a subsidiary concern.

Recognition of the changing society was evinced by the fact that this commission appointed a subcommittee on social studies (not history), which was charged with the task of recommending a scope and sequence that would reflect the changes. This committee's recommendations did not deviate greatly from those of the earlier commissions, for much of the historical emphasis was retained: American history at both the eighth and eleventh grade levels, European history at the tenth grade (becoming world history in the 1940–1950 decade, more like global history today), community civics at the ninth grade, and some type of geography at the seventh grade (Committee on Social Studies 1916).

This committee, dominated by professional educators and staff people who were familiar with actual school conditions, gave recognition to the growing power of the other social sciences, a factor indicated by both the ninth grade "community civics" course and the recommended course for the twelfth grade: "Problems of American Democracy." Both recommendations seemed clearly to recognize two salient notions: First, that as American society rapidly became an industrialized and increasingly urban one, its citizens were confronted with increasingly complex problems with which the social science components of social studies might lend some assistance. Second, the study of society (or social studies) focused on training citizens to make decisions about their lives—to help them deal with those complex problems. This potential ability to learn how to develop citizenship skills and thereby improve one's life was an outgrowth of pragmatism and its impact on educational thought through such people as John Dewey. Although not a member of the 1916 committee, Dewey's influence was strongly felt. (It is important to point out again, however, that twelfth grade social studies was not a requirement in any state; therefore, the recommended course did not have as great an impact as such a "problems" focus would have had at an earlier grade level.)

While the outbreak of war postponed the implementation of the committee's recommendations, they did become reality during the 1920s and 1930s, when the "Problems" course, for example, was given a major impetus by the efforts of Harold Rugg at Teachers College (Columbia University) to develop appropriate materials with which schools could implement the ninth and twelfth grade sequences. Another indirect outcome of the committee's work was the formation of a new professional association: the National Council for the Social Studies (NCSS)—which, for a long time, was singularly oriented toward secondary school programs and concerned with the broader aspects of citizenship.

The last major commission to have influenced the development of social studies was the American Historical Association's Commission on the Social Studies, which served from 1928 to 1934. While this commission made no scope-and-sequence recommendations and thus presumably had little or no impact on the curriculum as such (Hertzberg 1980; Jenness 1990; *James A. Michener* 1991), it nevertheless made a significant contribution by endorsing civic activism as a proper role for schools to play and social studies as probably the logical program in which to promote such activism. The commission's endorsement established a strong rationale for active citizenship, inspiring later educators to advocate greater participatory-type civics programs—a major emphasis that has been sustained by present-day social studies reformers. It would be a mistake, however, to assert that civic action programs—with the exception of a major project launched by Teacher's College in the 1950s—began to develop immediately. There is no evidence that such was the case, but it was due to such a rationale that one breed of social studies theorists emerged: the social reconstructionists. These theorists believe that the schools should be where students are trained to become social critics, learning how to actively improve society (Beard 1932; Commission 1935).

Up until the end of World War II, the secondary social studies curriculum remained what had been envisioned by the 1893, 1899, and 1916 commission reports: that is, a curriculum heavily oriented toward history, with some minor efforts to include a social science/civics orientation. It was not until the postwar and later periods that social science electives even began to be offered at the secondary level, and that was not a common feature of the curriculum. Even today, requirements in many states continue to be the three Carnegie units of social studies for grades nine to twelve: two of those are history, and one may be either geography or a government course of some type.

In the late 1970s, the Social Science Education Consortium conducted a major study of the status of social studies programs in the United States

(Project SPAN 1982). They discovered what most people already knew—there was a "national social studies curriculum," and its secondary school pattern looked like the following:

Grade 7: World Geography or History

Grade 8: American History

Grade 9: Civics, or World Culture

Grade 10: World History

Grade 11: American History

Grade 12: American Government.

Again, with regard to the twelfth grade course, the caveat is that "American Government" was primarily offered in school districts with elective programs; it was not (and still is not) a requirement in the vast majority of states, a few of which continue to require only two secondary social studies units for graduation.

If similar studies had been conducted in 1930, 1950, or 1970, the pattern would have looked the same. It can be said with some confidence that the same pattern has continued to prevail in the early 1990s—and, despite reforms, it will probably prevail in 2001. If one were to question why this is so, the reasons given would probably include the following: First, all nations expect their schools to inculcate the national heritage and the form of governance that dominates the nation; second, as with most social institutions, schools change slowly—they tend to be conservative in nature; third, social studies teachers (like teachers in general) seldom have the time or the opportunity to explore change (nor are they presently rewarded for doing so), and therefore, they tend to remain committed to the status quo; fourth, change to what? Even the most radical proposal for a "new" social studies scope and sequence, an NCSS effort of 1985–86, retained much of the "national" pattern described above—the objective was a totally different approach to its implementation (*Social Education* 1986). There appears to be an unshakable belief that history and geography are the core subjects for elementary and secondary school programs. All other disciplines as well as other configurations of knowledge (law-related, environmental or consumer education, etc.) are considered interesting but supplementary and, therefore, nonessential. From time to time, one of these other subjects may gain prominence for one reason or another, but that prominence is never sustained for long—especially in the face of budget-cutting and "back-to-basics" hysteria. Social studies—by name and by nature an integrative subject—especially secondary school social studies, remains a discipline-focused curriculum with little academic or societal propensity toward alternative syntheses of knowledge.

From the work of the various commissions and committees, and from the research of social studies educators over the years, several theories of what social studies education is, or should be, have emerged. According to one schema, those theories are subsumed under three major traditions: (1) social studies as citizenship or cultural transmission; (2) social studies as the interpretation of the social sciences for schools; and (3) social studies as reflective inquiry (Barr, Barth, and Shermis 1977).

The first tradition has translated into practice as the perpetuation of the "American" culture and tradition through transmitting information that supports and sustains the status quo in society. It has been suggested this tradition is signified by textbook and teacher-directed recitation methodologies and, pejoratively, that this tradition is best exemplified by chronologically oriented, fact-accumulation history and by "structure and function" government courses, with a minimum of social and behavioral science input.

The second tradition views people as behaving and interacting in the world—past and present—and this interaction is best interpreted by means of the various social sciences (including history, as a subject informed and empowered by the social sciences). This tradition, in a modified manner, may be best represented by Paul Hanna's (1963) "expanding environments" (or "horizons") model, which incorporates generalizations and concepts from the social sciences in a spiraling fashion, that is, students learn to understand the world first from their involvement with self and then with the increasingly larger worlds in which they live. This tradition has lasted the longest and been the most effective at the elementary level; except in rare elective courses, it has seldom found expression in secondary social studies.

The third tradition—that of reflective inquiry—posits the notion that students construct knowledge through constant involvement in the processes of investigating, organizing, and evaluating information. This may be translated as students' learning how to use the tools and assuming the role of the social scientist or historian. While this tradition has been embraced periodically over the years, its most significant impact occurred as part of the "New Social Studies" movement of the 1960s, when almost all projects entailed using primary source materials, case studies, data banks, and other information bases to involve students directly in their own learning.

CURRENT ISSUES AND TRENDS

Most of the change, or reform, in social studies today is occurring at the elementary level, and much of that effort is directed toward improving the base upon which the secondary school programs are built: that is, restoring history and geography to dominant positions in the K–6 grades and downplaying the social sciences or other content arrangements (such as Paul Hanna's "expanding environments" concept). Reform efforts at the secondary level have been directed toward improving the instructional delivery of history, geography, and government and toward instituting accountability measures that will establish whether or not students are meeting whatever standard has been set. Despite efforts to "track" or "group" students in less vigorous programs, the orientation of curriculum design for secondary school social studies remains that of college preparation—just as it was in 1893. The fundamental objective is the transmission of cultural knowledge (and less emphasis on the social construction of knowledge), and the two dominant modes of delivery are those practiced in the university: reading of texts and lectures (Wilen and White 1991; Ehman and Glenn 1991; Clegg 1991; Winitzky 1991). If there is any innovation, it lies in the area of citizenship—the extension of the school into forms of community action; but even that is not widespread, being more often accepted than adopted (Conrad 1991; Bragaw 1991).

One major effort to reform the delivery of social studies education that was primarily focused on the secondary program was the "New Social Studies" (NSS) projects of the 1960s and early 1970s. Financed almost entirely through government funding (National Science Foundation) and directed by university academics, each of the projects concentrated on one or another of the social science disciplines. While failing to involve classroom teachers in the development process, the projects in geography, history, anthropology, and so forth were presented in what was referred to as "teacher proof" form, ready to be implemented. All that the teachers needed to do was deliver the canned material to their students for instant successful learning (Fenton 1981, 1991; Haas 1977; Hertzberg 1981).

While generally rejected by the majority of teachers, the projects of the Sixties nevertheless contributed greatly to advancing the idea of teaching critical thinking through a variety of inquiry-and-discovery learning strategies, something which has only lately received widespread endorsement, but still limited implementation, in social studies (and other curricular areas). The other major contribution of these projects to the field of social studies was their emphasis on concepts and generalizations, thus bringing to the fore the need for teachers and students to concentrate on the "big ideas" rather than compiling and memorizing facts in isolation. Present day reform efforts focus on "depth" rather than "breadth" studies, which when translated into programs essentially means trying to intellectually grapple with major ideas—concepts and hypotheses that need to be tested and tried.

The NSS projects asked students to learn the investigative methods used by practitioners of the disciplines involved. The case studies, simulations, and problem-solving or decision-making exercises of such projects as the High School Geography Project, the Sociological Resources

Project, the Harvard Public Issues Project (the most successful and enduring of the projects), the Amherst and Carnegie Mellon History Projects, and the Georgia Anthropology Project were all conducive to critical and creative thinking and were keyed to "big ideas." The major problem with these projects was that teachers were treated as conduits, rather than as key participants in the process of student learning. Many assumptions were also made about the ability of teachers to conduct classroom inquiry operations, but perhaps the largest barrier to implementing these strategies was time: teachers felt hard-pressed to "cover" the course material as prescribed by state guidelines and by their own perceptions of what was needed by students. Furthermore, whatever teachers do not intellectually and emotionally own they cannot and will not seriously incorporate in their teaching repertoire.

After a brief spurt of successful school tryouts, publisher implementation efforts, and extensive explication in the pages of *Social Education,* the projects of the Sixties faded into obscurity, and textbook, teacher-directed recitations and lectures returned with a vengeance to the secondary social studies classroom. Some would have it that such traditional modes never left the classroom, even for a moment, and still prevail today. However, besides the delayed impact of the projects' emphasis on critical thinking in the classroom, they also influenced textbooks. Specific "Thinking" questions or sections began to appear with regularity in texts, and end-of-chapter and unit assignments frequently incorporated modified inquiry approaches (Haas 1977; Fenton 1991; Jenness 1990).

The enormous changes occurring in the United States during the 1960s with regard to civil rights, the women's movement, and especially the conflict in Vietnam, were further magnified by the successive assassinations of President John F. Kennedy, Martin Luther King, Jr., and Senator Robert Kennedy. The social studies community responded by calling for a greater emphasis on social issues. The pages of *Social Education,* the official journal of the National Council for the Social Studies, were full of articles proposing various approaches to social problems. But as with other ideas, the emphasis on social issues also had but a brief existence: it wasn't easily "textbookable" and, therefore, not easily adapted to the courses being taught. History was not perceived as a problem- or issue-focused subject.

These events, followed by the debacle of Watergate, which brought about a president's resignation, and problems associated with drugs and the presumed excesses of the sexual revolution, ignited a conservative reaction in the mid-1970s. Beginning with a call to return to the solidity of a history and geography curriculum, this reaction intensified during the 1980s with the election of conservative national administrations and the consequent appointment of similarly minded education secretaries. The social studies field found itself swept up in another movement to return to the "Golden Age," when the United States was great and powerful, and its glorious history dominated the classroom (Ravitch 1987; Weisberger 1987).

In an attempt to begin a rational discussion about the nature of social studies, in 1984 the National Council for the Social Studies (the professional educators) initiated a scope-and-sequence project in which the various perspectives on the nature of social studies education, K–12, would be explored (*Social Education* 1986, Task Force 1984). There were a total of six alternatives offered. Two of these were semi-radical, organized around the problem solving and critical societal analysis reminiscent of the 1916 committee's "Problems" course and the 1934 commission's social action approach. Two alternatives retained much of the "national" curriculum, although one strongly recommended that teachers be empowered to make the ultimate decisions as to where the emphasis would be placed and what methodologies would be used. Only two of the alternatives challenged the content organization of the prevailing social studies curriculum, but both presaged the "reform" movements in social studies of the late 1980s and the early 1990s. One secondary history-oriented curriculum proposed the following sequence:

Grade 7: World History: Early Industrial and Modern History

Grade 8: United States History, 1789–1914

Grade 9: Community Civics

Grade 10: The World in the Twentieth Century

Grade 11: The United States in the Twentieth Century

Grade 12: United States Citizenship in the Modern World.

This secondary social studies program was to be based on an elementary program covering the earlier historical periods. The social sciences were to empower these history courses with their concepts and suggestive generalizations. The second alternative that deviated from the norm emphasized a global systems approach based on five major conceptual themes (interdependence, change, culture, scarcity, and conflict), but retained the history and geography basics:

Grade 7: Major Global Systems

Grade 8: Human Values: Western Civilization focus

Grade 9: Global History

Grade 10: United States History in Global Perspective

Grade 11: Global Political Organizations and Policies

Grade 12: Application of previous learning to Global Problems.

The spirit of these two recommended programs was to be captured by the latest commissions convened to suggest a direction for social studies education. Both the Bradley Commission on History in Schools (1988), composed only of historians, and the National Commission on Social Studies in the Schools (1989), dominated by historians, determined that history and geography constituted the core of the future as well as the past. The Bradley Commission, decrying a perceived lack of emphasis on history in the public schools, proposed essentially the same design as the history scope-and-sequence recommendation described above—early history at the elementary level and modern history at the secondary. The Bradley Commission also recommended six "vital themes" to guide teacher selection of content:

Civilization, cultural diffusion, and innovation;

Human interaction with the environment;

Values, beliefs, political ideas, and institutions;

Conflict and cooperation;

Comparative history of major developments;

Patterns of social and political interaction.

These themes reflect a social studies model that incorporates the social sciences, major concepts, and significant social, political, and economic issues. It is somewhat extraordinary that this commission endorsed a great deal of the "new history" of the turn of the century, the issues orientation of the 1916 and 1934 commissions, and the conceptual themes and designs promoted by both historians and social scientists in the 1960s and 1970s. (While not totally incorporated into the new California *History-Social Science Framework* [1988], that state's full commitment to a historical core with a strong geographic base for social studies at least encourages many of the same worthy goals for which social studies strives.)

While not going the conceptual-theme route, the National Commission on Social Studies in the Schools Curriculum Task Force report, *Charting a Course,* emphasizes history from the kindergarten level through grade twelve and makes a provocative recommendation for a three-year global history sequence (in grades 9–11) with which the United States experience would be interwoven. The remainder of the report mainly reinforces previous commissions' history recommendations. The goals defined by this commission, which stressed civic responsibility and active civic participation, as well as cultural diversity and critical thinking, were never fully realized (National Commission 1989).

Both of these commission reports have yet to prove whether they have any more power to bring about change than those of the other commissions since 1916. Both commissions, however, did react to what they believed was a broad field of studies that de-emphasized history in favor of the social sciences. As Will Cartwright and Richard Watson, Jr., pointed out in 1973, during another period of history's de-emphasis,

A relative de-emphasis on history is necessary in order to make room for other social studies that are needed by individuals and society. In part, however, the deemphasis is the fault of historians who have not come to a vigorous defense of their subject, of teachers who have not developed skills in relating the present to the past and both to the future, and of "new curriculum" makers who have fallen victim to a recurrence of presentism. (Cartwright and Watson 1973:33)

The commentary is familiar and has been repeated throughout the past fifty or more years. Since the late 1940s, there has been a *New York Times* survey of student knowledge of American history dates, events, and people every twenty years or so. The results always prove that the students are not learning their American history—and that is enough to set off another round of "de-emphasis of history" hysteria, which brings on another surge of social-science bashing and pro-history fervor. A new round of curriculum reform usually results, with the same lack of long-term results. No commission since that of 1916 has had any major effect on social studies programs in the schools: viewing state social studies syllabi reveals how stable the 1893–1899–1916 curriculum remained. Neither the curriculum nor the instruction with which it was implemented changed. While society has experienced many changes since 1893 and again since 1916, these have not always been reflected in school social studies programs. University academicians quickly lose interest in the public schools and return to their research and teaching, not to emerge again until a new outcry against the de-emphasis of history is raised.

The Bradley Commission, with substantial foundation support, formed a history association, sought to influence state education officials, and generally made its members available for presentations. Major funding was provided by the federal government for a history reeducation center at UCLA where teachers could be retrained in new modes of instruction. These strategies for change have had their predecessors, and it remains questionable whether this time they will work. More promising are the "Teacher Alliances" instituted by geographers, the NCSS, and the historical associations in order to encourage cooperative content institutes and an ongoing relationship between a university history or geography department and social studies teachers in the local school system. Again, however, unless interest is sustained through sincere collaboration between the university faculty (who are seldom rewarded for such efforts) and the public school teachers (also usually only self-rewarded), the alliance effort may not prove successful. Despite the huge sums of money invested by the National Geographic Society in geographic alliances, these began to falter and some have since fallen on hard times—proving again that money is not enough, but it is certainly an incentive.

PROJECTIONS

Despite major advances in learning theory, and some in methodology as well, (particularly in cooperative strategies), secondary social studies remains in a static condition. Individual teachers and programs across the country try and often succeed in making social studies classes interesting, but the evidence continues to be overwhelmingly indicative of no real change in either content or methodology, nor does any change seem likely to occur in the near future (Shaver, Davis, and Helburn 1978). Until the culture of the schools encourages and rewards methodological improvement, especially in terms of student-focused learning strategies, those changes will not come easily (Lieberman 1988). The school and teacher-education reform efforts of Sizer (1991) and Goodlad (1984, 1990), among others, each of which is potentially significant for secondary social studies, have yet to make major inroads into schools and colleges. Recent research by Newmann (1991) reiterates the findings of 1970s research, showing that secondary social studies classes remain lecture- and text-oriented and still reflect a content organization very similar to that of 1916. Recent social studies reform reports offer little that is new; what they offer is a rearrangement of content—sometimes provocative. Most reform efforts are directed toward strengthening history content and instruction. There is, however, little to suggest that even these changes will reach into the classrooms of Pocatello, Paducah, or Peoria. Educational inertia and economic realties do not portend change. The brightest prospect lies in the middle school movement toward greater program flexibility and greater awareness of the need to match method to student profile. But that movement shows signs of foundering on budgetary inadequacy, state requirements, and accountability measures that run counter to the movement's goals.

In a 1991 end-of-the-year television program, Stephen Jay Gould, paleontologist extraordinaire, was questioned about how he saw the world changing, namely, for the better or for the worse. His prescient comment was that, over the long haul, the only certainty was unpredictability. Recent global and domestic events underscore the acuteness of that observation over a "shorter haul" than paleontologists usually consider. There is a need to evaluate how school programs in general (and ideas about reform and restructuring abound) and, perhaps, social studies in particular can best help students learn to deal more realistically with that unpredictability—the increasingly problematic nature of our existence demands it. It suggests that social studies programs need to emphasize critical thinking, that is, problem solving and decision making—whether in history, the social sciences, or any of the other combinations of knowledge called social studies (Newmann 1991). The wider acceptance of the need to teach critical thinking as an educational priority suggests that its short-term future, at least, is relatively assured. In all content areas, that priority entails in-depth studies, not the continued launching of canoe trips across huge oceans of time. That poses a major challenge for secondary social studies professionals, who must make decisions about what should or should not be "covered." We have been reminded of "the futility of trying to teach everything" (Wiggins 1986), but "everything" continues to be the goal of social studies: an objective that has carried, and continues to carry, its own genes of destruction. The search for different syntheses of content that is of the "most social worth" is but an embryonic educational enterprise which is difficult for even the social studies gurus to accept (Cherryholmes 1991; Bernstein 1976).

The computer revolution is still but a small ripple in the educational process. It promises, however, to fulfill one of the longtime goals of social studies education: uniting student minds with information in a truly symbiotic relationship. The advent of computerized data banks makes possible a more systematic implementation of a wider variety of inquiry-discovery types of learning strategies for social studies. Such banks have the potential to make the full resources of masses of raw data (demographic and other statistical data, biographical information, encyclopedia articles, the library, including the Library of Congress) accessible to students for use in an investigatory mode of inquiry. Full realization of this potential will, perhaps, eliminate the need for ponderous and bland textbooks, as they are now constituted and used. The future is clouded, however, by the difficulty of supplying schools with adequate technology, which depends on adequate budgets to support the enterprise.

The unpredictability of our existence also suggests that developing an increased sense of social consciousness and responsibility will be an important direction for the future. Environmental, social, and economic causes of societal dysfunction—often on a global scale—have become a critical focus for social studies programs, not just to encourage more intelligent voting, but also to increase the active participation of students in community service of some kind. With the passage of the National Service law, this type of school-community tie will be encouraged, and a return to citizenship programs in the public interest may well follow. Recent research supports the notion that such participation in community service does increase students' sense of responsibility (Conrad 1991).

The endorsement of greater global awareness, of the interdependency of the peoples of the world, in many of the current educational reform recommendations would seem to portend that global emphases in social studies will not fade quickly from the scene, despite evidence of increased nationalistic tendencies. This global consciousness is also evident in the educational and public debates over "multiculturalism." Rather than encouraging "balkanization," as envisioned by Arthur Schlesinger, Jr. (1991), the arguments over multiculturalism will, as with all new ideas, become more rational, and "multi-civility" will triumph once the educational community has found ways of discussing and expressing the universal needs of all races and ethnic groups. The national history and ethos—essential to maintaining national identity—should not be so rigidly constructed that it cannot incorporate the heritage of all those who contributed to that national identity. The question then becomes: How can this be done? More research on and practice in cooperative modes of learning, which can often more easily accommodate different learning styles and thereby reduce racial and ethnic tensions, are needed to develop these promising methodologies. Cooperative learning also fulfills several major goals of social studies: increasingly democratic social behavior, acceptance of diversity as a normal social condition, and recognition of the worth of individuals—both separately and in community. Making course content more multicultural does not require eliminating the European heritage.

Secondary social studies remains discipline-centered, just as the universities do, and continues to influence the upper elementary grades with that same focus. While suggesting that history is both interdisciplinary and interpretive, present teacher preparation gives too little recognition to either perspective. No amount of funding for training institutes will solve the basic inadequacies of teacher training, of liberal arts courses that are not effectively encouraging students to reflect on their learning and to make connections between and among bits of information. The conceptual power of learning cannot be realized when those who purvey information cannot themselves see, or help others to see, the conceptual linkages.

Charles Beard's (1932) idea of process truly reflects the history of social studies education. The process, however, is a slow one. What changes do occur tend to be generated outside the field—by commissions, committees, and critics. The process is a civic one, with public and professionals alike engaged in a constant search for a vision of citizenship that is compatible with the times. Citizenship was the emphasis of the 1916 Committee on Social Studies, as it was of Charles Beard, and as it is of Shirley Engle. As long as it remains the vision, secondary social studies will be vital and relevant to the world in which we live.

REFERENCES

Allen, Jack, ed. *Education in the '80's: Social Studies*. Washington, DC: National Education Association, 1981.

Barr, Robert D., James L. Barth, and S. Samuel Shermis. *Defining the Social Studies*. Washington, DC: National Council for the Social Studies, 1977.

Beard, Charles A. *A Charter for the Social Sciences*. New York: Charles Scribner's Sons, 1932.

Belok, David. "Schoolbooks, Pedagogy Books, and the Political Socialization of Young Americans." *Educational Studies* 12:1 (1981): 35–47.

Bernstein, R. J. *The Reconstruction of Social and Political Theory*. Philadelphia: University of Pennsylvania Press, 1976.

Bradley Commission on History in Schools. *Building a History Curriculum: Guidelines for Teaching History in Schools*. Washington, DC: Educational Excellence Network, 1988.

Bragaw, Donald H. "Scope and Sequence: Alternatives for Social Studies: Introduction." Special issue of *Social Education* 50:7 (November/December 1986): 484–85.

———. "Expanding Social Studies to Encompass the Public Interest." *Bulletin* (National Association of Secondary School Principals) 75 (January 1991): 25–31.

Cartwright, W. H., and R. L. Watson, Jr., eds. *The Reinterpretation of American History and Culture*. Washington, DC: National Council for the Social Studies, 1973.

Cherryholmes, Cleo H. "Critical Research and Social Studies Education." In James P. Shaver, ed., *Handbook of Research on Social Studies Teaching and Learning*. New York: Macmillan 1991.

Clegg, A. A., Jr. "Games and Simulations in Social Studies Education." In James P. Shaver, ed., *Handbook of Research on Social Studies Teaching and Learning*. New York: Macmillan 1991.

Commission on the Social Studies. *Conclusions and Recommendations of the Commission*. New York: Charles Scribner's Sons, 1935.

Committee of Seven. *The Study of History in the Schools*. New York: Macmillan, 1899.

Committee of Ten. "History, Civil Government, and Political Economy." *Report of the Committee of Ten on Secondary School Subjects*. Washington, DC: National Education Association, 1893.

Committee on Social Studies. *The Social Studies in Secondary Education*. Bulletin No. 28. Washington, DC: Government Printing Office, 1916.

Conrad, Dan. "School-Community Participation for Social Studies." In James P. Shaver, ed., *Handbook of Research on Social Studies Teaching and Learning*. New York: Macmillan 1991.

Educational Testing Service. *The U.S. History Report Card*. Washington DC: U.S. Department of Education, Office of Educational Research and Improvement, 1990.

Ehman, L. H., and A. D. Glenn. "Interactive Technology in Social Studies." In James P. Shaver, ed., *Handbook of Research on Social Studies Teaching and Learning*. New York: Macmillan 1991.

Elson, Ruth Miller. *Guardians of Tradition: American Schoolbooks of the Nineteenth Century*. Lincoln: University of Nebraska Press, 1964.

Engle, S. H., and A. S. Ochoa. *Education for Democratic Citizenship: Decision Making in the Social Studies*. New York: Teacher's College Press, 1988.

Fenton, Edwin. "What Happened to the New Social Studies: A Case Study in Curriculum Reform." Unpublished manuscript, 1981.
——— "Reflections on the New Social Studies." *The Social Studies* 82:3 (1991): 84–90.
Goodlad, J. I. *A Place Called School.* New York: McGraw-Hill, 1984.
———. *Teachers for Our Nation's Schools.* San Francisco: Jossey-Bass, 1990.
Goodlad, J. I., R. Soder, and K. A. Sirotnik, eds. *Places Where Teachers Are Taught.* San Francisco: Jossey-Bass, 1990.
Gutmann, A. *Democratic Education.* Princeton, NJ: Princeton University Press, 1987.
Haas, John D. *The Era of the New Social Studies.* Boulder, CO: Social Science Education Consortium, 1977.
Hanna, Paul R. *Assuring Quality for the Social Studies in Our Schools.* Stanford, CA: Hoover Institution Press, 1987.
———. "Revising the Social Studies: What is Needed?" *Social Education.* 27 (April 1963): 190–96.
Hertzberg, H. W. "The Teaching of History." In M. Kammen, ed., *The Past before Us: Contemporary Historical Writing in the United States.* Ithaca, NY: Cornell University Press, 1980.
———. *Social Studies Reform, 1880–1980.* Boulder, CO: Social Science Education Consortium, 1981.
History-Social Science Framework. Sacramento, CA: California State Department of Education, 1988.
James A. Michener on the Social Studies. Bulletin 85. Washington, DC: National Council for the Social Studies, 1991.
Jarolimek, John, ed. "The Status of Social Studies Education: Six Case Studies." *Social Education* 44 (November-December 1977): 574–601.
Jenness, David. *Making Sense of Social Studies.* New York: Macmillan, 1990.
Johnson, Henry. *An Introduction to the History of the Social Sciences.* Report of the Commission on the Social Studies. New York: Charles Scribner's Sons, 1932.
Lieberman, A., ed. *Building a Professional Culture in Schools.* New York: Teacher's College Press, 1988.
Longstreet, W. "The Social Studies: In Search of an Epistemology." *The Social Studies* 81:6 (1990): 244–48.
Lybarger, Michael. "The Historiography of Social Studies: Retrospect, Circumspect and Prospect." In James P. Shaver, ed., *Handbook of Research on Social Studies Teaching and Learning.* New York: Macmillan, 1991.
Mehlinger, H. D. "Social Studies: Some Gulfs and Priorities." In H. D. Mehlinger and O. L. Davis, Jr., eds., *The Social Studies.* 80th Yearbook of the National Society for the Study of Education. Chicago: National Society for the Study of Education, 1981.
Morrissett, I., and W. W. Stevens, Jr. *Social Science in the Schools: A Search for Rationale.* New York: Holt, Rinehart and Winston, 1971.
National Commission on Social Studies in the Schools. *Charting a Course: Social Studies for the 21st Century.* Washington, DC: National Commission for Social Studies in the Schools, 1989.
National Survey of Course Offerings and Testing in Social Studies, Kindergarten–

Grade 12. Washington, DC: The Council of State Social Studies Specialists, 1991.

Nelson, M. R. "The Rugg Brothers and Social Education." In V. A. Atwood, ed., *Historical Foundations of Social Studies. Journal of Thought* 17:3 (Fall 1982): 27–36.

Newmann, Fred M. "Promoting Higher Order Thinking in Social Studies: Overview of a Study of Sixteen High School Departments." *Theory and Research in Social Education* XIX:4 (1991): 324–40.

Olson, L. "Sizer Outlines Triumphs, Travails of 'Horace's School' in New Book." *Education Week* XI:15 (December 15, 1991): 3–4.

Parker, W. C. *Renewing the Social Studies Curriculum*. Alexandria, VA: Association for Supervision and Curriculum Development, 1991.

Project SPAN Staff and Consultants. *The Current State of Social Studies: A Report of Project SPAN*. Boulder, CO: Social Science Education Consortium, 1982.

Ravitch, D. "Tot Sociology: Or What Happened to History in the Grade Schools?" *American Scholar* 56 (Summer 1987): 343–54.

Schlesinger, A. M., Jr. *The Disuniting of America: Reflections on a Multicultural Society*. New York: Whittle Books, 1991.

Schwartz, B. "Social Change and Collective Memory." *American Sociological Review* 56:2 (1991): 221–36.

Shaver, J. P., O. L. Davis, Jr., and S. W. Helburn. *An Interpretive Report on the Status of Pre-Collegiate Social Studies Education Based on Three NSF-Funded Studies* (Report to the National Science Foundation). Washington, DC: National Council for the Social Studies, 1978. (ERIC Document Reproduction Service No. ED 164 363.)

Sizer, Theodore. *Horace's Compromise*. Boston: Houghton Mifflin, 1984

———. *Horace's School: Redesigning the American High School*. Boston: Houghton Mifflin, 1992.

Social Education 44 (October 1980): cover.

Social Education. Special issues on Scope and Sequence: Alternatives for Social Studies. 50 (November/December 1986): 484–542.

Task Force on Scope and Sequence. "In Search of a Scope and Sequence for Social Studies," 48 (April 1984): 249–73.

The United States Prepares for Its Future: Global Perspectives in Education. Report of the Study Commission on Global Education. New York: Global Perspectives in Education, 1987.

Weisberger, B. A. "American History Is Falling Down." *American Heritage* (February-March 1987): 26–32 (Reprint).

Wiggins, Grant. "The Futility of Trying to Teach Everything of Importance." *Educational Leadership* (47 November 1989): 44–8, 57–9.

Wilen, W. W., and J. J. White. "Interaction and Discourse in Social Studies Classrooms." In James P. Shaver, ed., *Handbook of Research on Social Studies Teaching and Learning*. New York: Macmillan, 1991.

Wiley, K. B., with J. Race. *The Status of Pre-College Science, Mathematics, and Social Science Education: 1955–1975*. Vol. 3, *Social Science Education*. Boulder, CO: Social Science Education Consortium, 1982.

Winitzky, N. E. "Classroom Organization for Social Studies." In James P.

Shaver, ed., *Handbook of Research on Social Studies Teaching and Learning*. New York: Macmillan, 1991.

Wronski, S. P. "Edgar Bruce Wesley: His Contributions to the Past, Present and Future of Social Studies Education." In V. A. Atwood, ed., *Foundations of Social Studies Education. Journal of Thought* 17:3 (Fall 1982): 51–57.

Wronski, S. P., and D. H. Bragaw, eds. *Social Studies and the Social Sciences: A Fifty Year Perspective*. Bulletin No. 78. Washington, DC: National Council for the Social Studies, 1986.

4

AMERICAN HISTORY IN THE SCHOOLS

Robert P. Green, Jr., and Richard L. Watson, Jr.

One of the most striking academic paradoxes of the last decade has been that, during a period in which American historiography has been "undergoing the most creative ferment in its entire lifetime" (Kammen 1980: 22), the teaching of American history in the schools has been widely perceived as sterile, moribund, and ineffective. While the "new social history" added exciting areas of study to the academic discipline and forced rethinking in many traditional historical fields, a growing sense of crisis characterized history in the schools. The 1987 publication *What Do Our 17-Year-Olds Know?* analyzed the 1986 National Assessment of Educational Progress (NAEP), one objective of which was to ascertain whether students had a command of background knowledge about American history, and brought this sense of crisis to a head. Coauthor Diane Ravitch later summarized the results and the authors' reaction:

We found it disturbing that two-thirds of the sample did not know that the Civil War occurred between 1850 and 1900, that nearly 40 percent did not know that the *Brown* decision held school segregation unconstitutional, that 40 percent did not know that the East Coast of the United States was explored and settled mainly by England and that the Southwest was explored and settled mainly by Spain, that 70 percent did not know that the purpose of Jim Crow laws was to enforce racial segregation, and that 30 percent could not find Great Britain on a map of Europe.... Plainly, a significant number of students are not remembering the history that they have studied; they are not integrating it into their repertoire of background knowledge, either as fact or as concept. (Ravitch 1989: 52)

The Ravitch and Finn study, although not without critics, seemed to support the dismal findings of earlier research on social studies teaching and learning, for which American history provides the core (Project SPAN 1982: 80). One prior study, that of Project SPAN, had supplemented its findings of poor student learning with a review of studies of student attitudes. These authors found that, for the most part, "students do not like social studies very much and do not believe that subject is very important to their lives after school" (ibid.: 81). Such findings led curricular critic Joe Kincheloe to write, "Students in contemporary social studies classes are learning less and disliking it more" (Kincheloe 1989: 2).

As these studies fueled the growing concern over the teaching and learning of history and the social sciences, they provoked renewed efforts toward reform. The end of the decade saw the publication of the recommendations of two prestigious groups, the Bradley Commission's (1988) "Building a History Curriculum: Guidelines for Teaching History in Schools" and the report of the National Commission on Social Studies in the Schools (1989), *Charting a Course: Social Studies for the 21st Century*. Before reviewing the potential for reform in the recommendations of these commissions and their relationship to developments in the discipline, however, it will be beneficial to reflect upon the teaching of American history over the last two decades. Such reflection should provide us with an overview of the problems facing the field.

REFLECTIONS

The typical curricular pattern in American schools finds United States history taught at the fifth, eighth, and eleventh grades. "In practice," argues David Jenness, "most schools and texts adopt a modified chronological-forward scheme," with much review and repetition (Jenness 1990: 267). This repetition, typically by means of a superficial survey, becomes one source of student dissatisfaction. "You can only hear about the Civil War so many times," one high school student complained. "American history does not go back very far, so you have to study the same stuff over and over again" (Downey 1985: 5).

Warnings against a superficial, "hurried survey of the whole field," which loses student interest, can be traced back at least as far as the 1909 American Historical Association Committee of Eight (Adler and Downey 1985: 19), but this longstanding problem of repetition does not mean that content has not changed over the years. At least as reflected in United States history textbooks—which are the single most influential factor in shaping the curriculum—content has expanded beyond traditional political and military history to include a wide range of social, economic, and cultural developments. The inclusion of a broader range of material has resulted from pressures both inside and outside the profession (Patrick and Hawke 1982: 43–47).

Developments within the various fields of historical study (which we shall treat in some detail in the next section) have influenced the content of textbooks. Historians contribute to these multiauthored texts and bring their knowledge of current research to the task. In recent years, for example, conceptual and analytical tools borrowed from the social sciences have influenced traditional political and economic history, while the "new social history," a movement among professional historians to write history "from the bottom up," has focused greater attention on groups that have been underemphasized in the past: women, Blacks, Native Americans, and immigrants, among others.

In a parallel development, advocacy groups, anxious to ensure that the cultural diversity of American society is adequately represented in textbooks, have exerted pressure on publishers, often through government agencies or branches. South Carolina's Education Improvement Act of 1984 required that "by the 1989–90 school year, each public school of the state must instruct students in the history of the black people as a regular part of its history and social studies courses" (South Carolina Act 1984). The Texas Education Agency, acting on a 1985 state legislative resolution, required United States history texts to recognize the contributions made by Bernardo de Galvez, a Spanish governor of Louisiana, to the American effort during the revolutionary war (S.C.R. 1985).

Conversely, some advocacy groups exert countervailing pressure to limit the treatment that texts might give to some issues. Religious fundamentalists, concerned over the spread of "secular humanism" in the schools, review textbook material for anything that they feel subverts authority or is anti-Christian, antifamily, or un-American. As one can imagine, a very broad range of topics in American history may be identified with one or more of these labels. For example, the portrayal of women in nontraditional roles may be—and has been—perceived as antifamily. The absence of any serious treatment of religion in American history textbooks—criticized by both the Right and the Left—may be attributed in part to publishers' fears of censure from fundamentalist advocacy groups.

Given the pressures imposed by various interest groups, it is no wonder that textbooks avoid controversial topics, limit analysis, and offer only bland, encyclopedic renditions of "facts." Of course, where teachers fail to adjust their presentations of content, to go beyond the text by adjusting course content to student age and interest or by adjusting methodology, student interest will decline. Disenchantment with "repetition," therefore, may reflect a more significant problem. "The reason [repetition is a problem], one suspects," Adler and Downey write, "is that a great many secondary students find that much of the content being repeated is uninteresting and largely meaningless. . . . The basic flaw is not repetition; it is the repeated encounter with a history that has little meaning to students struggling to learn it" (Adler and Downey 1985: 20).

There are certainly more "facts" now than in earlier texts, but more is not necessarily better. It is impossible for teachers to survey all of American history in any other way than superficially, yet teachers are hesitant to "leave anything out."

Superficiality of treatment coincides with the lecture-recitation or worksheet-recitation instructional format. In a typical social studies lesson, the teacher assigns students a section of the text to read, follows with a recitation based on the reading, informally lectures on the topic, engages students in a discussion that involves students' answering questions, or has students complete written worksheets in class or as homework. (Project SPAN 1982: 83)

Typical evaluation procedures also appear to reinforce superficiality. Examinations of assessment methods reveal that teachers tend to assess low-level cognitive skills. On tests, students are expected to regurgitate memorized facts. "Generally avoided in evaluation are synthesis and evaluation, reasoning skills, and critical and creative thinking. Although paper-and-pencil tests can measure higher-level thinking operations, most teacher-made tests in fact do not" (ibid.). Standardized tests, when they play a role, further reinforce this pattern.

Research in the history of teaching practices reveals that this pattern has been stable throughout the century, despite periodic efforts at reform (Cuban 1991: 199–203). As far back as 1893, the NEA's Committee on Secondary Social Studies had argued, "It is better to omit history altogether than to teach it . . . by setting pupils painfully to reproduce the words of a textbook" (Jenness 1990: 262). Rather, the committee recommended the use of probing questions and discussion; a wide range of sources, including literature and primary sources; visual aids; and student investigations. The American Historical Association's (AHA) 1899 "Committee of Seven" disparaged rote memorization and "advocated inquiry and critical thinking, written work using several books and a variety of narratives and viewpoints, original sources, audiovisual aids, collateral readings, and correlation with other subjects, both the humanities and social sciences" (Hertzberg 1989: 79). Historians of the 1934 AHA Commission wrote, "If the objective of history is to develop understanding and insight, the emphasis will have to be placed upon wide and critical reading, upon the interpretation of data, upon the synthesizing of diverse accounts, and upon the understanding of relationships" (Jenness 1990: 262). More recently, historian Edwin Fenton, guru of the "new social studies," has argued, "A student who learns facts and generalizations about the past without becoming involved in the process of inquiry—and most students in American schools do exactly this—does not study history" (ibid.).

Despite these warnings, the teaching of American history today continues to be characterized by superficial surveys, simplistic literal mindedness, and little emphasis on historical process or critical inquiry. To students, history appears meaningless and dead. Yet American history, as reflected in developments in the discipline, is alive and dynamic. Let us turn to those developments and their implications for enlivening the classroom.

CURRENT ISSUES AND TRENDS

It does not take more than a quick glance at the leading history journals of the 1980s and 1990s to realize that those decades are considered a lively, fascinating, and controversial period in historical writing.[1] Indeed, controversies have become so frequent and so intense that few historians would claim that they could be completely objective in their writing and teaching. Peter Novick (1988) has used the title of a famous article on objectivity by Charles A. Beard, "That Noble Dream," to survey historians' attitudes toward objectivity from the 1880s to the present. Novick notes the irony of the fact that, in the early years, objectivity could be established "as the accepted norm within the American academic community" largely because of its "extraordinary ideological homogeneity of ethnicity, class, gender and religion" (Noble 1989: 520). Novick points especially to the 1930s, when Charles Beard and Carl Becker challenged their colleagues' claims to objectivity. Neither Becker nor Beard became pessimistic about the future of the profession in spite of the questions they raised, but Novick is concerned about the credibility of historians since their interpretations often seem to shift with passing fads. Literary theorists and philosophers sometimes go even further than Novick, arguing that documents mean different things at different times and that it is therefore impossible to interpret any document from the past with assurance. In short, they insist that a "belief in a fixed and determinable past" is questionable, if not impossible (Harlan 1981: 581, 583, 608; Diggins 1989).

Another issue which has provoked extensive debate concerns the kind of history that is actually being written. Here the buzz word is "new": "new political history," "new economic history," "new diplomatic history." Gertrude Himmelfarb has ironically commented that "the entire discipline has gone so far beyond the old 'new history' that one is tempted to speak of the 'new new history' " (Himmelfarb 1981: 661). Undoubtedly these "new" historians have thoroughly shaken up the profession. In fact, meetings and conventions of historians in the 1960s sometimes echoed the sounds of "ferocious battles" that were threatening to tear the profession apart. What was happening, according to Jonathan Weiner, was "the formation of a new generation of history students, mobilized by the civil rights and antiwar movements to challenge prevailing conceptions of the American past" (Weiner 1989: 401). At the same time, Weiner noted, "the history profession . . . changed its definition of history to include issues and problems that had previously been described as non-history" (Weiner 1989: 402; see also Thelen 1989: 393). Such divisiveness was reinforced by a reaction against those writing a type of history which seemed to stress continuities and ignore change, "with an assumption that in the United States the fundamental problems had been solved" (Weiner 1989: 407; see also Bender 1984: 619–21).

Weiner has identified several sources of what he considers "radical history." One early source was William Appleman Williams's graduate seminar at the University of Wisconsin in 1957, in which Williams had argued that "the roots of American foreign policy lay in the imperial expansion of corporate capitalism."[2] Other young "radicals were being inspired partly by the work of Herbert Gutman and E. P. Thompson and partly by the reaction to Viet Nam and the civil rights movement. Whether political activists or not, a considerable number, upset by racism, sexism, poverty, and overseas adventurism, turned their professional attention to these subjects" (Weiner 1989: 405). They also began to organize their research around certain concepts. Himmelfarb, who warned that a concentration on these concepts might leave important matters out, observed, "Race Gender Class—word processors all over the country must be programmed to print that formula with a single touch of the key" (Himmelfarb 1989: 662).

In 1989, Lawrence Levine called these developments "perhaps the most important intellectual breakthrough by historians in the past two decades" (Levine 1989: 673). But others viewed them with alarm, appealing for some sort of unifying thesis or principle. Thomas Bender has warned of too narrow a degree of specialization, which, he says, "has destroyed the American past, leaving only many disconnected pasts" with which different historians associate themselves (Bender 1984: 619). Bender was not critical of each of the parts—he criticized only the lack of a whole. Richard Fox reacted in somewhat the same way, but he has also complained that the social historians de-emphasized the individual too much by "subordinating individual consciousness to social fact" (Fox 1987: 115). Others have not been particularly concerned about that lack of wholeness. Joan Scott, for example, has denied that history is in a state of crisis. Denouncing Gertrude Himmelfarb's criticism of the "new history" in no uncertain terms, Scott vigorously argued that "there will always be a plurality of stories," that "the historian's mastery is necessarily partial," and that history's "many different" stories may be "irreconcilable." At the same time, she concluded that there should be "a way to think coherently and systematically about the past . . . if we accept the notion that history is a changing discipline" (Scott 1989: 689, 691–92).

Eric Monkkonner has gone further than Joan Scott to insist that there is a danger in synthesizing. As he puts it, the historical profession "cannot survive without research published in monographs and articles"—the building blocks. "Research-oriented syntheses" may be written in the subfields, he adds, but these cannot "create a sense of the whole past." "Popular syntheses" that transcend these fields, he warns, "must resemble textbooks, and, as such, they cannot foster research" (Monkkonner 1986: 1147, 1152, 1156–57).

Bender is not so pessimistic about the trend toward synthesis, but neither does he question the value of monographic studies, however specialized. He urges, instead, that at least some of these studies be reoriented in their conceptualization. The goal would be a synthesis that analyzes the making and remaking of a "public culture," showing how different social groups have contributed to that process (Bender 1986: 120, 130–31, 135–36).

Although it may be that the controversies within the profession have become less bitter since the end of the 1980s, there is little evidence to indicate that historians have changed their views on such questions as the proper subjects to investigate, how to conceptualize them, and whether and how to synthesize them. As measured by publications, at least, there is little reason to believe that the professionals—either in the traditional or the "new" fields—have given up. A glance at the programs of professional meetings, at the topics of recent scholarship published in *The Journal of American History,* or at the contents of *Reviews in American History* would suggest that intellectual history, political history, and diplomatic history are alive and well, even as the newer fields are becoming increasingly visible.

The main challenge for intellectual historians in the Eighties was to recover from the attacks they suffered in the Sixties and Seventies. Traditionally, intellectual history involved the history of ideas—which might have a life of their own, a life "without behavioral consequences." The activists of the 1960s had little patience with such a concept and favored ideas, perhaps more accurately described as ideologies, which had clear social consequences, such as those of Darwin, Marx, and Dewey. Even more threatening to the traditional intellectual historian, as indicated above, was "post modern literary criticism," which questioned "our belief in a fixed and determinable past . . . and undermined our ability to locate ourselves in time" (Grob 1984: 286–87; Harlan 1981: 581).

Serious though these criticisms of intellectual history seem to have been, significant contributions continued to be made in that field. James Hoopes, for example, commented that "intellectual history was where the action was in the study of Puritanism in the 1980s" (Hoopes 1989: 533). Moreover, there has been an increasing interest in interdisciplinary studies among intellectual historians. Daniel Worthy Howe, for example, has praised recent works of intellectual history for being able to provide "rewarding new perspectives on party politics in the young American republic" (Howe 1981: 349). Hoopes obviously agrees, for in an otherwise favorable review of two books on Puritanism he criticizes them for not furthering "our understanding of the role of Puritanism as a public and political force in early American history" (Hoopes 1989: 533).

Hoopes's admonition to intellectual historians to explore relationships between intellectual and political history reflects another controversy of the decades since the 1960s. If any field of history has taken a verbal beating in the past ten years, it is surely political history. William E. Leuchtenburg briefly reviewed the pessimistic prophecies of the field's future in his 1986 presidential address to the Organization of American Historians. Leuchtenburg, however, refused to endorse this pessimism and even cited leading social historians who warned that the history of a people could not be written with the politics left out (Leuchtenburg 1986: 585–89, 599).

Some political historians had already changed their approach and had been turning out their own "new" brand for years. Samuel P. Hays dates this shift as having begun in 1948, with the publication of Thomas C. Cochran's article "The Presidential Synthesis in American History." Indeed, Hays himself, with Lee Benson and with colleagues and students at the University of Iowa (e.g., William Aydelotte, Joel Silbey, Allan Bogue), among others, turned to the social sciences in the 1950s for theory and quantitative techniques. This group and their disciples have since produced significant studies on political parties and voting behavior in general elections and in legislatures.[3]

One example of a work which answers those who have criticized political history for its narrowness as well as those who have called for synthesis is Eric Foner's magisterial volume in the New American Nation Series on Reconstruction. Foner avoided the dangers of compartmentalization, wanting to view "the period as a whole, integrating the social, political, and economic aspects of reconstruction into a coherent, analytical narrative." He organized his study around several "broad themes," the most significant of which is the "centrality of the black experience" during Reconstruction. At the same time, he treated that basic theme in terms of "its intersection with the issues of class, of southern society, the emergence of a national state with an ideal of a national citizenship, and the impact of changes in the nation's economy upon Reconstruction."[4]

In the ferment of historical controversy during the 1970s and 1980s, some historians of foreign relations, like political and intellectual historians, felt themselves under attack. They were sometimes charged with "elitism, narrowness, and methodological staleness" and with studying "what white, male diplomats have said to each other in official messages." That such criticisms were taken seriously is suggested by the fact that the editors of *The Journal of American History* devoted ninety pages of a recent issue to a roundtable on the subject in which some of the field's leading specialists described various approaches to the subject.[5] Such approaches include those labeled "national security," which concerns the goals of defending territorial and material interests and of "core values"; "corporatism," which emphasizes the goals of international economic growth based on private initiative and overseas expansion supported by the federal government; "world systems," which is based on the theories of Imanuel Wallerstein concerning a "core" country's attempts to gain and maintain hegemony over the countries of the "periphery" and "semi-periphery"; "dependency," which specifically emphasizes the relationship between the United States (the "core") and Latin America or perhaps Africa (the "periphery"); and "culture" (partly a response to those who accuse historians of foreign relations of narrowness), which has to do with "ideology, emotions, lifestyle, scholarly and artistic works, and other symbols."[6]

It is not surprising that there is considerable overlap among these approaches. Indeed, Thomas Patterson lists "ideology" as a separate approach, which Michael Hunt then defines as "sets of beliefs, and values, sometimes only poorly or partially articulated," going on to acknowledge that such an approach would overlap others, such as "corporatism" and "gender studies" (Hunt 1990: 109). With respect to the latter approach, Emily S. Rosenburg points out that women have "played important roles" in foreign relations and that "gender" may provide a deeper understanding of the cultural assumptions from which foreign policies spring (Rosenburg 1990).

These various approaches to the historiography of American foreign relations can be constructive when used to analyze a particular problem. There is a danger, however, that one of them may become an ideology and thus be emphasized to the exclusion of the others.[7] In the increasingly complex international system (or lack of system) of the 1990s, historians must be prepared to ask complex questions with an open mind. Perhaps enough has been said, however, to indicate that the history of American foreign relations is alive and controversial—in part because of the ongoing research of an older generation of American scholars and in part because of prodding from a younger generation determined to try new methods, apply different theories, and address different topics across the disciplines.

The same generalization, to be sure, can be applied to fields of history other than foreign relations. Undoubtedly, the prodding from social historians has forced all historians at least to consider different questions, but at the same time, it has resulted in the splintering that provoked the critiques of Himmelfarb and Bender as well as garnering the plaudits of Joan Scott and Lawrence Levine.

Women's history is one of those fields in which new questions are being asked, especially those that arise in relation to such issues as women's rights and feminism, women in the professions, course offerings, and women's history vis-à-vis other fields. The present generation of women historians was trained during the 1960s, when women in the profession were few. By 1985 the number of women historians in colleges and universities had increased, but still made up only fifteen percent of the total, and their salaries lagged significantly behind those of men. However, committees on the status of women were appointed by the American Historical Association in 1969 and by the Organization of American Historians shortly thereafter, and these committees fought with some success for more open appointment procedures, as well as for greater representation of women on advisory boards, committees, and lists of reviewers. By 1983 women constituted thirty-four percent of the elected officers of the AHA; Gerda Lerner and Anne Scott were elected to the OAH presidency in 1982, and 1984, respectively, and Natalie Davis was elected president of the AHA in 1987.[8] The decade of the 1970s also saw the development of women's history as a teaching field. One study had identified twenty-two courses being taught in women's history nationwide, but by 1972 Sarah Lawrence College was offering a masters program in women's history, and by 1988, some sixty institutions offered graduate programs.[9]

Clearly, women's history has established itself as an important subfield of social history. Its importance lies not only in its own inherent value, but also in the dimension that it adds to other fields, such as labor history, black history, ethnic studies, medical history, and family history, which was described in 1982, with perhaps some exaggeration, as having exploded after being a minor subfield for something more than a decade.[10]

One of the newest subfields of social history is that of gay and lesbian history. Serious work in this field did not begin until the mid-1970s, a delay owing no doubt to homosexuality being a sensitive issue even in the academic world. Although there are no statistics to show how many homosexuals held teaching positions in earlier periods, they certainly faced an uphill struggle to get such jobs. Gay scholarship at first concentrated on the repression of gays, with biographies of gay people as primary source material. Currently, an interdisciplinary effort is under way to recover the gay past—to "study how gay people have viewed themselves through time," to determine when a self-consciously homosexual identity began to emerge, and to discover how various world communities have treated homosexuals (Emilio 1989: 438, 441; Duberman 1988: 516–17, 521–23).

A much longer established field is that of Afro-American history. The civil rights movement of the 1950s and 1960s, when activists enlisted history to support their cause, saw a tremendous increase in consciously written Afro-American history. But, as was the case with social history in general, black history had had an honorable, though perhaps not well understood, ancestry. August Meier and Elliott Rudwick, themselves specialists in the field, date the beginning of Afro-American history to 1915, the year that Carter Woodson founded the Association for the Study of Negro Life and History (Meier and Rudwick 1986). John Hope Franklin, however, points to an even earlier beginning with the appearance in 1882 of George Washington William's *A History of the Negro Race in America from 1619–1880.* In those early years, Afro-American history was largely the work of Afro-Americans, of whom W. E. B. DuBois was the most notable (Franklin 1988), but during the past fifty years, many white as well as black historians have moved into the field, producing such work as the writings of John Hope Franklin and Benjamin Quarles, and Gunnar Myrdal's much publicized work in 1944, *An American Dilemma* (Quarles 1988; Franklin 1989). The publication in 1947 by Alfred Knopf, a leading publisher, of John Hope Franklin's *From Slavery to Freedom* renewed interest in Afro-American history, which was later bolstered by the publication of C. Vann Woodward's *Strange History of Jim Crow* in 1955 and Kenneth M. Stampp's *Peculiar Institution . . .* in 1956 (Harris 1987).

The decade of the 1960s saw an outpouring of writing about the black experience—"the New Negro history"—so enormous that it was, as John Hope Franklin put it, "staggering by any standards" (Franklin 1988: 167). The "new urban history" and the "new social history," with their emphasis on the entire community rather than its white leaders, developed at the same time as the civil rights movement and stimulated an interest in historical research on Afro-Americans. As a result, new courses were taught, black studies programs were established, and black historians began to be appointed to faculty positions in what had been predominantly white institutions. As in other areas of social history, the question of the relative importance of race and class was sometimes an issue. Was the disenfranchisement of black people, for example, a consequence of "race" or of "class"? (Meier and Rudwick 1986; Harris 1987: 1159).[11] Another, more emotional issue that has emerged concerns what some have designated a "black nationalistic" ideology. The basic question is whether Afro-American history should be regarded "as a teaching and research specialty, particularly suitable for blacks" (Harris 1987: 1160). There is no doubt where either Vincent Harding or Sterling Stuckey stand on that question. In 1987 Stuckey clearly set forth the nationalist position in his work, *Slave Culture: Nationalist Theory and the Founding of Black America,* while Harding has appealed fervently to black scholars not to forget that their "source" is "the great pained community of Afro-Americans of this land." (Harding 1970: 135) One question that has been long debated by black scholars concerns the degree of African influence on slave culture. Stuckey's answer, based on an examination of folktales and folk customs, such as dances and religious practices, was a very simple one, but powerfully argued: the African background, regardless of its ethnic variety, was the principal force behind the black cultural unity created in the United States.[12]

In spite of the variety and volume of publications in the field of black history, John Hope Franklin nevertheless believes that there are still several areas of slave culture which invite future research: small farms, violence directed at runaways, and black women as workers rather than sex objects. In addition, Franklin observes that little research has been done on such black institutions as churches, fraternal orders, and businesses; moreover, those interested in biography could still find worthy subjects.

Although Afro-American history might be technically and justifiably viewed as a subfield of ethnic history, it has taken on the qualities of a separate, major field and is usually considered as such. Actually, there is little agreement on what constitutes an ethnic group or how many different ones there are (Thernstorm, Orlov, and Handlin 1980; Daniels 1981). Ethnic history is a field nonetheless and one in which the theories and the research of other disciplines, as well as such concepts as race, class, gender, and culture, can be widely applied. But theorizing, however helpful, may create its own hazards by suggesting that a generalization can be found to explain the actions of people and groups in all places and time periods. Nevertheless, ethnic historian Joel Perlman effectively avoided this hazard in his study of the educational experiences of several ethnic groups in Providence, Rhode Island. Perlman, in short, found it impossible to generalize. As one reviewer put it, "Multiple forces had to be at work. Family structure, class, cultural orientation, and hostility in the job market all were at work in varying ways and degrees."[13]

For years, Oscar Handlin's 1951 work, *The Uprooted,* served as a beacon for immigration history, as did its thesis that immigrants were virtually cut off from their previous cultures, namely, family, school, and church, as well as homeland. According to John Bodnar, however, recent research has substantially modified that thesis. He has argued that "far from a leap into the unknown, immigration presented an intelligent strategy for dealing imaginatively with the situation brought on by the emerging new order" (quoted in Kessner 1986: 975). In other words, immigrants did not necessarily retain unmodified a culture that they might have brought with them from abroad, nor did they create an entirely new culture. Instead, immigrant cultures reflected transformations of certain dynamic qualities of the original cultures. Yet Bodnar does not see such transformations as taking place in any particular way, and he insists on the diversity to be found in any group of immigrants. In short, "immigrant streams and communities were not huddled masses sharing a common orientation towards some future, but divided masses debating life goals and strategies."[14]

Roger Daniels, in reviewing the *Harvard Encyclopedia of American Ethnic Groups,* praised it in general, but also criticized its Eurocentrism and, particularly, its underemphasis of Asian-Americans and Native Americans. The editors, he noted, "assigned all American Indians to one author in one essay," despite their having been hundreds of tribes in different geographical environments. Such a focus is, of course, not unique (Daniels 429). Richard Berkhofer commented in 1973 that, to Native Americans, "whites just stole their lands and later robbed them of their history." He added, to be sure, that well-meaning whites had taken various approaches to the history of Native Americans, some of which were no longer based upon the racist premise of a completely degraded "red skin," but most of which generally viewed Native Americans as "passive objects." Berkhofer described these approaches as "white centered" and perfectly "legitimate," provided that authors and readers were conscious of the fact that only one side of the story was told. Berkhofer urged, however, that "a new Indian centered history" be developed in which Indians would be presented "as individuals within their cultures and tribes."[15] More than fifteen years later, James Merrill still found at least three divisions among scholars of Native American history: one group either bashed or ignored the Indian; another group took the Indians' side; and a third group, influenced by anthropology, produced the nearest thing to Berkhofer's "Indian centered history."[16]

Controversies also exist in another thriving field, that of labor history, although the boundaries between the new and the old, in practice, are sometimes not clear. Moreover, it is easy to become confused by the "labor history" label because of this field's interrelationships with other areas of social history. After all, women, blacks, and various immigrant groups may be laborers. Indeed the patron saints of labor history, E. P. Thompson and Herbert Gutman, provided much of the original stimulus for a polite declaration of independence by the new labor historians of the "Wisconsin School" of John R. Commons and Selig Perlman. This "school" stressed the "workers' collective response to changing labor-market conditions, most importantly the shift from anti-monopoly struggles to 'a stable and job-conscious unionism' " (Schatz 1984: 94).

Thompson had defined the laboring class in "cultural terms" and promoted an emphasis on such topics as "religion, rituals, kinship, and community," rather than on "strikes, trade unions, and political movements." Gutman and others also adopted this cultural focus and drew on the methodologies of anthropology and sociology in order to understand the culture of a labor group. Gutman's study of the black family, for example, was of great significance in showing how a distinctive slave culture had developed and "was passed from one generation to another." In later work, he applied this thesis to the "working class," showing "the ideals workers expressed in prose and poetry," as well as their work patterns, leisure habits, and the organizations in which they were involved (Buhle and Buhle 1988: 151–52).

But the kind of analysis inspired by Thompson and Gutman also inspired controversy, so their work does not seem to be the last word on what labor historians do or should be doing. John P. Diggins, for example, has faulted both of them for using what workers said (i.e., their rhetoric), rather than what they did, as evidence of the "real group motives of the workers." Diggins further questioned whether such historians were sufficiently careful in using theory to develop their arguments. The theory at issue was Antonio Gramsci's concept of hegemony and particularly its application to the organization of blocs to challenge the hegemony of the ruling class (Diggins 1988: 141; see also Lipsitz 1988: 146–47; Buhle and Buhle 1988: 153–55). The differences among labor historians, as among historians in general, have inspired a longing for synthesis, but there is apparently little agreement on how to synthesize (Schatz 1984: 93–94).

There is, of course, no logical place at which to end an essay on the subject of American history in the 1980s and 1990s. The choice of which fields to discuss inevitably displays a bias, and with more space, more topics could have been covered. One field that ideally should have been included here, is what's known as "new urban history," to distinguish it from the histories of the city written sixty years ago (see, e.g., Schlesinger 1933). Other necessary but unfortunate omissions are the well-established fields of economic and business history and a relatively new field that is rapidly expanding, environmental history, which allows specialists in political, economic, intellectual, and social history to join forces.[17]

One growing subfield based on the earlier work of a few historians and scholars in other disciplines is the history of medicine and health. In March 1940, Henry Sigerist, then director of the Johns Hopkins Institute of the History of Medicine, called on his colleagues to recognize that medical practice involves not only the physician but the patient and, thus, that medical history should be viewed as part of the social context from which the patient comes. The response to Sigerist's challenge was clearly positive. According to one historian, three types of medical historiography can now be identified: (1) books on healers and their institutions, (2) books that describe the process of health care, and (3) books that "use race, class, and gender to enhance our understanding of the range of healing practices and interactions" (Leavitt 1990: 1472).

Other fields, likewise springing from social history, come under the rubric of "popular culture," wherein one of the liveliest subfields is sports history. The relationship between sports and many other history fields is close. Indeed, Stephen A. Riess, whose *City Games: The Evolution of American Urban Society and the Rise of Sports* appeared in 1989, argues that "sports history is a chapter in urban history," which covers such subjects as city politics, urban development, and space utilization (ibid.). But sports history can also be a species of business history or the history of public health. Harold Seymour, who has earned the title of "dean" of baseball historians, has written one volume covering the history of professional baseball up to 1930 and another which is a detailed history of baseball outside of the organized leagues. Seymour has argued that "professional baseball is not a sport," but actually "a commercialized amusement business" (Tygiel 1991: 109). Others look at sports as a route to good health. Harvey Green, for example, has studied nineteenth-century experiments in nostrums and diets and has pointed out that German immigrants introduced gymnastics to the United States as a means of keeping fit (Green 1986).

The dynamism in academic history did not go ignored in the literature on history teaching in the schools. In fact, that literature, while suggesting strategies for incorporating elements of the "new social history" into the school curriculum, explicitly recognized the shortcomings of traditional history teaching and sought to use the new materials as a vehicle for redressing them. As Matthew T. Downey argued in *Teaching American History: New Directions,* the new research in history potentially had "the capacity to revitalize the teaching of history," offering teachers "the possibility of helping students construct a new definition of history, as well as new perspectives on the past" (Downey 1982: 3). The essays in Downey's collected volume demonstrate such revitalization by various means, such as strategies for teaching women's history that included students' comparing obituaries they wrote for themselves with those they wrote (using census reports) for women of the 1880s, allowing students to detect changes in women's roles over the past 100 years; the use of artifacts from the 1920s to encourage students to formulate hypotheses about the changing status of women in that decade; and the use of tabular data (statistics) to draw inferences about women's increasing participation in the labor force as well as to foster a critical awareness of the degree to which statistical data can be used as historical evidence. (With regard to statistical data, it is important to note that the introduction of computers into the classroom allows students to manipulate data bases containing social statistics—as well as many other kinds of data—to illustrate concepts, define trends, test hypotheses, and draw conclusions. In this fashion, historical study is truly "active learning" [Laughlin, Hartoonian, and Sanders 1989].)

A further benefit associated with incorporating the new social history in classroom instruction is that it provides a more comprehensive vision of America's past, thereby better meeting the needs and interests of an increasingly diverse student population. James A. Banks, writing for the Educational Equality Project of the College Board, makes this argument:

Students of all cultural and ethnic groups need to see their history mirrored in school history. Too often in the past women, working people, and ethnic and racial minorities—among them Native Americans, Hispanics, and blacks—have seen little of their historical experience in study. Social history gives attention to these groups and others that usually have been left out of historical accounts, including, as [historian Robert] Darnton puts it, "the oppressed, the inarticulate, the marginal." (Banks 1986: 21–22)

Thus the new social history can provide more meaningful content, that is, content related to the experiences of a diverse student body, while it exposes students to, and enables them to work with, "relevant source materials and 'survivals' from the past. . . . Once students have experience in working with the actual survivals from the past," argues Banks, "they begin to see that history is less a familiar series of names and incidents to be memorized than a challenge to critical thought, less standard answers than a number of significant questions open to diverse treatment and interpretation" (45).

That the schools are blessed with a number of teachers who take these ideas to heart and develop meaningful learning experiences for their students, there is no question. Vincent Rogers, Arthur D. Roberts, and Thomas P. Weinland (1988) have collected a number of examples in their *Teaching Social Studies: Portraits from the Classroom*. These portraits reflect the use of a wide range of strategies and activities. In the teaching of history at the elementary level, for example, we see a historically rich community used to actively involve students in "doing" history, the study of names and family histories illustrating cultural diversity and teaching a variety of skills, and the study of ecology organized around Native Americans' strong connections with Mother Earth. At the secondary level, we see critical reasoning fostered through historiographical treatments of major topics in American history, the controversial nature of the Vietnam war explored through a wide variety of sources, and a U.S. history course organized around such enduring issues as freedom and authority, unity and diversity, stability and change. As the editors argue, such strategies are characterized by a "clear sense of purpose" on the teachers' part that goes "far beyond the listing of narrow, relatively low-level objectives" and includes the devotion of "an enormous amount of thought to the importance of process as well as product in the act of teaching." In short, "students are consistently asked to think" (94–95). Yet the teachers who describe their work in this volume are exceptional. How can the profession foster more of this kind of effort? Two sources of recommendations at the end of the decade were the Bradley Commission on History in Schools and the National Commission on Social Studies in the Schools.

Composed of both history teachers and historians, the Bradley Commission was formed in 1987 "in response to widespread concern over the inadequacy, both in quantity and in quality, of the history taught in American elementary and secondary classrooms" (Bradley Commission 1989: 16). The commission's recommendations, issued in its 1988 report, *Building a History Curriculum: Guidelines for Teaching History in Schools*, include returning to a more history-centered curriculum in social studies at both the elementary and secondary levels. As its title suggests, the major thrust of the report is curricular. Criticizing the "expanding environments" approach to social studies in the elementary schools for being grounded neither in research on how children learn nor in developmental studies, the commission called for the infusion of historical and literary subject matter at that level: "folk tales of different cultures; novels that vividly portray important events and people, and the experiences of ordinary people in extraordinary times; poetry; songs, stories of immigrants; and books that bring complicated subjects such as the U.S. Constitution within the understanding of young children" (33). For the secondary level, the commission recommended that considerably more curricular time be devoted to history—at least four of the six years from seventh to twelfth grade, with two dedicated to American history.

The commission's recommendations also included a number of suggestions that could help to remedy the problems identified in this essay. For example, teaching the two years of American history back-to-back, as in one pattern recommended by the commission, with the Civil War as the dividing point, might solve the problem of repetition at the secondary level. Furthermore, devoting more curricular time to history could help with the problem of superficial coverage. However, evidently recognizing that more time in itself is no solution to superficial coverage (one could use the extra time simply to "cover" more disconnected "facts"), the commission declared that "to develop judgment and perspective, historical study must often focus upon broad, significant themes and questions, rather than the short-lived memorization of facts without context. In doing so, historical study should provide context for facts and training in critical judgment based upon evidence, including original sources" (23). The commission then went on to identify "vital themes" and topics "central to the history of the United States" that could guide teachers in making decisions about what material to emphasize and what to leave out.

Because of limited time and resources, the commission restricted its report to the curriculum (19). Fortunately, however, the commission also published a companion volume, *Historical Literacy: The Case for History in American Education*. Through a series of essays by commission members and others, this volume provides a wide-ranging discussion of history's place in a liberal education, as well as highlighting new ideas in a variety of historical fields and offering suggestions for better teaching. The last section includes discussions of obstacles to better teaching, methodological suggestions, and recommendations for better teacher preparation.

The major curricular report issued by the National Commission on Social Studies in the Schools, *Charting a Course: Social Studies for the 21st Century* (National Commission 1989), is also characterized by a limited focus. Born of the contemporary recognition by both professional historians and history teachers of a malaise in social studies teaching, the commission and its task forces comprised a broad coalition of historians, social scientists, educators, and others involved in public policy, business, and the professions (Jenness 1990: 430). It was the first major commission to study the social studies in over fifty years. As originally conceived, the commission had three major objectives: (1) the recommendation by its Curriculum Task Force of an overall scope-and-sequence design, (2) the creation of an Advisor-Responder Schools Network to tap opinion in the field, and (3) the publication of a major background work (David Jenness's excellent *Making Sense of Social Studies*), which would, in turn, "feed into full-scale and sustained deliberations of the Commission." These deliberations would be further informed by "a census and critical assessment of distinctive or 'exemplary' current practices in existing social studies programs; a group evaluating recent developmental, cognitive, and sociological research in terms of pedagogy and school and classroom procedures; some consideration of tests and texts in relation to curriculum; and consideration of what implications the commission's recommendations would hold for teacher education, pre- and in-service" (ibid.). Unfortunately, lack of funding forced the commission to limit its work to the three original objectives.

Like those of the Bradley Commission, the recommendations of the National Commission's Curriculum Task Force addressed some of the problems identified in the teaching of American history. However, the absence of support from the planned supplementary work leaves this commission's main document open to criticism. While placing history and geography at the core of the social studies, thus providing a "time and place matrix" as an organizing instrument, the task force also repeatedly emphasized the importance of selectivity, to allow study in depth of certain issues, individuals, and groups, and the importance of incorporating concepts from the social sciences. Recommending a three-year sequence of United States history combined with "the general story of humanity" for the secondary grades, the task force suggested that "the way to see human history as a whole is to pay special attention to the cultural, economic and political links that ran across different civilizations" (National Commission 1989: 14). The second and third years of the sequence would therefore trace the development of "three dominant transformations of modern times" in the nineteenth century to see how they "worked themselves out" in the twentieth (15–17).

Although in its list of "Characteristics of a Social Studies Curriculum," the task force emphasized that "content knowledge from the social studies should not be treated merely as received knowledge to be accepted and memorized," and although a wide range of teaching strategies and materials received explicit endorsement, the absence of a thorough treatment of these issues leaves *Charting a Course* open to the criticism that its recommendations will readily devolve into "the chronological exposition and memorization of history" that so undermines the social studies today (Engle 1990: 431). If that devolution were to occur, then the work of the commission would certainly be vulnerable to the criticism that the "proposed curriculum . . . does not engage students in critical study of history and geography, only in the study of sterilized, prescribed mainstream content" (Nelson 1990: 437).

PROJECTIONS

Lester Stephens defined history as "a mental construction of the past based on evidence which has been carefully subjected to tests of validity and then critically and systematically ordered and interpreted to present a story of man's interaction with other men in a society" (Jenness 1990: 269). A key idea here is that history is *constructed* by the historian—the result of an interactive process between the historian and whatever remains of the past. History is alive; it is not composed of inert and arid facts. It is critical to the subject's future in the schools that teachers of history understand this and embody this understanding in their teaching. As historian Gordon Craig argues,

It is vital that our emphasis be as much upon thinking about history as describing what happened in it. For above all we need living ideas to correct inherited myths and conventional assumptions about the historical process and to provide a basis for the political competence that so often seems in short supply today. General factual knowledge about the past is not enough, whether we consider the role of history in the schools, or in public affairs of the society at large. (McNeill, Kammen, and Craig 1989: 115)

The idea of history as being constructed is clearly reflected in the work of today's academic historians. However, it is, of course, dangerous to attempt to forecast the future of historical writing, especially on the basis of a survey like the one made here. For example, a considerable controversy may now be brewing over a suggestion to de-emphasize American "exceptionalism" (i.e., a national framework) in the writing of history and to attempt instead a "transnational" approach—one that "transcends national boundaries."[18] At the same time, it is clear that the quality of historical investigation and writing is in no way declining. The call to write history "from the bottom up" and to include groups that have been previously underemphasized has in fact contributed to the health of the profession. Moreover, the increased emphasis on analysis, on "conceptualizing," and on theory will continue to inspire historians to study other disciplines for what they can contribute to an understanding of the past.

Even those who have questioned whether the writing of history is even possible, given the impossibility of understanding documents from the past, can serve as a stimulus to good historical writing. Although their position is extreme, it should be viewed as a challenge by researchers to accept the impossibility of complete objectivity and, recognizing their own biases, to study the sources as best they can in the context of the times. James Kloppenberg put it powerfully, saying that "through a combination of imagination, technology, and diligence, historians have compiled hard data that now make impossible some versions of the past that once passed as truths" and, thus, that "only within this realm of the verifiable can competing interpretations survive the scrutiny of the community of professional historians."[19]

The demand for a great synthesis can be premature; building blocks for such an ambitious structure must come first. The principal question then becomes: What is this great structure to be? Obviously, a synthesis of the work done on women's history or black history or on a relatively brief period of time would be more feasible than an attempt to integrate all of the findings from all fields and subfields into one grand synthesis, the result of which would probably be either a hodgepodge or something like a textbook with a chapter devoted to each field. Yet the fact remains that a course purporting to be a course in a period of U.S. history should somehow do more than touch base with the important fields, but then the question is: What is important?

The profession should now be at the point of recognizing such questions, of accepting them as a challenge, and of resisting ideological involvement in any one approach to the extent that others appear to be unacceptable. The "new history" has served a useful purpose, and a "new, new history" will make useful contributions, but the "new historians" must recognize, if they have any historical perspective, that the "old" history continues to be valuable. At the same time, those who still write narrative history or political history or another type that some might label "old" history should profit from criticism, but continue to do their research without questioning the goals and methods of their colleagues who like to think of themselves as "new."

It is critical for teachers of history to understand that their subject is a *scholarly* activity. Scholars ask questions. Their answers are necessarily tentative and susceptible to revision. "History is, among other things, a forum for inquiry—in this sense, inquiry driven by puzzlement, the fallibility and ambiguity of evidence, the nonknowability of the past" (Jenness 1990: 285). To teach history merely as a body of information to be set to memory is an injustice to the discipline itself, as well as to the students.

American History is—in terms of the demands it places on the knowledge of the practitioner—one of the most difficult subjects to teach well. As Lee Shulman argues in a broader context, to teach well, teachers

must understand the structures of the subject matter, the principles of conceptual organization, and the principles of inquiry that help answer two kinds of questions. ... What are the important ideas and skills in this domain? and How are new ideas added and deficient ones dropped by those who produce knowledge in this area? (Shulman 1987: 9)

Central to Shulman's thinking is the concept of "pedagogical content knowledge." Most of the evidence available suggests that, generally, teachers of American history do not have this knowledge and, consequently, the subject is not taught well.

What can be done? Suzanne Wilson and Gary Sykes argue that the challenge is one of professional resocialization of history teachers (Wilson and Sykes 1989: 279). Years of exposure to inappropriate models must be overcome. Such an effort would require the cooperation of teacher educators and college history professors, as well as institutional support for continued professional development. Fortunately, research is under way (Wineburg and Wilson [in press]) on the teaching of American history, using Shulman's concepts, that offers a promising base. This work explores the means by which teachers integrate their knowledge and pedagogical skills to get students excited about history and about the way that historical knowledge is created.

Such an approach to the teaching of American history facilitates the citizenship education most appropriate to democracy. The criticism of historical study in the schools as shallow "citizenship transmission" that stands in the way of a truly critical, informed analysis of social issues misses its mark. One cannot conduct a solid study of history without addressing such issues. In conclusion, we note the comments of historian Allan Nevins:

The most important part of history is really a series of problems. ... The way to penetrate beneath the petty superficialities and come to grips with historical realities is to propound one incisive question with another, until the past ceases to look like a smooth record and becomes instead a rough and puzzling set of difficulties. (Nevins 1970: v)

NOTES

1. Note some of the titles in *The Journal of American History*'s table of contents for issues published between 1980 and 1990: "A Round Table: Synthesis in American History" (June 1987); "Intellectual History: A Time for Despair?" (March 1980); "The Discipline of the History of Technology: An Exchange" and "The Pertinence of Political History" (December 1986); "Labor, Historical Pessimism and Hegemony" (June 1988); and "Explaining the History of American Foreign Relations" (June 1990).

2. This theme was exemplified by Gabriel Kolko's 1963 work, *The Triumph of Conservatism, 1890–1916* and by Eugene Genovese's *Political Economy of Slavery*, of 1965.

3. Thomas C. Cochran, "The Presidential Synthesis in American History," *American Historical Review* 53 (July 1948): 748–59; Lee Benson, "Research Problems in American Political Historiography," in Mirra Komorovsky, ed., *Common Frontiers in the Social Sciences* (Glencoe, IL: Glencoe Press, 1957). Hays's contributions are conveniently collected in *American Political History as Social Analysis Essays*. (Knoxville, University of Tennessee Press, 1980).

4. Eric Foner, *Reconstruction: America's Unfinished Revolution, 1863–1877* (New York: Harper and Row, 1988).

Richard Kirkendell has also suggested that an approach such as that taken in Robert Kelley's *Battling the Inland Sea: American Political Culture, Public Policy, and the Sacramento Valley, 1850–1986* (Berkeley: University of California Press, 1989) provides the kind of revitalization of political history that Leuchtenburg called for in his presidential address (Richard S. Kirkendall, "Water and the Revitalization of Political History," *Reviews in American History* 18 [December 1990]: 568, 572).

5. Thomas G. Patterson, "A Round Table: Explaining the History of American Foreign Relations," *The Journal of American History* 77 (June 1990): 93–182. Walter LaFeber has also attempted to respond to critics in his stimulating survey, *The American Age: United States Foreign Policy at Home and Abroad Since 1750* (New York: Norton, 1989).

6. Melvyn Lefler, "National Security," *The Journal of American History* 77 (June 1990): 144–46; Michael J. Hogan, "Corporatism," *The Journal of American History* 77 (June 1990): 154–56; Thomas A. McCormick, "World Systems," *The Journal of American History* 77 (June 1990): 125–32, and Imanuel Wallerstein, *The Modern World System: Capitalist Agriculture and the Origins of the European World Economy in the Sixteenth Century* (New York: Academic Press, 1974). Wallerstein credits Fernand Braudel's work with having stimulated his interest in such a theory. (It seems clear that the complex background of Wallerstein's theoretical work would also include Karl Marx and Antonio Gramsci.)

Louis A. Perez, Jr., "Dependency," *The Journal of American History* 77 (June 1990): 133–42; Akira Iriye, "Culture," *The Journal of American History* 77 (June 1990): 99–101, 107.

7. Robert J. McMahon, in reviewing Thomas J. McCormick's *America's Half Century: United States Foreign Policy in the Cold War* (Baltimore: Johns Hopkins Press, 1989), accused McCormick of recognizing only "one driving force behind American diplomacy, a relentless expansionist capitalist system . . . while dismissing all explanations . . . that introduce non-economic factors into the policy question" (Robert J. McMahon, "Hegemony and Its Problems," *Reviews in American History* 19 [March 1991]: 139–40).

8. Gerda Lerner, "A View from the Women's Side," *The Journal of American History* 76 (September 1989): 452–53.

Anne Scott was also elected president of the Southern Historical Association in 1988. The contributions made by an earlier generation of women historians are also evident in the bibliographies of such works as Dixon Ryan Fox and Arthur S. Schlesinger, Jr., *A History of American Life,* 13 vols. (New York: Macmillan, 1927–1948).

9. Gerda Lerner, "A View from the Women's Side," *The Journal of American History* 76 (September 1989): 454. In June 1972, the bibliography of *The Journal of American History* included its first listing of articles (six of them) on the subject of women; in March 1991, there were forty-three.

10. Mary P. Ryan, "The Explosion of Family History," *Reviews in American History* 10 (December 1982); Tamara K. Harevan, "The History of the Family and the Complexity of Social Change," *American Historical Review* 96 (February 1991): 96, 98. Harevan, who asserts that "systematic historical study of the family" began in the mid–1960s, also mentions it roots in social science disciplines. But examples of earlier work, such as A. W. Calhoun's *Social History of the American Family,* 3 vols. (Cleveland, 1917–1919) and the bibliography of works on the American family in Dixon Wector's *Age of the Great Depression* (New York, 1948, 325–26), can also be found. Harevan's notes provide a superb bibliography as well.

11. This issue is also addressed in Richard L. Watson, Jr., "Furnifold M. Simmons and the Politics of White Supremacy," in Jeffrey J. Crow, Paul D. Escott, and Charles L. Flynn, Jr., eds., *Race, Class and Politics in Southern History* (Baton Rouge: Louisiana State University Press, 1989).

12. Sterling Stuckey, "Twilight of Our Past: Reflections on the Origin of Black History," in John A. Williams and Charles F. Hartes, eds., *Armistad 2: Writings on Black History and Culture* (New York: Random House, 1971).

This question is also addressed by Margaret Washington Creel (*The Journal of American History* 75 [March 1989]: 1281–83); Wilson J. Moses (*American Historical Review* 93 [December 1988]: 1397–98); and Colin A. Palmer (*Reviews in American History* 16 [June 1988]: 241–44).

13. Hosea B. Diner, "Ethnic Differences in the Class Room: The Search for Answers," *Reviews in American History* 18 (December 1990): 518, reviewing Joel Perlman's *Ethnic Differences: Schooling and Social Structure among the Irish, Italians, Jews, and Blacks in an American City* (Cambridge: Cambridge University Press, 1988).

14. John Bodnar, "Symbols and Servants: Immigrant America and the Limits of Public History," *The Journal of American History* 73 (June 1986): 144. This article questions the appropriateness of the Statue of Liberty as a symbol of what

is sought newly arrived immigrants, since that symbol could not represent all of the aspirations of all immigrants.

15. Richard Berkhofer, "Native Americans and United States History," in William H. Cartwright and Richard L. Watson, Jr., eds., *The Reinterpretation of American History and Culture* (Washington, DC: National Council for the Social Studies, 1973), 37–55.

16. James H. Merrill, "High Priests and Missionaries," *Reviews in American History* 17 (June 1989): 178–81 (review of James Axtell's *After Columbus: Essays in the Ethno-History of Colonial North America* [New York, 1988]).

The scholar who perhaps best represents this "Indian centered history" is James Axtell. Merrill describes Axtell as a "missionary" who insists that Indians are "indispensable" for understanding America's past. (Another example of Axtell's work is his article, "Colonial America without the Indians," *The Journal of American History* 73 [March 1987]: 982–83.)

17. In Donald Worster's words, environmental history can show "how humans have been affected by their natural environment through time, and . . . how they have affected that environment and with what results" ("Transformation of the Earth: Toward an Agroecological Perspective in History," *The Journal of American History* 76 [March 1990]: 1089).

18. The issues in this controversy are well argued in an *American Historical Review* forum: Ian Tyrell, "American Exceptionalism in the Age of International History," *American Historical Review* 96 (October 1991): 1031–55; Michael McGerr, "The Price of New Transnational History," *American Historical Review* 96 (October 1991): 1056–67; and Tyrell's response, pp. 1068–72.

19. James T. Kloppenberg, "Objectivity and Historicism: A Century of American Historical Writing," *American Historical Review* 94 (October 1989): 1019, 1028–29.

REFERENCES

Adler, Douglas D., and Matthew T. Downey. "Problem Areas in the History Curriculum." In Matthew T. Downey, ed., *History in the Schools*. Washington, DC: National Council for the Social Studies, 1985.

Banks, James A. *Academic Preparation in Social Studies*. New York: College Entrance Examination Board, 1986.

Bender, Thomas. "The New History-Then and Now." *Reviews in American History* 12 (December 1984): 612–22.

———. "Wholes and Parts: The Need for Synthesis in American History." *The Journal of American History* 73 (June 1986): 120–36.

The Bradley Commission on History in Schools. *Building a History Curriculum: Guidelines for Teaching History in Schools*. Washington, DC: Education Excellence Network, 1988.

Buhle, Mari Jo, and Paul Buhle. "The New Labor History at the Crossroads." *The Journal of American History* 75 (June 1988): 151–57.

Cuban, Larry. "History of Teaching in Social Studies." In James P. Shaver, ed., *Handbook of Research on Social Studies Teaching and Learning*. New York: Macmillan, 1991.

Daniels, Roger. "The Melting Pot: A Content Analysis." *Reviews in American History* 9 (December 1981): 428–33.

D'Emilio, John D. "Not a Simple Matter: Gay History and Gay Historians." *The Journal of American History* 76 (September 1989): 435–42.

Diggins, John P. "The Misuses of Gramsci." *The Journal of American History* 75 (June 1988): 141–45.

———. "Language and History." *Reviews in American History* 17 (March 1989): 1–9.

Downey, Matthew T. "The New History and the Classroom." In Matthew T. Downey, ed., *Teaching American History: New Directions.* Washington, DC: National Council for the Social Studies, 1982.

———. "The Status of History in the Schools." In Matthew T. Downey, ed., *History in the Schools.* Washington, DC: National Council for the Social Studies, 1985.

Duberman, Martin. "Reclaiming the Gay Past." *Reviews in American History* 16 (December 1988): 515–25.

Engle, Shirley. "The Commission Report and Citizenship Education." *Social Education* 54 (November/December 1990): 431–35.

Fox, Richard. "Public Culture and the Problem of Synthesis." *The Journal of American History* 74 (June 1987): 113–16.

Franklin, John Hope. "Afro-American History: State of the Art." *The Journal of American History* 75 (June 1988): 162–73.

———. *Race and History: Selected Essays, 1938–1988.* Baton Rouge: Louisiana State University Press, 1989.

Gorn, Elliott J. "Doing Sports History." *Reviews in American History* 18 (March 1990): 27–32.

Green, Harvey. *Fit for America: Health, Fitness, Sports, and American Society.* Baltimore: Pantheon Books, 1986.

Grob, Gerald N. "Sidney Fine on the Intellectual Origins of the General Welfare State: Or What Happened to Social and Intellectual History?" *Reviews in American History* 12 (June 1984): 286–95.

Harding, Vincent. "Beyond Chaos: Black History and the Search for the New Land," in John A. Williams and Charles F. Harris, eds., *Armistad 1: Writings on Black History and Culture.* New York: Random House, 1970.

Harlan, David. "Intellectual History and the Return of Literature." *American Historical Review* 94 (June 1981): 581–609.

Harris, Robert L. "The Flowering of Afro-American History." *American Historical Review* 92 (December 1987): 1150–61.

Hertzberg, Hazel W. "History and Progressivism: A Century of Reform Proposals." In Paul Gagnon, ed., *Historical Literacy: The Case for History in American Education.* Boston: Houghton Mifflin, 1989.

Himmelfarb, Gertrude. "Some Reflections on the New History." *American Historical Review* 94 (June 1989): 661–70.

Hoopes, James. "Puritanism and Puritans." *Reviews in American History* 17 (December 1989): 529–34.

Howe, Daniel Worthy. "Virtue and Commerce in Jeffersonian America." *Reviews in American History* 9 (September 1981): 347–353.

Hunt, Michael. "Ideology." *The Journal of American History* 77 (June 1990): 108–15.

Jenness, David. *Making Sense of Social Studies*. New York: Macmillan, 1990.

Kammen, Michael. "Introduction: The Historian's Vocation and the State of the Discipline in the United States." In Michael Kammen, ed., *The Past before Us: Contemporary Historical Writing in the United States*. Ithaca, NY: Cornell University Press, 1980.

Kessner, Thomas. *The Journal of American History* 72 (March 1986): 974–75.

Kincheloe, Joe. *Getting Beyond the Facts: Teaching Social Studies in the Late Twentieth Century*. New York: Peter Lang, 1989.

Laughlin, Margaret A., H. Michael Hartoonian, and Norris M. Sanders, eds., *From Information to Decision Making: New Challenges for Effective Citizenship*. Washington, DC: National Council for the Social Studies, 1989.

Leavitt, Judith Walzer. "Medicine in Context: A Review Essay on the History of Medicine." *American Historical Review* 95 (December 1990): 1472–73.

Leuchtenburg, William E. "The Pertinence of Political History: Reflections on the History of the State in America." *The Journal of American History* 73 (December 1986): 585–99.

Levine, Lawrence. "The Unpredictable Past: Reflections on Recent American Historiography." *American Historical Review* 94 (June 1989): 671–79.

Lipsitz, George. "The Struggle for Hegemony." *The Journal of American History* 75 (June 1988): 146–50.

McNeill, William H., Michael Kammen, and Gordon A. Craig. "Why Study History? Three Historians Respond." In Paul Gagnon, ed., *Historical Literacy: The Case for History in American Education*. Boston: Houghton Mifflin, 1989.

Meier, August, and Elliott Rudwick. *Black History and the Historical Profession*. Urbana, IL: University of Illinois Press, 1986.

Monkkonner, Eric H. "The Dangers of Synthesis." *American Historical Review* 91 (December 1986): 1147–57.

National Commission on Social Studies in the Schools. *Charting a Course: Social Studies for the 21st Century*. Washington, DC: National Commission on Social Studies in the Schools, 1989.

Nelson, Jack L. "Charting a Course Backwards: A Response to the National Commission's Nineteenth Century Social Studies Program." *Social Education* 54 (November/December 1990): 437–39.

Nevins, Allan. "The Gateway to History." In John A. Garraty, ed., *Interpreting American History: Conversations with Historians*, Part II. New York: Macmillan, 1970.

Noble, David. "Perhaps the Rise and Fall of Scientific History in the American Historical Profession." *Reviews in American History* 17 (December 1989): 519–22.

Novick, Peter. *That Noble Dream: The Objectivity Question and the American Historical Profession*. New York: Cambridge University Press, 1988.

Patrick, John J., and Sharryl Davis Hawke. "Curriculum Materials." In Irving Morrissett, ed., *Social Studies in the 1980s: A Report of Project SPAN*. Alexandria, VA: Association for Supervision and Curriculum Development, 1982.

Project SPAN Consultants and Staff. "Six Problems for Social Studies in the 1980s." In Irving Morrissett, ed., *Social Studies in the 1980s: A Report of Project SPAN*. Alexandria, VA: Association for Supervision and Curriculum Development, 1982.

Quarles, Benjamin. *Black Mosaic: Essays in Afro-American History*. Amherst: University of Massachusetts Press, 1988.

Ravitch, Diane. "The Plight of History in the Schools." In Paul Gagnon, ed., *Historical Literacy: The Case for History in American Education*. Boston: Houghton Mifflin, 1989.

Ravitch, Diane, and Chester E. Finn, Jr. *What Do Our17-Year-Olds Know?* New York: Harper and Row, 1987.

Rogers, Vincent, Arthur D. Roberts, and Thomas P. Weinland, eds. *Teaching Social Studies: Portraits from the Classroom*. Washington, DC: National Council for the Social Studies, 1988.

Rosenburg, Emily S. "Gender." *The Journal of American History* 77 (June 1990): 116–24.

Schatz, Ronald W. "Review Essay: Labor Historians, Labor Economics, and the Question of Synthesis." *The Journal of American History* 71 (June 1984): 93–100.

Schlesinger, Arthur M., *Rise of the City, 1878–1898*. New York: Macmillan, 1933.

Scott, Joan Wallach. "History in Crisis? The Other Side of the Story." *American Historical Review* 94 (June 1989): 680–92.

S.C.R. No. 56, 69th. State Legislature of Texas (1985).

Shulman, Lee. "Knowledge and Teaching: Foundations of the New Reforms." *Harvard Educational Review* 57 (1987): 1–22.

South Carolina Act 512, Section 59–29–55 (1984).

Thelen, David. "What Has Changed and Not Changed in American Historical Practice?" *The Journal of American History* 76 (September 1989): 393–98.

Thernstorm, Stephen, Ann Orlov, and Oscar Handlin, eds. *Harvard Encyclopedia of American Ethnic Groups*. Cambridge, MA: Belknap Press of Harvard University, 1980.

Tygiel, Jules. "A Very Peculiar Business." *Reviews in American History* 19 (March 1991): 109–15.

Weiner, Jonathan. "Radical Historians and the Crisis in American History." *The Journal of American History* 76 (September 1989): 399–434.

Wilson, Suzanne M., and Gary Sykes. "Toward Better Teacher Preparation and Certification." In Paul Gagnon, ed., *Historical Literacy: The Case for History in American Education*. Boston: Houghton Mifflin, 1989.

Wineburg, Samuel S., and Suzanne M. Wilson. "Subject Matter Knowledge in the Teaching of History." In J. E. Brophy, ed., *Advances in Research on Teaching*. Greenwich, CT: JAI, in press. (An earlier version of this essay, "Models of Wisdom in the Teaching of History," appeared in *Phi Delta Kappan* 70 [September 1988]: 50–58.)

5

WORLD HISTORY IN THE SCHOOLS

Burton F. Beers

World history moved into the mainstream of American secondary education during the 1980s. By the decade's end, a year-long course in the subject was not just an elective for college-bound youth. Rather, world history increasingly became a course that nearly every student should take—almost as vital as that old standard, American history. Some states, such as Texas and California, made world history a graduation requirement. Elsewhere, students were steered toward world history and away from other electives. Sensing the trend, textbook publishers produced perhaps as many as half a dozen new books and updated some older titles.

Early in the 1990s the debate that had previously swirled around the issue of making world history a standard part of the curriculum abated somewhat. Such new questions as how to organize the curriculum so that world and American history might reinforce each other, what the content of world history ought to be, and how the quality of instruction and learning might be improved began to command attention. The first rounds of debate on these questions suggested that answering them would be neither quick nor easy.

REFLECTIONS

The swing toward world history came at a time when Americans were once again locked in a sometimes bitter, far-reaching controversy over the quality of public education. Charges that standards in American education were "shockingly low" echoed similar criticisms made during the Sputnik crisis of the 1950s. On that earlier occasion, Americans had been jolted by the Soviet Union's ability to launch a satellite well in advance of any similar accomplishment by the United States. National outrage touched off reform efforts that focused initially on instruction in math and science. Later, the reform movement spread to social studies. The renewed furor over public education in the 1980s, however, highlighted deficiencies in social studies from the outset. One highly publicized study after another charged that American students were undereducated in virtually everything that social studies were supposed to teach: history, geography, government, and economics.

A number of thoughtful critics of American education had begun to call even earlier (i.e., by the mid-1970s) for strengthening social studies through more emphasis on history (Kirkendall 1975–76; see also Boyer 1983; Finn 1984). In North Carolina some historians—chiefly members of the Historical Society of North Carolina—took up the cause, and early in the 1980s the state's education agency approved curriculum changes that clarified and strengthened history's role in the schools. This occurred well in advance of any significant movement on the national level. The American Historical Association, which had played no significant role in efforts to reform social studies in the 1960s and 1970s, waited until 1985 to join the National Council for the Social Studies in taking some initial steps toward reform (Link 1985). By that time the Organization of American Historians had also begun searching for ways to encourage the teaching of history. In 1987, a privately funded organization, the Bradley Commission on History in the Schools, was established "to review the status of history in United States school curricula and to make recommendations for its improvement." The Bradley Commission itself was composed of respected historians and master classroom teachers from elementary and secondary schools. Under the commission's direction, staff—and sometimes commission members—developed model curricula, defined standards of "historical literacy," and collaborated with local and state school systems in promoting history's cause (Bradley Commission 1988).

This commission promoted history as vital to citizenship education and the training of future generations of American leaders. Such education required not only a mastery of the basics of American history, but also a familiarity with the nation's links to the larger world. Historian Paul A. Gagnon, who was listed by the Bradley Commission as its "Principal Investigator," made the case for Western Civilization courses in these terms:

If students have done no systematic study of the history of Western Civilization before the 9th or 10th grade, it must become the heart of whatever course is then offered. Why emphasize Western Civilization? Simply because American history and ideas, and the vision and fate of democracy on earth, are not intelligible without a prior grasp of the life and ideas of Greece and Rome, Judaism and Christianity, Islam and Christendom in the Middle Ages, feudalism, the Renaissance and the Reformation, absolutism, the English Revolution, the Enlightenment, the French Revolution, and the comparative experiences of Europe and the United States in the 19th and 20th centuries. (Gagnon 1989: 38–39)

Later, it would become evident that the members of the Bradley Commission, like almost any gathering of academicians, did not unanimously subscribe to Gagnon's assertions. One of the most distinguished commission members, William H. McNeill, has been an articulate proponent of a fundamentally reorganized approach to world history. McNeill's approach, unlike Gagnon's, would not make Western Civilization central to the study of history.

The world history textbooks most commonly found in the nation's schools, however, have followed the pattern that Gagnon described. While these books may differ significantly in terms of reading levels, quality of scholarship, and the aids offered for teaching, virtually all of them target tenth graders, and virtually all present a narrative stretching from prehistory and the early river valley civilizations to the present. Chapters covering the development of Western Civilization account for about two-thirds of the total text; the pre-Columbian Western Hemisphere, Africa, the Middle East, and Asia are covered in the remainder. This organization has enabled textbook writers to indicate the variation in patterns of civilization and the interaction between the modern West and the larger world. If students have had little opportunity in such books to dig deeply into Indian and Chinese civilization, given the four or five chapters assigned to all of some 4,000 years of Asian history, they have nevertheless been able to learn a great deal about the origins of many American institutions and traditions as they were formed in and then transferred from Europe to the United States.

The sameness among, and similarities within, competing textbooks have drawn sharp criticism. The nature of these complaints was best captured by one world history teacher in her extended review of several newly published texts: "It is certainly an ironic tragedy," she wrote, "that in a free society where choice is theoretically available, the result has been much like the results in the Soviet Union—a one textbook history. One suspects that behind some of this is heavy politicization of the textbook production and acquisition process" (Hitchens 1990: 10). Other critics, while supporting this teacher's complaint about limited choice, have fixed the blame on the economic clout exercised by education agencies employing statewide textbook adoption practices. Under this system short lists of textbooks for each subject area are drawn up by a state agency which examines each publisher's offering against rather detailed sets of specifications prepared by the state. Local school districts must then choose books from the approved list if they are to qualify for funds from their state's book budget. While twenty-two states employ these procedures, two in particular—Texas and California—have been most frequently cited as the ones that allegedly determine what choices the nation's schools will have. These two states have had very large student populations and generous book budgets, circumstances which have become ever more important as the costs of publishing and marketing textbooks have gone up and corporate mergers have brought the number of competing publishers down. Publishers, the critics have claimed, point to good sales in Texas and/or California as the essential baseline for national sales campaigns that will bring solid returns on their investments. Anyone watching the hard-driving sales campaigns in Texas can scarcely doubt the importance of brisk sales there to the fortunes of publishers and their sales representatives. Yet the evidence seems to support the publishers—certainly in terms of world history textbooks—when they deny that they are targeting a single state.

The criteria that publishers must meet in all statewide adoption systems have been virtually identical (California has recently become an exception); nor have sales representatives found the requirements to be any different as they have moved from one school to another in the "open adoption" states. In effect, the market has persuaded publishers that there is a broad consensus on the nature of the world history that American students should study. Moreover, while calls for something different have been heard, the alternatives have yet to become clearly enough defined or sufficiently attractive to undermine broad support for world history texts organized around Western Civilization. Hence, publishers revise established textbooks or commission new ones in circumstances that prompt them to look more closely at the competition than at standard state or local adoption guidelines. Publishers have found it useful to observe carefully what others have done with the student editions, teacher editions, and the ancillary texts that serve as teaching aids. By bringing narratives up to date, freshening the prose, and adding attractive features to any or all of a book's components, each publisher hopes to enlarge its market share. Radical departures from accepted content have been rare (Van DeVen 1990).

While Gagnon and other publicists have undoubtedly helped nudge the Western-centered world history course into the mainstream in American schools, the course more likely owes its current popularity among curriculum designers to the fact that it is one of the most time-tested components of social studies education. For untold numbers of educators, that course—or something akin to it—was an essential feature of their own collegiate experience.

The rise of "Western Civ" is one of the great success stories in the history of the historical profession in America. For a time between the First World War and the campus protests of the 1960s, all roads led to the Western Civ class. Compulsory enrollment requirements at many institutions brought liberal arts students from every discipline, and from science programs and professional schools came others in mass numbers to brush with "culture" in a class renowned for grand ideas and great books. Classrooms filled, budgets bulged, teachers multiplied. In discussion sections that became a feature of the course virtually everywhere, three generations of "teaching assistants," the best and the brightest graduate students in European history, began their apprenticeship in college instruction. Western Civ, more than any other academic invention, brought European history to power in the college curriculum, and the easy acceptance of the class in colleges across the country indicated that it represented an idea about the Old World whose time had come. (Allardyce 1982: 695)

This trend was to be taken up more gradually in public education, but the success enjoyed by Western Civilization in higher education was eventually reflected in the high school curriculum. By the 1930s a year-long version of this course, followed by American history, was becoming commonplace in high schools.

Western Civilization was a course that met distinctive American needs. This nation had inherited from Europe the idea that civilization originated in the ancient Near East, evolved through classical Greece and Rome, and then moved on to medieval and modern Europe. But Americans departed from the practice of nineteenth-century European historians, who, preoccupied with ever more vibrant nationalisms, split this heritage up into the histories of particular states. American historians searched for the common elements in that European culture which had been transmitted to the United States. By so doing, these historians endowed the nation's history with an antiquity reaching far beyond Columbus in time and beyond the dimensions of the North American continent in space.

Historians at Harvard and Columbia were the first to capture these ideas in a single course. The impulse at Harvard was generated by efforts to fill a void in the undergraduate curriculum after introductory studies in the classics had been discarded. Harvard's faculty moved to fill the freshman and sophomore years with a new program in general education. There, beginning as early as the 1870s, form was given to a course that eventually became "Western Civilization": one which swept across time, but centered on Europe and its roots; teaching which combined large lecture sessions with small discussion groups; and assignments drawn from textbooks and primary sources.

A major problem with this course at Harvard and on other campuses was that it initially lacked any organizing principles that would determine which facts from an ocean of data were taught and which were omitted. The Harvard faculty dealt with the problem by gradually reducing their general history to a study of Europe's Middle Ages. Likewise, Columbia responded to criticism that its survey was overburdened, chaotic, and unteachable not only by bringing its content under control, but also by infusing it with a rationale that eventually captured the American mind.

James Harvey Robinson proved to be a key figure in reducing Columbia's survey to manageable proportions. As the author of several successful college and high school texts, and as a popular teacher, Robinson had the authority to confront and resolve the problem of selection.

Only gradually did the writer [Robinson recalled] come to conceive of history as something far more vital than the record of bygone events and the description of extinct institutions. He then saw that if history was to fulfill its chief function and become an essential explanation of how our own civilization came to take the form it has, and present the problems that it does, a fresh selection from the records of the past would have to be made. Much that had been included in historical manuals would of necessity be left out as irrelevant or unimportant. Only those considerations would properly find a place which clearly served to forward the main purpose of seeing more and more distinctly how this, our present Western Civilization, in which we have been born and are now immersed, has come about. (Allardyce 1982: 705)

In short, Robinson's conception of the "living past"—that part of the past which continues into the present—laid the foundation for a simplified, thematic, and interpretive version of European history for introductory courses in high schools and colleges. Such courses, it must be added, would not be restricted to the subject of past politics only. As a leading popularizer of the "New History," Robinson infused his narratives with economics and with social and cultural events. By so doing, he became an innovator in still another significant way: he presented history as an integrating discipline, one which could draw upon other disciplines to portray the whole panorama of civilization.

Many of these innovations spread beyond the Harvard and Columbia campuses in the century's early years, altering to some degree the kind of teaching done in colleges and high schools. Yet, not until the United States entered World War I did the Western Civilization course begin to sweep the country's schools. During the war years, over five hundred colleges were designated centers for training military officers. A War Department directive required each school to assemble its best men from history, government, philosophy, economics, and literature to design and teach officer candidates a "War Issues" course which would inculcate an understanding of the way of life and the society they were to defend as well as the enemy they were to destroy. At the beginning of this enterprise, critics predicted that academic rivalries would produce tumult, but, drawn together by patriotism, these professors made the course work. For many faculty the "War Issues" course provided practical illustrations of how a general education course stressing the heritage of liberty might serve students in peacetime: namely, as a compulsory, interdisciplinary exercise in common training for the duties of citizenship. Moreover, Columbia's courses in Western Civilization provided proven models for colleges that did not already have general introductory programs of their own.

Few students who attended college during the half century after World War I escaped Western Civilization. Yet, soon after the Second World War, even as the nation's battles against "world communism" provided a context that seemed to favor continuing studies in the West's heritage of liberty, faculty support for Western Civilization courses began to fade. New generations of academics, who became ever more numerous as college enrollments expanded in the postwar years, were less inclined to accept the generalizations upon which the survey course was built. Young Europeanists were often skeptical of attempts to portray European history as a narrative of liberty and reason. Fascism and Bolshevism belied those images. Moreover, as a generation educated in social history, these younger faculty members deplored Western Civilization's emphasis on the "high" history that told only of great political figures, ideas, and institutions. Where were the women, children, Jews, and peasants? In short, in reality, there was no single history of Europe, as presented in Western Civilization, but rather many possible histories. Such criticism was magnified by the Third World specialists, who argued that Western Civilization fell far short of offering what Americans needed to know. In an age when the United States was deeply involved with people who represented so many civilizations around the world, it was essential, these specialists said, that Americans learn about the world beyond the West.

These dissenting voices soon made an impact, both on the way Western Civilization was taught and on the content of the course itself. In the post–World War II era, as the commanding lecturers of Western Civilization's glory days disappeared, the relative importance of the lecture hall and discussion sections was reversed. No longer did large groups of students listen to great ideas expounded from the lectern, and no longer did they seek to amplify what they heard by reading from a common textbook and discussing the week's assignment in section meetings. Instead, the section leaders took charge of the course. Decisions to replace textbooks with collections of documents opened the door to the possibility that section leaders might teach quite different things; the likelihood that this would happen increased when collections of documents were in turn supplanted by paperback books; and these developments cumulatively eroded the links between the lectures and the discussions. Since section leaders also assigned the grades, the unified view of knowledge that had once characterized Western Civilization evaporated. In the late 1960s and early 1970s, few faculty were willing to rise to the course's defense when student protestors, angered by the Vietnam War and skeptical of the West's claim to world leadership, demanded the abolition of the Western Civilization requirement. The course remained on the lists of departmental offerings, but almost everywhere it became only one of many introductory courses (Allardyce 1982).

In the nation's high schools, world history—in effect, Western Civilization—rose and then fell, much as it had in the colleges. As was indicated earlier, this year-long course had made its way into school curricula during the 1920s and 1930s. Public educators were attracted by the same elements in the course that had been so appealing to college faculty: namely, the essential knowledge for citizenship. Thus, while not all students were required to take it, world history was usually offered in the tenth grade, where it served as an introduction to the subsequent required year of American history. Bracketing these two courses in most schools were a ninth grade course in "civics" and a twelfth grade course called "Problems of Democracy." No doubt educators viewed world history as an ever more essential element in this sequence of courses during the late 1930s, as the nation entered a period of international crisis, and students did in fact take the course in ever increasing numbers. One prominent figure in educational circles, Edgar B. Wesley, in an article entitled "The Potentialities of World History in a World Society," described the course as a "model offering next in popularity to American history" (West 1949: 1). By 1961, sixty-nine percent of tenth-grade students were enrolled in world history.

Both praise of the course and its swelling enrollments, however, proved to be facades, thinly veiling serious flaws. Students, perhaps unprepared for the challenges of such a course, professed themselves bored rather than stimulated by world history; teachers complained that the focus of a course covering so much time and space eluded them; and curriculum designers, apparently influenced by the growing discontent with the course in higher education, began to doubt that world history was serving its intended purpose. Dorothy McClure, then president of the National Council for the Social Studies, whose views were published in the same volume as Edgar B. Wesley's, reminded her colleague that the elegance of a curriculum model, in the instance of world history, was not matched in the classroom: "Random surveys of opinion among teachers and students alike indicate that perhaps no part of the social studies program is more criticized than the one-year, elective world history course" (ibid.: 25). Even as enrollments were approaching their zenith in the early 1960s, education critic Martin Mayer found high school world history to be the course that "everyone hates" (Mayer 1963: 22).

To appreciate fully the developments still to come, it should be emphasized at this point that in promoting the world history course as part of the school curriculum from the 1930s on, public educators were operating largely on their own. While college professors appeared frequently as the authors of student texts, and teachers had often been enrolled in Western Civilization as undergraduates, little contact occurred between college-based historians and social studies teachers. Whatever institutional links had been established during the formative years of the modern high school became strained in the early 1920s. Public schools began to break away from a curriculum that had been devised some thirty years earlier by leaders of the American Historical Association. Acting on the historians' advice, the schools had instituted in grades nine through twelve a four-year sequence of courses: ancient history, medieval and modern history, English history, and American history. By the World War I years, however, the emerging social sciences were clamoring for a place in school curricula and public educators were reacting positively to the possibilities that these disciplines offered. The formation of the National Council for the Social Studies in 1921 marked a significant step by reform-minded educators who were trying to find ways to draw upon a number of disciplines in constructing a school curriculum that would serve both those students for whom a high school diploma was a terminal degree and the relatively few who were college bound. It was in this context that high schools began to shift toward a two-year sequence in world and American history as well as in other subjects.

Representatives of the American Historical Association deplored the departure from a social studies curriculum based exclusively on history. Public school educators defended themselves by saying that their own professional expertise enabled them to devise appropriate courses of study. In one sense, such heated exchanges, which became a standard feature of the American educational scene, changed little. School teachers and college professors were not in the habit of consulting one another anyway, so these tensions did not destroy any existing interchange at the classroom level. Fortunately, no organizational ties were broken because the American Historical Association and the National Council for the Social Studies established and maintained some cooperative efforts. Yet the continuing crossfire did not encourage professional historians to cultivate much interest in the public schools, and classroom teachers in turn seldom looked to these historians. Not surprisingly, when the reform of social studies was first attempted in the 1960s, social scientists, not historians, led the way (Robinson and Kirman 1986).

This reform process was set in motion by the Sputnik crisis alluded to earlier. Allegations that in a time of great international crisis American education was failing to match the Soviet Union's system resulted in generous federal funding, with which the universities and public schools were to introduce a new rigor to secondary education. University-based math and science projects were given priority. These generated new curriculum materials and provided master teachers with assistance in introducing these materials into the schools. Similar collaborative efforts were undertaken in the social studies when they became eligible for funding under the National Defense Education Act in the mid-1960s. One result was the development of the "new social studies," which organized instruction by the guiding principles of history, political science, sociology, and other relevant academic disciplines. This affirmation of social science disciplines as appropriate in the schools became one weapon deployed in the attack on the old Western Civilization course. A second weapon was created by the contention that school curricula must be relevant to the time. As the K–12 curriculum was examined anew, reformers looked for opportunities to introduce studies having a truly global dimension. Given the worldwide reach of American society, educators could ill afford to allow only the study of a Eurocentric heritage:

For over one hundred years there has been some form of teaching about people outside America's geographic borders in both elementary and secondary schools. All of us have traced the storied Nile to its source while learning that Egypt is her gracious gift. We have memorized the Plantagenet kings and sung about the Alps. Events of the 1960s, however, changed all that. The Soviet launching of Sputnik had set the USA on her ear. . . . When most of us try to recall what we were taught about human cultures from kindergarten through grade 12, we remember only United States history, the history of our own home state, and what was lumped into a bag known as "world" history, namely European, emphatically Western culture, commencing in Mesopotamia and the Nile Valley. Suddenly out of the 1960s, sprang Africa, Asia, Latin America, and Canada. (Bullard 1979: 1)

Such was the rhetoric that justified the collaborative efforts of specialists from higher education and public school teachers to produce teaching units on Chinese communes, Indian villages, African arts, and the like for junior and senior high school students. Much of this work was campus-based, but not infrequently groups of teachers discovered that curriculum building could land them in South Asia, Sub-Saharan Africa, or some other place that they had previously seen only in the pages of *National Geographic*.

Curriculum reform went forward across the nation without much centralized direction or planning. North Carolina surprised many who were unaccustomed to looking toward the South for educational leadership by taking the lead over most states in adopting the "new social studies" and in attempting to globalize its curriculum. Guidelines approved in 1972 called for year-long study of the Americas (North and South) in grade five, Europe (as well as the Soviet Union) in grade six, and Africa, the Middle East, and Asia in grade seven. While the disciplinary base of these courses was not initially specified, they eventually came to be organized as cultural geography. A similar lack of specificity characterized the tenth through twelfth grade courses, where state guidelines called for a "World Studies Program" (American and North Carolina history were to be combined and offered in grades eight and nine). Local systems were free to retain the established Western Civilization course, but the list of suggested courses issued by the state education office favored the "cultures" approach, which encouraged students to move intellectually inside societies and thereby to gain knowledge and an understanding of a diversified world. North Carolina, it should be added, enjoyed enough success in actually implementing this curriculum in the classroom to attract the attention of other states (Grubbs 1982: 150–223).

The stress placed on "cultures" rather than history was not uncommon in the 1960s and 1970s. From many quarters came evidence (college enrollments in history, for example, declined dramatically) that history was generally losing favor and that, in global studies especially, history was not an appropriate discipline. One reformer, however, historian Leften Stavrianos of Northwestern University, spoke out against this trend. He rejected "cultures"-based curricula on the grounds that the lessons they taught were less essential than those of global history, which he described as embodying a perspective of civilizations as seen from the moon. He decried Western Civilization's masquerading as world history because it encouraged Americans to believe that the West's hegemony in the world would be everlasting. What young Americans really needed to prepare them for life in a dynamic world were studies that examine the changing fortunes of civilizations as societies met and interacted with one another. Stavrianos's Global History Project reaffirmed the value of historical studies in the 1960s. His textbooks for college and high school courses attracted considerable attention while the global studies movement was at its height (Allardyce 1990).

But Stavrianos's project and all the others in global studies rapidly lost support in the 1970s. The nation's agonies over the Vietnam War seem to have been a catalyst, redirecting popular attention inward. Educators found public opinion to be focused on crime, violence, and family problems; Americans no longer gave a high priority to education with an international flavor. It was in this new climate of opinion that North Carolina again took the lead over most states, reexamining its curriculum and deciding on retrenchment: while the fifth, sixth, and seventh grade units in cultural geography of the world were retained, courses in the grades above were reorganized in a manner that gave greater emphasis to history as the base of instruction. North Carolina history was to be studied in grade eight; the American governmental, legal, and economic systems would be covered in grade nine; world studies (from which students might elect history, geography, or "cultures") were assigned to grade ten; and United States history was restored to grade eleven.

CURRENT ISSUES AND TRENDS

Reform along these lines throughout the nation marked the demise of the "new social studies." Their passing was scarcely mourned. In 1989, the National Commission on Social Studies in the Schools, a body of distinguished public school educators, historians, and social scientists assembled by the National Council for the Social Studies and the American Historical Association, issued a harshly worded obituary. The "new social studies" were seen by the National Commission as having failed to produce students who had a fundamental grasp of "basic facts and issues of local, state, national and world history, of American political traditions, institutions, and processes, and of geography." It was a failure, moreover, born of a "focus upon discrete social science and humanities disciplines without considering their relationship to the whole curriculum" (National Commission 1989: v).

These blunt statements were made in the preface to a rather detailed blueprint indicating how, according to the National Commission, curriculum designers in all fifty states should recast their social studies programs. Published under the title *Charting a Course: Social Studies for the 21st Century,* the National Commission's recommendations deserve some detailed attention here because they encourage the continued development of world history. The five goals articulated for the K–12 curriculum by the National Commission include the following one: "An understanding of other people and the unity and diversity of world history, geography, institutions, traditions and values." This "understanding" would be achieved through programs offering

selective studies of the history, geography, government, and economic systems of the major civilizations and societies [which] should together receive attention at least equal to the study of the history, geography, government, economics and society of the United States. A curriculum that focuses on only one or two major civilizations or geographic areas while ignoring others is neither adequate nor complete. (3)

Elsewhere, the National Commission indicated its conviction that the contributions to knowledge made by several social sciences should be incorporated into the curriculum through history and geography, "the twin disciplines on which the content of social studies can be organized" (x).

The recommendations retained one key element of the global-studies reforms: Schools were advised to begin students' introduction to the world in the early grades. Primary school teachers would find that a "good rule of thumb would be to balance material about the United States with about an equal number of stories about other times and places." Grades four through six should include the study of United States and world history as well as geography. But it was at the high school level that the National Commission's recommendations took an especially dramatic turn, proposing a three-year sequence in which the history and geography of the United States would be merged with the world's, thereby "teaching our nation's history as part of the general story of humanity." The sequence would start at grade nine, with "World and American History and Geography in 1750"; 1750–1900 would be covered in tenth grade, and 1900 to the present in eleventh grade. Each of these courses was to focus on topics and themes that, when knitted together, presented a coherent view of an emerging world. At grade twelve, a course in government and economics, which ideally would compare the American systems with those of other nations, was recommended (7–20).

By introducing world history early, identifying key topics and themes, and establishing courses that required students to wrestle with the subject at different points in their intellectual development, the schools, declared the National Commission, could provide a much improved context for linking studies of the world with those of the United States. The students emerging from such a unified curriculum would be "prepared to live well and wisely in a changing world, better able to play their part as citizens of our country, as members of their local community and as sharers in the human adventure on earth" (National Commission 1989: 58). While the reforms intended to produce these results were presented as a solution to the problems associated with the "new social studies," the members of the commission seemed aware that a history-based curriculum could potentially generate a chaos of its own. The knowledge explosion set off by historical research extended the range of possible answers to some enduring questions: What history is to be taught? How is it to be structured and to fit into curricula? And what purpose does history teaching serve? The history profession had by no means achieved consensus on how these questions were to be answered. Hence it was essential that curriculum reform not be undertaken in a piecemeal fashion. The model curriculum produced by the National Commission was intended to demonstrate the wisdom of focusing on a core of knowledge and understanding. It was not essential, however, that this core be identically constructed everywhere; details might vary from place to place. The crucial matter was for curricular design to be based on agreement and for that agreement to be reflected in the schools.

The National Commission's own report, however, also provided an inkling of the difficulties that curriculum designers would probably encounter. William H. McNeill, University of Chicago Emeritus Professor of History, was cochair of the commission and the key figure in shaping its recommendations on world history. In his hands, the commission's model curriculum and its accompanying rationale became a vehicle for advocating histories that eschewed the convention of focusing on civilizations and their achievements. Rather, "world history ought to be more organized around major breakthroughs in communication that, step by step, intensified interactions within ever larger regions of the earth until instant global communications became a pervasive reality of our own time" (55). Here was an organizing theme, moreover, that broke with other well-established conventions. Western Civilization could never be central to this conceptualization simply because it was conceived as culminating in the shaping of the United States. Rather, it would be considered one of several, roughly equal civilizations which had in turn made contributions to a heterogeneous world that the United States shared with many nations. Finally, this was a model of history that could probably be best implemented through wholesale reorganization of time-honored topics and chronology along the lines of the high school courses outlined above (53–58).

NcNeill's approach was not his alone, but also had the organized support of an able group of college faculty and school teachers. This group, who had been working together to introduce a new model of world history into schools and higher education, had become large enough by the early 1990s to produce an excellent journal and to meet regularly at national and regional conferences. Yet its cause was still that of a minority.[1] Richard E. Sullivan, Professor of History at Michigan State University, predicted in 1985 at a conference session entitled "Western Civilization or World History?" that historians would be slow to discard specialized courses and embrace world history because of their skepticism toward some of the concepts needed for writing or teaching in the field, such as

long-term processes in place of assertive events; commonalities in human experiences in place of uniqueness; comparison in place of linearity; collectivities in place of individuals; structure in place of conscious choices; problems in place of shared values. To reshape thinking in these directions and to rearrange data according to their dictates does indeed suggest a revolution. (Sullivan 1985: 262–63)

Moreover, even teachers shifting from Western to world civilization would be obliged to jettison vast amounts of information hitherto "held sacred in terms of defining what anybody . . . should know." The retooling to be required of college faculty and school teachers alike "will be excruciating; perhaps the pain endured in the process will deserve its own circle . . . in a future version of the *Divine Comedy*" (ibid. 263).

Although Professor Sullivan was describing his personal vision of possibly tortured teachers, it became clear that efforts to settle on a core of knowledge and understanding could certainly involve curriculum specialists and teachers in heated public debates. By the early 1990s, for example, "multicultural education," a phrase that referred to teaching about the heritages of minorities in American society, was catching educators everywhere in a crossfire. A report to New York's Commissioner of Education, *Minorities: Equity and Excellence,* charged that African Americans, Asian Americans, Puerto Ricans/Latinos, and Native Americans were "victims of an intellectual and educational oppression." The "systematic bias toward European culture and its derivatives," the report claimed, had "a terribly damaging effect on the psyche of young people of African, Asian, Latino and Native American descent" (New York State 1989: 5–6, 9). The allegation prompted Professor Arthur Schlesinger, Jr., to respond that the report was a call not for "intellectual challenges," but for "psychological therapy," and he went on to say,

Let us by all means teach women's history, black history, Hispanic history. But let us teach them as history, not as a means of promoting group self-esteem.... Let us by all means learn about other continents and other cultures. But... we inherit an American experience, as America inherits a European experience. To deny the essentially European origins of American culture is to falsify history.[2]

For Professor Schlesinger, a renowned holder of distinguished university appointments, author of acclaimed books, advisor to presidential aspirants, and member of President John F. Kennedy's White House staff, this plunge into the politics of New York's social studies curriculum was remarkable. Even more remarkable has been the increasing amount of space in the publications of the American Historical Association, the Organization of American Historians, and other historical societies that has been devoted to a wide range of issues related to teaching history in the schools: curriculum revision, the formation of teaching alliances, summer institutes for teachers, and curriculum materials.[3] A growing number of historians have begun to work with schools and to find practical ways to collaborate with teachers. This has been in marked contrast to the American Historical Association's first, clumsy efforts to strengthen history in the schools beyond nominally cooperating with the National Council for the Social Studies. Between 1958 and 1965, the AHA's Service Center for Teachers published some seventy pamphlets on various aspects and fields of history. While these little publications were excellent in some ways, the historians responsible for writing and publishing them were so unfamiliar with public school classrooms that they missed their intended audience. To be sure, the pamphlets sold, but they sold to graduate students, who used them to prepare for Ph.D. exams, and to college instructors for use in course preparation.

In short, the National Commission's call for strengthening the teaching of history in schools was issued at a time when more and more bridges were spanning the gulf between colleges and secondary schools—quite a few of which seemed strong enough to carry traffic. This meant that secondary school teachers would not be left, as they had been from the 1930s through the 1950s, to wrestle by themselves with some version of world history. This also meant that, given the many voices speaking to college professors, curriculum specialists, and school teachers, the National Commission's recommendations—insofar as they were accepted— would assume a distinctive form in every state. In 1987, California adopted wholesale reforms in social studies that embodied many, but not all, of the changes that were to be proposed by the National Commission. North Carolina's practice of introducing world studies at the fifth through seventh grades also anticipated the National Commission's recommendation that such studies start early, but these courses, unlike California's, employed geography rather than history as the central organizing discipline (*History-Social Science Framework* 1988; *Teacher Handbook* 1985). Indeed, there seemed little reason to doubt that, in one way or another, curriculum designers throughout the nation would continue to favor history and geography as the bases for instruction and that they would press for introducing study of the larger world in the early grades. World history also seemed to have become a fixture of high school curricula, but chronic complaints about the quality of teaching and curriculum materials promised to become more acute as world history was required of an increasingly heterogeneous student body. Moreover, given the failure of the historical profession to reach a consensus on the scope and content of the course, as it had after World War I, the debate in public education, already heated by citizen concerns, over what lessons were to be learned from world history promised to become even more intense. If public education were to be served, historians, it seemed, needed to build bridges not only to the schools, but also within their own profession.

PROJECTIONS

Early in the 1990s only a few colleges and universities were advertising positions for assistant professors of history who specialized in "world history." Such a small number of openings made a return to some equivalent of the once universally required survey seem improbable. More likely, these institutions were seeking individuals to teach one or two courses which, unlike most standard department fare, would sweep across time and space. It was also possible that some of these institutions were attempting to reach students in teacher education tracks, since several of them were once state-supported "normal schools." If that were indeed the case, these institutions were at the forefront of a movement that could potentially strengthen instruction. One of the most frequent and persistent complaints made by teachers as world history returned to the curriculum in the 1980s was that the course required them to deal with content for which they were unprepared.[4] Some veteran instructors, whose under-graduate curriculum had required Western Civilization, called up old memories in teaching their own students. Such teachers generally ignored those chapters in the text that dealt with the world beyond the West. Younger teachers, who had missed the sweeping survey courses, but had profited from more specialized studies in their undergraduate years, some-times describe their courses as a collage of topics on ancient Rome, modern Europe, China, and the like, all of which were presented without much of a connective structure. Perhaps the most unfortunate product of such tactics was that teachers, resenting requirements which they could not satisfy, were often less than enthusiastic about being assigned to teach world history. These indications of sagging morale were reminiscent of the 1960s, when disaffected teachers had to cope daily with Western Civ-ilization.

In these circumstances, efforts to recruit faculty to teach world history might well be evidence that a few institutions have become aware of teachers' problems and have begun to respond to them. At other cam-puses, historians and teachers have been making at least some use of the teaching alliances, summer institutes, and professional conferences that have become increasingly available to address issues in teaching world history. The significance of these activities should not to be measured by the degree to which they have resolved problems. The outcome of all such activities scarcely approaches the need. They seem to herald, how-ever, the emergence of coalitions of educators, who share a concerned citizenry's conviction that world history—regardless of how its dimen-sions may be defined—has an essential place in social studies education and that problems associated with the course should not be allowed to destroy it ("To Teach History" 1990).

The diminished role of the textbook, as no longer the key to instruction, seems likely in the 1990s. New technologies are rapidly making available an array of resources and classroom tools that will give teachers many more ways to reach a diverse student body. Publishers who target college freshman-level courses began early in the decade to market textbooks as components of much larger instructional packages. Available to instruc-tors now are audio cassettes of speeches by twentieth-century figures and of actors reading from diaries, letters, interviews, and speeches, recreating voices from the more distant past, as well as video discs that can bring preprogrammed still and motion-picture footage to the classroom. Many students now have access to computerized tutorial software, map work-books for self-directed projects in historical geography, and self-help study guides. One publisher has even added to all of this instructional material ten slim volumes containing, under different titles, biographical sketches, primary sources, documents on everyday life, and short essays that pres-ent conflicting interpretations of an issue. Nothing akin to this has made its way into secondary school history-teaching materials yet, but multimedia packages are already available in math and science. Moreover, despite their tight budgets, California, Texas, and Florida are in the vanguard of states allocating funds for such materials.

Some teachers, especially those who have advocated dispensing with textbooks and teaching exclusively from significant documents, are likely to welcome the arrival of this rich variety of teaching tools. However, textbooks are probably still not threatened with extinction. Even if they had the financial resources to purchase these new multimedia packages, many teachers have become too accustomed to textbooks to be likely to surrender them quickly. Some of the prospective materials might require class time to be devoted to self-instruction; others might depend on the "inquiry" methods so much in vogue in the 1970s; and still others might require skills in "reading" visual documents. In short, teachers who lack the time, the opportunity, or the inclination to revamp their classroom procedures, develop new skills, or familiarize themselves with all manner of new historical topics will probably be turned off by elaborate multimedia packages. A seasoned curriculum specialist, commenting on a university professor's proposal that textbooks be abandoned and that teachers assist students in constructing their own histories from original documents, probably put his finger on the reason why abandoning familiar textbooks would draw mixed reactions: "To do this kind of thing," he said, "a teacher has got to be a pretty good historian" (Crabtree and Symcox 1991: 15).

Finally, the 1990s promise to be a decade in which historians are more determined to exercise leadership in shaping school curricula than any time in the previous century. In 1988, for example, a "National Center for History in the Schools" was established at the University of California, Los Angeles, with a generous grant from the National Endowment for the Humanities. While the center is based in UCLA's School of Education, much of its leadership has been drawn from the ranks of professional historians. Among the center's key projects are (1) defining what knowledge should be acquired by students as they move through a sequence of historical studies; (2) designing research that will reveal what is actually being taught in the nation's history classes; and (3) developing and disseminating instructional materials by means of which teachers can bring their instruction into line with the center's definition of what students should know. These are certainly neither modest goals nor projects of the type to avoid controversy. Indeed, perhaps the clearest sign that the historical profession as a whole did not anticipate the California center's resolving all problems appeared in 1991 when the American Historical Association and the Organization of American Historians collaborated to establish the National History Education Network (NHEN). The NHEN describes itself as an alliance that brings together history's advocates across the professional and political spectrums, from learned societies to organizations for teachers and public historians, from advocates of a history-centered curriculum to the champions of the interdisciplinary approach of social studies. Some have special interests such as the use of material culture in the classroom or the adoption of a world history curriculum, but all share a basic determination to promote and enhance history teaching and learning. (Gardner 1991: 9)

The NHEN's leadership expect the network to sustain itself on membership fees ranging from $25 to $2500, and it certainly has attracted a substantial following. Nearly thirty organizations have already paid their annual fees since the first announcements of the NHEN's formation were published in 1991. Given world history's long and often troubled career, word that the UCLA center and the NHEN were up and running has perhaps raised hopes not only for the course's survival but also for the fulfillment in the nation's classrooms of its much vaunted promise. These hopes are not based on the prospect of a quick resolution to a long-standing controversy. Rather, they spring from the potential for such organizations to expand, sustain, and keep focused their collaborative efforts to resolve the complex problems of teaching world history.

NOTES

1. The World History Association claimed a membership of about one thousand in 1991. Both of the association's major publications, *Journal of World History* and *World History Bulletin,* have published extensive discussions on new models for teaching world history in colleges and public schools.

2. Arthur Schlesinger, Jr., "When Ethnic Studies Are Un-American," *Wall Street Journal* (April 23, 1990). In this instance, the debate swirled around courses that were designated "multicultural." The public debate, however, frequently concerned the nature and content of U.S. and world history courses, on which educators, journalists, and politicians urged the public to take a stand. For example, a nationally syndicated column by Georgie Anne Geyer, "Students Must Learn Their Own Culture First," *News and Observer* (Raleigh, NC) (Dec. 12, 1990), concluded: "Should there be first a profound education in America's own civic culture? Or should we send our children off on a spurious 'multicultural' goose chase that does not have even one chance in hell of catching a real goose?" Some of the complexities of the increasingly divisive and bitter debates among college and school faculties were captured in "Upside Down in the Groves of Academe" (*Time* [April 1, 1991]: 66–69). Alan Singer's "New York State: Multicultural Education Is Good Education—But It Can't Perform Miracles," in the American Historical Association's newsletter, *Perspectives* 28 (December 1990): 14–16, defended the concept of multicultural education and urged that materials for developing it be built into social studies. Proponents of multiculturalism, however, were said to be overselling the idea. Schools attended by minorities

were so starved of resources that they were unlikely to reach the students most in need of multicultural education.

3. *Perspectives,* the American Historical Association's newsletter, was devoting by the late 1980s and early 1990s approximately one-third to one-half of its pages to discussions about undergraduate and public school teaching.

4. *Perspectives,* which published the American Historical Association's job registry, carried advertisements for about a dozen openings in "World History" in 1991–92. Previously, openings for survey courses had almost always been listed as "Western Civilization." None of the advertisements in the more recent issues, however, indicated the way in which world civilization was defined.

Some of the problems faced by young teachers are reflected in the experience of graduates from the author's institution, North Carolina State University. Undergraduates seeking certification as secondary school social studies teachers are registered in the College of Humanities and Social Sciences, where they major in history, political science, sociology, or economics. Their curriculum is coordinated with the College of Education, and they register in that College for enough courses to meet certification requirements. While graduates are solidly grounded in the humanities and social sciences, none will have had an opportunity to study world history. History majors take courses that individually provide grounding in some elements of the course; social science majors are likely to have had only three or four courses in history of any kind. Yet world history was often the course to which they were assigned for practice teaching. In 1992, acting on requests from graduates and advisors in the College of Education, the history department established a seminar in teaching world history for the prospective teachers.

REFERENCES

Allardyce, Gilbert. "The Rise and Fall of the Western Civilization Course." *The American Historical Review* 87 (1982): 695–725.
———. "Toward World History: American Historians and the Coming of the World History Course." *Journal of World History* 1 (Spring 1990): 23–76.
Boyer, Ernest L. *High School: A Report on Secondary Education in America.* New York: Harper and Row, 1983.
Bradley Commission on History in the Schools. *Building a History Curriculum: Guidelines for Teaching History in Schools.* Washington, DC: Education Excellence Network, 1988.
Bullard, Betty. "Personal Statement to the President's Commission on Foreign Language and International Studies." *President's Commission on Foreign Language and International Studies: Background Papers and Studies.* Washington, DC: United States Department of Health, Education, and Welfare, Office of Education, 1979.
Crabtree, Charlotte, and Linda Symcox. "The National Center for History in the Schools." *Perspectives* 29 (April 1991): 15–16.
Downey, Matthew T., ed. *History in the Schools.* Washington, DC: National Council for the Social Studies, 1984.
Finn, Chester E., Jr., Diane Ravitch, and Robert T. Fancher. *Against Mediocrity:*

The Humanities in America's High Schools. New York: Holmes and Meier, 1984.

Gagnon, Paul A. *Democracy's Untold Story: What World History Textbooks Neglect*. Washington, DC: Education for Democracy/American Federation of Teachers, 1987.

Gagnon, Paul A., ed. *Historical Literacy: The Case for History in American Education*. New York: Macmillan, 1989.

Gardner, James B. "National History Education Network." *Perspectives* 29 (November 1991): 9.

Grubbs, Carolyn Barrington. "Historical Development of Social Studies Education in the Public High Schools of North Carolina." Ph.D. diss. North Carolina State University, 1982.

Hertzberg, Hazel Whitman. *Social Studies Reform, 1880–1980*. Boulder, CO: Social Studies Education Consortium, 1981.

History-Social Science Framework for California Public Schools: Kindergarten through Grade Twelve. Sacramento: California State Department of Education, 1988.

Hitchens, Marilynn Jo. "World History Textbooks for High Schools: A Review." *World History Bulletin* 7 (Spring/Summer 1990): 8–15.

Jenness, David. *Making Sense of the Social Studies*. New York: Macmillan, 1990.

Kirkendall, Richard S. "The Status of History in the Schools." *Journal of American History* 62 (1975–76): 557–70.

Link, Arthur S. "The American Historical Association, 1884–1984: Retrospect and Prospect." *The American Historical Review* 90 (1985): 1–17.

Mayer, Martin. *Where, When, and Why? Social Studies in American Schools*. New York: Harper and Row, 1963.

New York State Special Task Force on Equity and Excellence in Education. *A Curriculum of Inclusion: Report of the Commissioner's Task Force on Minorities: Equity and Excellence*. New York: Department of Education, 1989.

National Commission on the Social Studies. *Charting a Course: Social Studies for the 21st Century*. Joint Project of the American Historical Association, Carnegie Foundation for the Advancement of Teaching, National Council for the Social Studies, and Organization of American Historians. Washington, DC: National Council for the Social Studies, 1989.

Ravitch, Diane. *The Troubled Crusade: American Education, 1945–1980*. New York: Basic Books, 1983.

Reilly, Kevin, ed. *The Introductory History Course: Proceedings of the AHA Annapolis Conference on the Introductory History Course*. Washington: American Historical Association, 1984.

Robinson, Paul, and Joseph M. Kirman. "From Monopoly to Dominance." In Stanley P. Wronski and Donald H. Bragaw, eds., *Social Studies and Social Sciences: A Fifty Year Perspective*. Washington, DC: National Council for the Social Studies, 1986.

Sullivan, Richard E. "Summary Statement." In Josef W. Konvitz, ed., *What Should Americans Know: Western Civilization or World History?* Proceedings of a Conference at Michigan State University, April 21–23, 25–70. East Lansing: Michigan State University, 1985.

Teacher Handbook—Social Studies: Grades K–12, North Carolina Competency-Based Curriculum. Raleigh, NC: Department of Public Instruction, 1985.

"To Teach History, Go Back to the Source, Professor Says." *Education Daily* 23 (October 4, 1990): 1.

Van DeVen, Susan Elizabeth Kerr. "State Production of Middle East Chapters in World History Textbooks." Ph.D. diss., Harvard University, 1990.

Werner, Walter. *Whose Culture? Whose Heritage?* Vancouver: Center for the Study of Curriculum and Instruction, Faculty of Education, University of British Columbia, 1977.

West, Edith, ed. *Improving the Teaching of World History.* Washington, DC: National Council for the Social Studies, 1949.

Wronski, Stanley, and Donald H. Bragaw, eds. *Social Studies and Social Sciences: A Fifty Year Perspective.* Washington, DC: National Council for the Social Studies, 1986.

6

INTERNATIONAL STUDIES IN THE SCHOOLS

Betty M. Bullard

The present situation in international studies for elementary and secondary grades is a paradox: seldom, if ever, has so well documented an educational need been so summarily ignored by the education sector. As the United States reassessed itself after World War II and later experienced the nationally embarrassing Soviet coup of successfully launching Sputnik, the American public demanded to know who these other peoples of the world were, how they had gotten ahead of us, and how we could catch up with our competition. It was in this context that international studies at the precollegiate level began to take on new importance. International studies has had many definitions over the years, but the root understanding in all of them is that international studies encourages the pursuit of greater knowledge about the world and the relationships among various peoples and nations.

REFLECTIONS

From time to time in the first half of the twentieth century, efforts were made by professional associations and blue-ribbon committees to encourage more interest in international studies. The 1916 report of the National Education Association (NEA) Commission on the Reorganization of Secondary Education recommended, through its Committee on the Social Studies in Secondary Education, that greater emphasis be given to developing international mindedness, especially an awareness of the increasing interdependence among nations, and to teaching more about Japan and Latin America (Shane 1969: 272–73). Little happened over the next twenty years, with the exception of a joint statement issued by the National Council for the Social Studies and the Association for Supervision and Curriculum Development in 1948 urging teachers to redefine their teaching responsibilities in light of the changing world scene (277).

In 1967, Edwin Reischauer wrote, in *Beyond Vietnam,* of the major problem faced by advocates of an increased emphasis on international studies:

The problem essentially is that our educational system remains geared to the political and cultural conditions of the nineteenth century. We educate our children only about ourselves and our own cultural heritage and then expect them to grow up and live successfully in a unitary world of many cultures. By dealing only with the western tradition, we unconsciously indoctrinate our children with the idea that all other traditions are aberrant or not worth knowing. This may have been adequate for the nineteenth century when distances were great and the imperialist hold of the West on other regions made the occident the only part of the world that really counted for us. Today, however, this approach to education is dangerously outdated, and it will get more unrealistic with each passing year. (Reischauer 1967: 234)

Thoughtful scholars and educators reflected on how to initiate lasting changes. For the first time, renowned university scholars worked hand in hand with school teachers to develop dynamic and effective ways of conveying sound world knowledge to modern students. To this end, also for the first time, federal funds were made available to develop projects that would yield new and appropriate methods and materials. The "New Social Studies" urged that more knowledge related concepts and generalizations be taught through the processes of inquiry and discovery. Characteristic features were new content in the curriculum, new strategies and techniques for presenting the content, and new materials to be used in the instructional process.

Of these new materials, one of the most outstanding came from a project developed with federal funding during the 1960s and 1970s, "Man: A Course of Study (MACOS)." MACOS was a prime example of what could be produced by scholars and teachers working together. Lavishly funded at approximately one million dollars by the National Science Foundation, "Man: A Course of Study" examined different aspects of culture, using different cultures as examples. Overall, the program developed substantive knowledge, in a sequential structure, about how humans live on the earth. Nevertheless, the program experienced sudden death when a child in an irritable mood came home from school to his mother, who was also having a bad day. In the heated exchange that ensued, the student told his mother that he wished he could put her on an ice block and send her off to the horizon (as had been the practice of some Inuit groups with the older members of the population). The mother, thinking such material inappropriate for a young student to be taught, contacted her Congressman, who brought the matter before the House of Representatives. As a result, the program was withdrawn from the curriculum (*Congressional Record*). The public was not ready in 1975 for a curriculum that represented value systems so alien to those of their local communities.

Other projects of the same period, such as, "The High School Geography" project, "The High School Anthropology" project, and "The Minnesota Project Social Studies," focused on cultural understanding, new knowledge, more effective materials, and a wide variety of instructional processes largely derived from the discrete disciplines involved. These had faded out by the 1980s due to lack of promotion and, in one case, to lack of a commercial publisher. Only fragments of these projects remain in the curriculum today.

Fortunately, it was during this same time that curriculum reform was under way in the schools of every state. The predominant reform effort was to restructure the curriculum in accordance with conceptual frameworks based largely on the tenets of the major disciplines. That is, reformers strove to organize learning by synthesizing knowledge so as to distill major concepts and generalizations from the data. The knowledge gained could then be applied in order to broaden understanding of other concepts and generalizations. International studies became a useful vehicle for the new approach because the dimension was new to teachers and students alike. Therefore, there were no "sacred cows" to be protected, making it easier to introduce changes into traditional teaching and subject matter.

Most of the new curriculum organization divided the world into regions, which were then to be examined in terms of their history, geography, culture, society, and economics. These regional studies would depart from traditional world history by integrating not only history and geography, as had been done in the past, but sociology, anthropology, and economics as well. Rather than being organized around a standard chronological focus, the new studies in world cultures would delve deeper into each of the selected regions by concentrating on significant concepts, themes, and generalizations, as opposed to amassing factual data. In this way it became possible to devote more time to each region than was the case when Europe was the primary focus. All of this in-depth study was to proceed through discovery and reflection, greater use of instructional media, and pilot program materials.

However, teachers and administrators found that in order to achieve a lasting institutionalization of the new curriculum and instruction in international studies, it would be necessary to effect real change on three fronts:

1. teachers' beliefs about how education takes place;
2. the content and methods of teaching;
3. instructional materials. (Fuller 1982)

Furthermore, consideration had to be given to the fact that few social studies teachers had a broad-based background in international studies or were state-certified as competent to teach that subject. The teaching of world cultures would require further education and training in new methodologies for most of them. Also, in most places it would be difficult to find a local mentor to assist and encourage the teacher who might feel inadequate and lose self-confidence.

Where, then, could educators look for help? Three prominent sources were available: (1) university-based centers for area studies and/or private, nonprofit, regionally focused organizations; (2) companies that marketed media-based instructional packages; and (3) institutions providing opportunities for cultural interchange among scholars and teachers of different countries, to increase their knowledge and to design instructional materials for their countries' schools.

University centers for area studies (e.g., Asia, Africa, Latin America, Canada, China, Japan, or India) included Duke University's South Asia Studies Center, the University of Michigan's East Asia Studies Center, and Stanford University's centers for several different area studies, among others. In addition, educators were assisted by a number of private, nonprofit organizations whose mission is to help Americans learn more about a particular country. For example, in the years following World War II, the Japan Society, an arts organization based in New York, broadened its mandate to include an educational function, helping educators gain the background needed for competent teaching. There was much to be learned about other Asian nations as well, so philanthropist John D. Rockefeller III satisfied a number of needs by forming the Asia Society in the mid-1950s which, as one of its major functions, promoted education on Asia. Other regionally oriented organizations served similar functions, such as the outstanding African-American Institute. Several regionally focused associations of scholars (e.g., the Latin American Studies Association, the Asian Studies Association, the African Studies Association, and Canadian Studies, to name a few) appointed outreach committees to assist teachers in locating appropriate materials and in learning more about a specific region.

The second source of help for teachers was a group of companies that marketed a number of instructional media packages. These were designed by entrepreneurs who had first-hand knowledge about other countries. The popular and clever artifact-filled steamer trunks called "Village Trunks" produced by Henry Ferguson's InterCulture Associates represent an outstanding example of these media packages. A private company, InterCulture Associates, whose founder was a widely traveled scholar, designed and produced trunks containing teaching materials for different regions. One trunk "held" a village in India, for example, including typical artifacts of village life in India—clothing, turbans, cooking and eating utensils, books, implements used to perform marriage ceremonies, and religious objects—as well as demographic data. Other trunks represented a variety of sites, such as villages in Africa. These materials fit well with the new approaches to instruction and the new content to be taught.

The third resource for educators was a group of institutions that were created to provide scholars and teachers from different countries with opportunities for cultural and educational interchange. In the early 1960s, the East-West Center, located on the campus of the University of Hawaii in Honolulu, was chartered. The center brought teachers, students, and scholars from all of the Asian nations and from the United States together for a year-long program of intensive study. Following this year of study together, the U.S. and Asian teachers went to each others' countries for an on-site practicum. Many of today's leaders in international studies have come through this program. Another example of this kind of interchange was New York State's instructional studies center in New Delhi, India. There, teachers and scholars from the United States could work with Indian scholars on projects intended to produce authentic media and other instructional materials to be used in U.S. classrooms.

State and federal agencies were instrumental in encouraging the development of international studies in the schools. Many states, including North Carolina, New York, California, and Michigan, recommended a broadened study of the world, primarily through social studies. These endorsements came from the highest official levels, the heads of state education departments. Their support made change possible, creating a climate of cooperation between the colleges and universities and the public schools.

By endorsing the Helsinki Accords of 1975, the United States agreed to promote more scholarship and language acquisition in order to create a competent national pool of experts on other nations. The United States did not want to find itself again in a position where, as at the outbreak of World War II, only six non-Japanese people in the country spoke Japanese. Therefore, through the National Defense Education Act (NDEA, 1958), Title VI, which later became the United States Department of Education, Title VI, centers were established on university campuses for foreign language and area studies. One of the mandates for each center was to conduct an "outreach" operation to assist nearby schools with intensive staff, curriculum, and instructional-materials development in an effort to add a genuinely international component to school programs.

However, the path toward realizing this goal was not smooth. Sometimes serious interference by influential people frustrated efforts to accomplish change. For example, from 1970 to 1974 a North Carolina educational television program called "World Cultures in Africa and Asia" was broadcast. Intended to promote televised classes for students and to provide teachers with adequate background on other countries (until the transition to international studies had been completed), this tame and politically innocuous program was castigated by a conservative North Carolina broadcasting executive who has since become a prominent national figure.

One of the pivotal studies of the 1970s was *Other Nations, Other Peoples: A Survey of Student Interests, Knowledge, Attitudes, and Perceptions* by Lewis Pike and Thomas E. Barrows (1979). The survey concluded that students' perceptions of other countries were influenced by regular course work, reading, movies, teachers, travel, and international events. The authors surveyed students in grades four, eight, and twelve, with questions about countries in Europe, Asia, Africa, and North and South America. At all three grade levels, the survey's results were dismal and pointed to the need for reform in the curriculum, teacher education, instruction, and instructional materials. The study was an important nationwide stimulus to strengthen teaching about other lands and other people at all grade levels. In his foreword to this landmark study, Robert Leestma, then Associate Commissioner for Institutional Development and International Education, wrote that the work would significantly contribute to focusing our efforts on helping the United States carry out its commitment to the Helsinki Accords of 1975. As a result of the Conference on Security and Cooperation held in Europe that year, all signatory nations agreed to "encourage the study of foreign languages and civilizations as an important means of expanding communication among peoples for their better acquaintance with the culture of each country, as well as for the strengthening of international cooperation" (xvi).

The study also made a contribution to the work of the President's Commission on Foreign Language and International Studies, which was appointed by President Carter in the fall of 1978 and issued its report in 1979. The President's Commission found that American capability in languages and knowledge of international affairs at all educational levels were woefully low. In the area of precollegiate education, the commission's report noted that

a major hurdle to teaching children for the world that lies ahead is that teachers learn, and therefore mostly teach, about the world that lies behind. . . .

If our schools are to teach more effectively about other countries and cultures, we must provide our teachers with the knowledge and tools this task requires. ... International content should be part of the teaching of all subjects, and within the capabilities of all teachers. (*United States* 1979: 48–49)

The commission recommended that foreign language instruction be encouraged to shift its focus from proficiency in reading to speaking the language and that the states designate flagship schools to lead the way in developing an internationally oriented curriculum and instructional materials.

All of this support and activity—university-school cooperation, federal and state monies, and assistance from private foundations—has resulted in new content and instructional materials, such as the following:

—elective social studies courses in international affairs;
—studies of cultural regions employing television programs and other media aids, with assistance from foreign visitors and Americans who have traveled in the areas studied;
—courses initiated by interested (and well-traveled) teachers;
—courses designed to integrate geography, anthropology, sociology, and economics.

The courses were most often organized chronologically within a region, such as Asia or Africa, but some were organized around a topic or concept, while others were problem-focused or globally-oriented. Staff development took the form of student and faculty travel courses, exchanges, and a combination of intensive study, travel, and instructional-materials development. Little by little, teachers assigned to international courses became more competent, but they still often needed sensitivity training, as the following anecdote shows. I observed a class taught by a teacher in a small, rural community of only a few hundred people, including one barber, one dentist, two doctors (one of whom was a surgeon), three preachers, and a handful of merchants and service workers. This teacher decided to present the subject of India in a very compelling way to his students, the liveliest and most talkative of whom was the barber's son. The teacher, in his ignorance, thought he saw a way to quiet the student down, so, as he explained the Indian social system's lowest classes and outcastes, the teacher gave the barber as an example because he worked with hair. This was, of course, an inappropriate interpretation; the young student was crushed and became withdrawn. Such instances may be rare, but they illustrate the need for intensive, ongoing staff development.

Despite all the progress made during the 1960s and 1970s in the development of international studies, there were still episodes of bickering and hostility. Even as the training of international studies teachers improved, some kinds of ignorance were still evident. I can recall a conversation, for example, in which a male history teacher declared, "Only men should teach world cultures. They would teach the tough stuff like wars, rulers, etc., not soft stuff like art, values, cultures, civilizations, and religious influences." Sometimes it seemed as if the progress of international studies was a matter of one step forward, two steps back. For example, while New York State's instructional-materials center in India proved to be very useful to teachers, the nature of these materials upset some legislators. Therefore, the state education agency was forced to withdraw its support and participation in 1976, according to its director, Ward Morehouse.

How has the public at large influenced the course content? The road to better international understanding and knowledge has never been a smooth one largely because, in the final analysis, the public has control over education; therefore, educational efforts rise and fall according to the public's desires and expectations. Typically, the public is conservative and, perhaps, egocentric. When Africa was included in one state's curriculum, for instance, I received a call from a citizen who said, "We don't have nothing in common with those Africans, and I don't want my kids studying them." Another caller was concerned by efforts to teach *about* Asian religions in order to enhance understanding of social, cultural, and economic influences, declaring, "I'm not going to let my children be contaminated with such teaching." School board members have also been known to cry out against the teaching of values, especially those of a region half a world away, in school. Additionally, there have always been persistent voices calling for, orally and editorially, schools to adopt a U.S.-centered curriculum so that students will "know America first." Fortunately, such incidents as these have been uncommon. Thoughtful citizens throughout the country want their children to become more knowledgeable about the world. Attesting to this fact was a 1979 Gallup poll which indicated that seventy-eight percent of parents wanted schools to offer more courses with more international content.

In the 1980s, the findings of various surveys, blue-ribbon committee reports, and other studies led to the creation of international magnet schools. Such schools had already been established during the late 1970s in a few cities—Philadelphia, Pittsburgh, New York, and Washington— and today there are more than 150 international magnet schools throughout the country. Drawing students from an entire school district, these schools are the best sites for implementing real curricular and instructional reform. Some international magnet schools are entirely dedicated to an international orientation, while others are schools within schools. What they all have in common is a curriculum designed to include an international dimension in every course. These special schools require students to take two or more foreign languages, and they offer a wealth of international courses per se, such as those on international economics, global issues, and particular nations. They also provide opportunities to travel and participate in projects abroad, as well as exchange programs and specifically targeted international programs. International magnet schools support the proposition that we can provide our children with an international perspective and at the same time ensure that schools are responsive to other educational needs.

CURRENT ISSUES AND TRENDS

In the present period of shrinking budgets, discipline-focused reform, and an increased emphasis on basic skills, international studies has been presented with new challenges related to content. Since its inception, international studies has been beset by semantic problems, with a number of competing terms used to define the field. Entire issues of journals and conference agendas have been devoted to defining the terms of international studies. Whether the content and the teacher-preparation materials are labeled "international," "global," "intercultural," "transnational," or "multicultural," the thrust of international studies is the same: a focus on relationships among different peoples. Each term can be given a working definition, such as the following:

International: a term designating relationships among separate, independent nation-states, rather than the unified interrelatedness of all humankind.

Global: a space-age word reflecting a view of the earth from outer space, the term connotes transcendence of international politics while stressing human interrelatedness on one planet, Earth, which is viewed as a "life-support" system.

Intercultural: a term originating in the work of social scientists and humanist scholars that stresses the sociological, anthropological, and cultural relatedness of people generally.

Transnational: a term linking international and global concerns and referring to the study of topics that cross the boundaries of nations.

Multicultural: a term whose meaning has shifted from simply studying the impact of different cultures to including the study of all ethnic groups in the school curriculum.

Translating the various terms employed by a particular school district will in effect define the specific content of international studies. As states blend the teaching of basic skills with course content or define a curricular framework, new questions arise.

The most pressing questions are where to place the emphasis and how to insure an international dimension in education. William H. McNeill's essay "World History," in *Charting a Course: Social Studies for the 21st Century,* offers the following response:

Our country has become part of an intensely interactive world system that no longer revolves solely upon events in Europe, as was (or at least seemed to be) the case so recently as the 1930s. To deal effectively with Asians, Africans, Latin Americans and Europeans we need to know how the historical past has shaped their diverse outlooks on the world. In the second place immigrants from Asia, Africa and Latin America have filled our classrooms with students whose ethnic and cultural background is not "Western." They need a past they can share with Americans of European descent; and equally, Americans of European descent need a past they can share with all their fellow citizens, including the indigenous Indian population that got here before anyone else. (National Commission 1989: 53)

If an international dimension in education is to be realized, then three things must happen: First, school systems must move to institute the kind of internationally-focused curriculum now found in magnet schools. Second, the trend among more and more states to emphasize history and geography in the social studies must be reversed. Third, experts on international studies must be part of curriculum-designing teams. In brief, the social studies must be redefined in such a way as to include, as a given, international studies.

Other significant influences on curricular content have evolved from areas once perceived as fads and fashions. In the early 1980s, for example, global education was seen as a fad, but today, it has become a standard part of social studies teacher preparation. The advocates of global education have worked hard over the years to help educators understand the curricular advantages of global understanding.

One consistent influence on the various definitions of international studies has been a classic work in the curriculum field, Robert G. Hanvey's (1976) *An Attainable Global Perspective*. Hanvey defines the different facets of this perspective as follows:

1. Perspective consciousness—the student analyzes "his opinions, and usually unexamined assumptions, evaluations, conceptions of time, space, causality, etc.," to achieve a more conscious perspective;

2. "State of the Planet" awareness—an awareness of current and emerging trends in migration, disease, population statistics, science, technology, and the like;

3. Cross-cultural awareness—a consciousness of the diversity of ideas and practices in societies throughout the world and the perspectives from which they may be viewed;

4. Knowledge of global dynamics—an understanding of world systems as contexts of global change;

5. Awareness of human choices—a conscious recognition of some of the major choices affecting the human species as knowledge of world systems expands.

The most recent and demanding concern (whether it becomes an enduring issue or is just a faddish trend remains to be seen) related to the international studies curriculum is that of "centrism." Advocates of centrism believe that the curriculum should center, or give equal time to, the study of a particular national or ethnic group, a view that New York state curriculum designers have debated. Education officials in California, (California 1988), on the other hand, seem to have decided that the curriculum and textbooks should be organized around studies of all the cultures represented in the state. Although textbooks have been revised to take this requirement into account, they have still been criticized by some cultural groups who argue that they are not properly or equitably represented in the textbooks. Presently, several cultural groups are negotiating with textbook publishers in an effort to reach a solution that will satisfy all of these groups.

Even though curriculum reform and new curricular frameworks have reflected the return of international topics and perspectives to school programs, little, if any, material related to the content or process of international studies is included on skills tests, despite the fact that many of the skills were refined in the early years of the international studies curriculum. Curiously enough, the back-to-basics movement has amounted to a setback for courses with an international emphasis.

Growing opportunities that hold promise for those engaged in international studies include expanded programs for student and teacher travel as well as for participation in development projects overseas. There are more travel and exchange programs now in addition to the Fulbright and American Field Service programs, which helped to define the field years ago. Schools and communities seem to be enthusiastic about the opportunities these exchange programs offer.

The National Council for the Social Studies recently published two outstanding works, *Charting a Course: Social Studies for the 21st Century,* the report of the National Commission on the Social Studies (1989), and *Social Studies and the Social Sciences: A Fifty Year Perspective,* edited by Stanley Wronski and Donald Bragaw (1986). How have these publications influenced international studies? In William McNeill's essay "World History," in *Charting a Course,* several salient points were made concerning the lessons to be learned from international studies. The use of art and literature from each of the four great Eurasian civilizations, for instance, can help students grasp ideas and institutions "from the inside," giving them such insights into the spirit of particular civilizations as the following:

1. *Ancient Greece:* Territorial state is the institution and natural law is the idea (this is applicable both to humans in the Polis and to inanimate nature).

2. *China:* Extended family is the institution and decorum is the idea (this is applicable to the behavior of human beings and the whole cosmos).

3. *India:* Caste is the institution and transcendentalism is the idea (the reality of the spiritual realm above and beyond the illusory world of the senses).

4. *Middle East:* Bureaucratic monarchy is the institution and monotheism is the idea. (National Commission 1989: 55)

Likewise, McNeill argues that two "imperatives" underlie the need to teach world history: (1) our country has become part of an intensely interactive world system, and (2) immigrants from other parts of the world do not have "Western" cultural backgrounds. Given the number of related pasts to be explored, McNeill sees world history as needing "to organize itself around a pattern of major breakthroughs in communication" that intensified interaction within ever larger regions of the earth (53).

In another significant work, *Social Studies and the Social Sciences: A Fifty Year Perspective,* David Van Tassel's chapter, "Trials of Clio," discusses the excitement that has been recently generated by radical historians (New Left, or neo-Marxist, as typified by Fred Harvey Harrington and William Appleman Williams). These historians believe that true history is made not by the dominant elite groups, but by "the people," the "inarticulate masses." Black studies, women's studies, Asian studies, "area" studies, and minority studies have all contributed to the fragmentation of and confusion in the traditional discipline of history. To this is added the new phenomenon of social science historians, who lean heavily on statistical techniques and other methods used by social scientists. As a result, international studies is currently in a state of ferment. Nevertheless, as the field matures and continues to take shape, an important and distinct field of knowledge is certain to emerge.

PROJECTIONS

International studies faces the future with confidence. Surely, it will become increasingly apparent that conservative isolationism is harmful to the best interests of the United States, as is a myopic emphasis on an exclusively American or Western tradition. Courses with a truly international focus will deal creatively with the great world civilizations and their historical interactions, thereby placing Western studies in a proper perspective. United States history will emerge from such a context with a much sharper focus and a greater appeal and interest than when it is taught in isolation and as an end in itself.

The increasingly diverse ethnic, cultural, and racial composition of contemporary American society will be reflected by increasingly diverse classrooms. The content of disciplines in international studies will easily adapt to this cultural diversity and will help to eliminate student assumptions about the inferiority of non-Western cultures.

The current knowledge explosion will certainly have a serious impact on curricular content, leading to the production of more diverse and useful auxiliary materials for teaching. Both greater knowledge and rapidly developing pedagogical technology augur improved instruction in international studies.

Should the current curricular trend of focusing on history and geography continue, international studies could still survive by drawing on the content of these two disciplines. Instructional materials, including media packages, with which to design effective international studies courses or modules for inclusion in more traditional courses are now available. International studies have an advantage over other social sciences in being based on a holistic view of the world. For students who have studied nations, regions, and otherwise defined places, the global view ties what they have learned together into a gestalt.

REFERENCES

Alexander, Francis, and Diane Brooks. *The Changing History-Social Science Curriculum: A Booklet for Parents*. Sacramento: California Department of Education, 1990.

Anderson, Lee. *Schooling and Citizenship in a Global Age: The Meaning and Significance of Global Education*. Urbana, IL: Foreign Student Development Center, 1979.

Asia Society. *Asia in American Textbooks*. New York: Asia Society, 1976.

Asian Studies in American Secondary Education. Washington, DC: U.S. Department of Health, Education, and Welfare, 1971.

Balk, Alfred. *The Myth of American Eclipse*. New Brunswick, NJ: Transaction Publishers, 1990.

Barber, Elinor G., and Warren Ilchman. *International Studies Review: A Staff Study*. New York: The Ford Foundation, 1979.

Becker, James M., ed. *Schooling for a Global Age*. New York: McGraw-Hill, 1979.

Becker, James M., and Howard D. Mehlinger, eds. *International Dimensions in the Social Studies*. 38th Yearbook. Washington, DC: National Council for the Social Studies, 1968.

Berelson, Bernard, and James E. Preston. *The Social Studies and the Social Sciences*. Sponsored by the American Council of Learned Societies and the National Council for the Social Studies. New York: Harcourt, Brace and World, 1962.

Black, Robert, ed. *Education and the World View*. New Rochelle, NY: Change Magazine Press, 1980.

Bonham, George, ed., "Educating for the World View." *Change Magazine* Special Issue 12 (May–June 1980): 2–47.

Bradburn, Norman M., and Dorothy M. Gilford, eds. *A Framework and Principles for International Comparative Studies in Education.* Washington, DC: National Academy Press, 1990.

Brislin, Richard. *Topics in Culture Learning,* Vol. I. Honolulu: East-West Center Press, 1973.

Bullard, Elizabeth Moore. "Conceptualizing South Asian Culture: A Pedagogical Approach to a Problem in Social Studies." Ph.D. diss. Duke University, 1975.

California State Board of Education. *History/Social Science Framework for California Public Schools: Kindergarten through Twelfth Grade.* Sacramento: California State Board of Education, 1988.

Congressional Record. H2588 (April 9, 1975).

"Contemporary Issues: Global Education." *Educational Leadership.* Special Issue 48 (April 1991): 44–67.

deBary, William Theodore, and Ainslie Embree. *Approaches to Asian Civilizations.* New York: Columbia University Press, 1964.

Dinnman, Andreas, and Burkart Holznes. *Education for International Competence in Pennsylvania.* Pittsburgh: Pennsylvania Department of Education and University of Pittsburgh, 1988.

Dula, Annette, Michael Fultz, and Andrew Garrod, eds., "Education as Transformation: Identity, Change, and Development." *Harvard Educational Review* Special Issue 51 (February 1981).

Fleming, Dan B. "Social Studies Reform and Global Education." *The Social Studies* 82 (January/February 1991): 11–15.

Fuller, Michael. *The Meaning of Educational Change.* New York: Teachers College Press, 1982.

Groennings, Sven, and David S. Wiley. *Group Portrait: Internationalizing the Disciplines.* New York: American Forum, 1990.

Hanvey, Robert G. *An Attainable Global Perspective.* New York: Center for War/Peace Studies, 1976.

Hsu, Francis L. K. *Inter-Cultural Understanding: Genuine and Spurious.* Evanston, IL: Northwestern University Press, 1974.

International Dimensions of Education. Washington, DC: Council of Chief State School Officers, 1985.

Jenness, David. *Making Sense of Social Studies.* New York: Macmillan, 1990.

Juncker, Sigfield, and Jo Ann Larson. *Civic Literacy for Global Interdependence: New Challenge to State Leadership in Education.* Washington, DC: Committee on International Education, 1976.

Merryfield, Merry. *Teaching about the World: Teacher Education Programs with a Global Perspective.* Columbus, OH: Mershon Center, Ohio State University, 1990.

National Commission on Social Studies in the Schools. *Charting a Course: Social Studies for the 21st Century.* Washington, DC: National Commission on Social Studies in the Schools, 1989.

Phillips, Craig, ed. *Education for International Understanding.* New York: Asia Society, Education Department, 1977.

Pike, Lewis, and Thomas E. Barrows. *Other Nations, Other Peoples: A Survey of Student Interests, Knowledge, Attitudes, and Perceptions.* Washington, DC: U.S. Office of Education, 1979.

Reischauer, Edwin O. *Beyond Vietnam: The United States and Asia.* New York: Alfred A. Knopf, 1967.

Rosenfeld, Erwin M., and Harriet Geller. *Global Studies: Asia, Africa and Latin America.* New York: Barron's, 1987.

Scaneon, David T., and James J. Shields, Jr., eds. *Problems and Prospects in International Education.* New York: Teachers College Press, 1968.

Schultz, Fred, ed. *Annual Editions: Education 91/92.* Guilford, CT: Dushkin Publishing Group, 1991.

Seager, Joni, ed. *The State of the Earth Atlas.* New York: Simon and Schuster, 1990.

Seelye, H., ed. *Teaching Culture: Strategies for Intercultural Communication.* Lincolnwood, IL: National Textbook, 1984.

Shane, Harold G. *The United States and International Education.* Chicago: National Society for the Study of Education, 1969.

Smith, Elise C., and Louise Fiber Luce, eds. *Toward Internationalism.* Rowley, MA: Newbury House, 1979.

Strazicich, Mirko, and Diane Brooks, eds. *History-Social Science Framework for California Public Schools.* Sacramento: California State Department of Education, 1988.

Tonkin, Humphrey, and Jane Edwards. *The World in the Curriculum: Curricular Strategies for the 21st Century.* New Rochelle, NY: Change Magazine Press, 1981.

Tye, Kenneth A., ed. *Global Education: From Thought to Action.* Alexandria, VA: Association for Supervision and Curriculum Development, 1991.

United States President's Commission on Foreign Language and International Studies. Strength Through Wisdom: A Critique of U.S. Capability. Washington, DC: U.S. Office of Education, 1979.

Weatherford, Robert, ed. *A Report to the Council of Chief State School Officers.* Pinehurst, NC: U.S. Office of Education, 1977.

Wronski, Stanley P., and Donald H. Bragaw, eds. *Social Studies and the Social Sciences: A Fifty Year Perspective.* Washington, DC: National Council for the Social Studies, 1986.

7

SCHOOL GEOGRAPHY

Robert N. Saveland

REFLECTIONS

To understand where geography is going, one must examine not only where it is now, but where it has been. This inevitably involves the use of history. Geographers sometimes feel that within the public schools the discipline of geography has often been usurped by history, so it is with temerity that a geographer attempts to do history, particularly knowing that after examining primary sources the historian formulates an interpretation of history that is essentially subjective, despite all efforts to be objective and analytical.

To predict the course of geography as a discipline in the educational system of the twenty-first century requires first looking briefly back at geography in the United States prior to 1900 (Buttimer and Claval 1987). In the first fifty years of the new nation, school geography was rather rudimentary, although the subject was taught at Harvard College. From textbooks of the time, such as those of Jedediah Morse (1796), it is clear that the geography taught in the schools was often catechismal, stressing creationism and dividing the world's people into four races—black, white, red, and yellow. The textbook writers were often clergymen who depended on ships' captains and other travelers for information about remote areas of the world. Thus originated the term "capes and bays geography," from the books' frequent descriptions of the land as seen from the deck of a ship.

From 1825 to 1850, and beyond, school geography, often taught in one-room schools, was much influenced by the textbooks of Samuel G. Goodrich and William C. Woodbridge. Goodrich utilized the fictional character of Peter Parley to appeal to students' natural curiosity about the world. Both Goodrich and Woodbridge had traveled to Europe, where they apparently came in contact with the ideas of Pestalozzi, a Swiss educational reformer who stressed learning by observation (Palmer, Smith, and Davis 1988). Woodbridge was also influenced by the German concept of *Heimatkunde,* or home geography, which emphasized early study of the child's home surroundings. His books advocated a progression from the simple to the complex and the utilization of classification and comparison (Woodbridge 1826). Both Goodrich and Woodbridge sought to avoid the rote-learning, catechismal approach of earlier geographies.

The second half of the nineteenth century saw a great many changes in the United States. Waves of immigrants arrived, many of whom had to learn the language, while all had to be assimilated into the evolving American economy and culture. As the Civil War determined the supremacy of the federal government and freed the slaves, the westward movement and a nationalistic spirit put their stamp on the geographic concepts that would influence thinking about geography even to this day. For instance, the abundance of land and the wealth of America's natural resources have contributed to an educational mindset in which ourselves and our nation are assumed to be more important than the rest of the world.

School geography in the latter half of the nineteenth century was greatly influenced by Arnold Guyot, who came to the United States from Switzerland after studying with the German geographer Carl Ritter. Like Ritter, Guyot emphasized the unity of the earth and the importance of the scientific method (James 1967). In his schoolbooks, he stressed cause/effect relationships. For example, a mountain chain affects land transportation by constituting a natural barrier or boundary. Guyot was followed by Matthew Fontaine Maury, better known as a naval officer and an early oceanographer, whose *Manual of Geography,* a high school physical-geography text, was adopted by sixty percent of the states (Maury 1871; James 1969: 475).

In the early years of the twentieth century, the physical-geography taught in the high schools was often based on a widely used textbook by William Morse Davis (1904), a professor at Harvard. Through his writing and his service on national commissions, Davis exerted considerable influence on education. This was reflected in two reports issued by the National Education Association, that of the "Committee of Ten" in 1894 and that of the "Committee of Seven" in 1904. Not surprisingly, both committees strongly recommended a course in physical geography at the high school level (Stoltman 1986) since, with Davis as a committee member, it would have been difficult to support a program which lacked a geography component. This disciplinary structure of national commissions would soon create concerns for geography, however, as new disciplines entered the curricular fray and some old ones, history and science, began to flex their collective muscle.

During the early 1900s, as courses in science were becoming more a part of the curriculum, they began to usurp some of the content of physical geography. At the same time, such social issues as labor unrest, women's suffrage, and debate over entry into World War I were commanding increased attention. Subsequently, a reaction against physical geography occurred, and the National Education Association appointed yet another commission to study the reorganization of secondary education.

Although the 1916 report of the Sub-Committee on the Social Studies refrained from offering detailed outlines of courses, it did emphasize curriculum continuity. The report's authors subscribed to a topical approach, rather than one of chronological sequence, and offered specific suggestions for grade placement of topics. Although these recommendations were intended as suggestions, the Report had a prescriptive impact on many in the education profession. For instance, a study of the geography of South America and Africa was suggested for the first half of the sixth grade, followed by a study of the United States in the second half. While such topical divisions would continue to be employed throughout the twentieth century, geography as a separate subject would slowly disappear.

One of the more enduring recommendations of the Sub-Committee on the Social Studies was the sequence of studying American history in grades 5, 8, and 11; civics in grade 9; European history in grade 10; and the introduction of a new course, "Problems of Democracy," in the twelfth grade. Although much can be said for these recommendations, they left little room in the curriculum for geography. As textbooks based on this proposal were published, this sequence became the standard fare in most states for several decades (Superka, Hawke, and Morrissett 1980).

The Geography/Social Studies Debate

The committee report of 1916 was also significant in that it gave recognition to the term "social studies," defining it as those subjects related to the direction and organization of human society and to man as a member of social groups. The emergence of the social studies was a logical outgrowth of the progressive education movement, which was closely associated with Teachers College, Columbia University, John Dewey, and William Heard Kilpatrick. This movement grew out of concerns about the education of the "whole child." Probably because of the time lag between the introduction and the dissemination and subsequent adoption of new ideas in the school curriculum, geography and history continued to be taught as separate subjects during the first third of the twentieth century.

Geography books were marked by their large format, which was needed to accommodate Mercator maps. (Cartoons and movies sometimes showed students using these big books to hide from the teacher.) "Home geography" was taught in the primary grades, and by the fourth grade students would have been taken pedagogically on a trip around the world, learning about Eskimos in igloos, Pygmies in Africa, and Dutch children in wooden shoes.

The 1930s may be thought of as a period of strength for geography in the schools. Wallace W. Atwood and Helen Goss Thomas (1932) teamed up to write a series of elementary geography books while Harlan Barrows and Edith Parker (1941) at the University of Chicago, wrote a second geography series for the elementary school. These series were both widely used into the 1940s. Another series of textbooks, written by J. Russell Smith (1938), Professor of Economic Geography at Columbia University, followed the Ritter/Guyot tradition of emphasizing the study of the home community. During most of these two decades economic geography was being taught in vocational courses at the secondary level, often in separate vocational schools in the large cities. A leading textbook for these courses was *Economic Geography for Secondary Schools* by Charles Colby and Alice Foster (1931).

Into this arena came the social studies textbook series authored by Harold Rugg of Teachers College, Columbia University. One of the most vocal proponents of the social studies, Rugg wrote textbooks that reflected the cultural and social milieu of the times. Just as the Stock Market Crash of 1929, followed by the Great Depression, then by Franklin D. Roosevelt's "New Deal" profoundly affected American political, economic, and social life, so did Rugg's books affect American education. Authored in the 1930s, they were attacked by veterans' organizations and other groups as being too socialistic. While school systems responded to such attacks by withdrawing them from use, Rugg's textbook series did serve as a forerunner to the emerging social studies movement, which, in turn, led to the decline of geography as a separate subject area.

The debate over whether to teach history and geography as separate subjects or together in a social studies course was a protracted one, continuing to a certain extent to this day. Geographers felt then and still feel that in a fused course their subject becomes subsumed by history. Teachers and school administrators are attracted to the economies of time and money realized when only one class period and one set of textbooks are needed to fulfill a combined social studies requirement. At the heart of the matter lies the problem of finding the time for separate social studies disciplines in an already crowded curriculum. Geography was often the casualty of such competing demands.

As a result of World War II, large numbers of Americans, who had previously viewed the world myopically, suddenly became aware of such places as Melanesia and Micronesia. Professional geographers were called to Washington to serve on boards that would plan the strategy and logistics for carrying on the war. New recruits needed training in geography and in the customs of places where they might be sent. World War II also gave particular emphasis to "Air-Age Education" popularized by George Renner at Teachers College, Columbia. Renner, as well as J. Russell Whitaker, at Peabody College, wrote books on conservative education. The polar projection map, upon which great circles could be drawn, was not only introduced into the schools, but would also become the symbol of the United Nations. George Renner, at Teachers College, Columbia, as well as J. Russell Whitaker, at Peabody College, wrote books stressing issues of conservation education. These were the forerunners of a late-twentieth-century focus on environmental education, with its strong geography component.

Immediately after the war ended, several new series of elementary social studies textbooks appeared on the market. Concomitantly, the teaching of geography and history as separate subjects in the elementary schools began to fade away. However, at the junior high school level the traditional emphasis on geography was maintained by the introduction of a seventh-grade book, *Eurasia,* written by Robert M. Glendinning of the University of Southern California. While John Hodgdon Bradley's *World Geography* became the textbook of choice in the tenth grade, geography was mainly taught as an alternative to world history for the "less able" students. (As of yet, no one has satisfactorily explained why world geography was considered easier or more suitable for these students.) The Bradley book introduced a unique series of perspective maps by Richard Edes Harrison, one of which, "Europe from the East," attracted a great deal of attention when it first appeared in *Fortune* during World War II (Bradley 1968: 370–71). The Harrison maps also incorporated detailed hill shading to depict land relief by showing the shadows of mountains. This technique, which had been used in German schools and by Edwin Raisz, has become a common feature (though sometimes sloppily done) of social studies textbooks.

The "knowledge explosion" has been a much used phrase since the postwar period. Presumably, information, like the world's population, is expanding at an exponential rate. This new knowledge has been "shoe-horned" into the existing curriculum along with driver education, sex education, drug education, and other add-ons. One result appears to be less and less time for geography.

The sight of the man-made mini-star, the Soviet Union's *Sputnik,* arching across the night sky in 1957 shook up the government and the educational community of the United States. The Space Age had dawned, and with it came the notion that America's schools were lagging behind those of the Soviet Union. In response, Congress appropriated funds for various projects to stimulate changes in American education. The High School Geography Project (H.S.G.P.) was initiated in 1961 with financial support from the Fund for the Advancement of Education. A unique feature of the project was that academic geographers from the Association of American Geographers worked with public school teachers from the National Council for Geographic Education on the development of geography materials for the American classroom (Natoli 1986). During this time textbooks were being de-emphasized, while instruction was focusing on concepts and theories rather than isolated facts. By the end of the decade, the H.S.G.P. had produced materials and conducted field trials for several units of study, most notably *Portsville,* emphasizing urban geography, *Japan,* emphasizing cultural geography, and *The Game of Farming.* The latter used simulation and role-playing to illustrate the precarious nature of farming the Great Plains during different historical periods, along with the human adjustments required to live and prosper in a semiarid climate zone. Over several class periods, *The Game of Farming* could demonstrate the crises of drought, dust, and isolation depicted in John Steinbeck's *Grapes of Wrath* or the classic, award-winning documentary, *The Plow That Broke the Plains.* These same ideas which were "covered" in about two pages of Bradley's *World Geography* now provided enough material for several class periods of discussion and activity.

While opinions differ on the overall influence of the High School Geography Project, going by sales figures and other data on usage, its impact was minimal (Winston 1986). This was due in large part to the fact that H.S.G.P. materials were not neatly bound in a single package. Instead, the materials needed for the various lessons were too often separate bits and pieces that could be easily lost in the typical classroom. However, the project did attract attention, and it also provided food for thought and debate when it came time to conduct teacher education courses and to construct future textbooks. The H.S.G.P. focused attention on the need for better teacher preparation by funding workshops to assist teachers in using the materials. Unfortunately, these workshops reached only a relatively small number of teachers. Amazingly, throughout this period it was possible to graduate from college and to become certified to teach social studies without having completed a course in geography. During the two decades between 1955 and 1975, geography was not required for graduation from high school in any state (Natoli 1986). So it is little wonder that the impact of the H.S.G.P. was minimal at best.

Geography and Technology

Throughout this chapter the thread of history has been used to weave the story of developments in the evolution of school geography. School systems do not operate in a vacuum, but rather are conditioned by events taking place around them, such as the Vietnam War and the tumultuous social changes of the 1960s and 1970s. The tragedy of Kent State demonstrated the emotional involvement of college students in major issues of that time. Television, having been rapidly developed as a result of advances in radar technology made during World War II, became a household staple in the 1950s. The ability to broadcast scenes and events from around the world in people's living rooms suddenly became a factor in the formation of public attitudes. This visual medium also proved to be particularly effective for geography instruction. From the time of silent films, documentaries had enabled students to "travel" to faraway places while sitting at their desks or in a movie theater. Newer, more sophisticated films now treat serious issues and stimulate reasoning processes. What was once captured in still form by the camera is now being filmed in motion by camcorders, and the linkage between the VCR and the television set has become ubiquitous.

To specify the effect of television on school geography would be extremely difficult. Studies have shown that children spend much of their time in front of the "tube," and analyses of program offerings have revealed a predominance of television shows depicting sex, violence, and the seemingly inevitable "chase scene." Teachers feel that television has had an effect on students' attention spans and has made it more difficult to motivate students. Certainly, television both mirrors and shapes our culture, so it seems particularly unfortunate that this medium has been underutilized for the purpose of improving geographic literacy. However, the major network news programs have recently begun to incorporate more and better maps in their nightly news coverage, and one major network, ABC, has hired geographer Harmon De Blij to be a commentator on its morning show.

As we entered an era of school and business consolidation, we witnessed the growth of the electronics and computer industries. While IBM at first dominated the market in government and business computers, Apple Computers, Inc., took over a large segment of the educational market. Computers were soon appearing in classrooms everywhere, and professors, teachers, and students began to create their own software. Some of the early efforts to adapt geography instruction to the computer environment marked a return to the rote-learning of the past, with exercises in matching states to their capitals. But other, more creative and stimulating software was also produced, such as *National Inspirer* and *Where in the World is Carmen San Diego?*

National Inspirer arouses the spirit of competition to promote inter-active learning. The program assigns resources to each group of students. Then, through a series of planned activities, students use maps and graphs to find and visit the state(s) where the largest amount of the assigned resources is produced. The goal is to reach the "cash in" state with the assigned area, population density, or elevation (Hass 1989). Besides being effective in this type of direct instruction, computers can also be used to produce a variety of maps and to store immense quantities of information. Thus they can serve as both as atlas and an encyclopedia, with the further advantage of being readily updatable. While the computer can give students instant access to thousands of facts, the student must make inferences and draw conclusions from this data. Good computer programs guide students through this process.

Satellite imagery, especially through infrared photography, has amassed a great deal of new data about the planet Earth, allowing scientists and geographers to gain new insights into global systems. One result has been the recognition that the size and shape of the Earth needed to be recalculated. Other findings that have attracted much public attention include the denudation of the tropical rain forests, the spread of acid rain, and the discovery of holes in the ozone layer which could lead to global warming and possibly to rising sea levels. These recent discoveries have focused new attention on the importance of environmental geography for the future of the planet.

CURRENT TRENDS AND ISSUES

Educational reform movements have periodically swept through American education. Once each movement has passed, it often seems as if little has changed, as when the "new math" was introduced in the 1960s, then abandoned a decade later. However, blockbuster books which reach the general public seem to be one avenue of change. For instance, Rudolph Flesch's *Why Johnny Can't Read* did bring about a renewed emphasis on phonics in primary schools (Flesch 1955, 1986). Unfortunately, no one has written a book on "Why Johnny can't learn geography." Yet we are all aware that the geographic knowledge of most people is woefully inadequate.

Educational researchers and writers have contributed to changed ways of perceiving the learning process in geography instruction. David Paul Ausubel advocated the use of "advance organizers," whereby students are apprised of their task at the outset. Jerome Bruner popularized the idea that any subject or topic could be taught at any level if presented in an understandable manner. The work of Jean Piaget in defining distinct stages of development had a particular application to geography since his experiments dealt with childrens' comprehension of spatial relationships.

A new reform was ushered in at the beginning of the 1980s when Secretary of Education T. H. Bell created the National Commission on Excellence in Education. After conducting hearings and visiting schools around the country, the commission, whose membership comprised college presidents, superintendents of schools, school board members, principals, a former governor, and a National Teacher of the Year, issued its report, *A Nation at Risk* (National Commission on Excellence in Education 1983). The report immediately became the subject of newspaper editorials and TV talk shows as everyone expressed concern over declining test scores, widespread functional illiteracy, high dropout rates, and deficiencies in writing, mathematics, and science. The report made specific recommendations for curriculum content (especially at the high school level), the grading system, textbooks, time in school, and teacher preparation. Although recommendations were also made on foreign language and computer science instruction, references to geography were noticeably lacking.

When William Bennett succeeded T. H. Bell as Secretary of Education, some assumed that he had been appointed by President Reagan to dismantle the department, but, to the contrary, Bennett became a vocal advocate of educational reform, especially in the area of geography instruction. His report, *First Lessons,* focused on the elementary schools and contained explicit recommendations for the content of geography courses. The prevailing "expanding environments," or home-school-neighborhood mode of organizing instruction in the first three grades was particularly called into question (Bennett 1986).

Many of the recommendations made in *First Lessons* were repeated in the California History-Social Science Framework of 1988. The California Framework created consternation among publishers by departing from the customary social studies content in its scope and sequence. California, because of its statewide textbook adoption policy, has a significant national impact. Among the innovations in the California scope and sequence was the provision that history in grades five, eight, and eleven would concentrate on three separate, major chronological periods rather than the prevailing sequence of repetitious survey courses. The intent is for geography to be taught in conjunction with history and civics (Hergesheimer and Hobbs 1989). Studying the state of California is proposed for grade four, and electives for grade nine include geography. While many of the major publishers declined to submit books for adoption, Houghton Mifflin prepared and submitted a series of textbooks corresponding to the California Framework, and these books were adopted. It still remains to be seen what the national impact will be.

During much of the 1980s the National Council for the Social Studies as well as many educators struggled with the problem of content in the social studies. A new answer was being sought to the question "What shall we teach?'' There was obvious dissatisfaction with the scope and sequence that had prevailed for many years, especially since repetitious survey courses appeared to contribute to student apathy. Africa, Asia, and Latin America were not receiving sufficient emphasis, and the emerging Pacific Rim and Caribbean Basin areas were especially neglected— all of which seemed to indicate that more geography was needed in the social studies curriculum.

With funding from the Carnegie Foundation, the National Council for the Social Studies, together with the American Historical Association, formed the National Commission on Social Studies in the Schools to study the matter. The report of the commission's curriculum task force, *Charting a Course: Social Studies for the 21st Century,* was issued in November of 1989 and included specific content recommendations which showed an increased attention to geography:

K–3—A balance of local, national, and *global* concepts of the immediate *environment,* the local community, diverse people, and *models* of the *physical* world;

4–6—Introduction of United States History, World History, *global patterns and regional land-use;*

7–8—Local community: economic and political development of the United States [the in-depth study of the local community would involve geography, but the traditional world regional study at seventh grade is eliminated];

9–11—World and American History *and Geography* to 1750, 1750–1900, since 1900;

12—Government/Economics. (National Commission on Social Studies in the Schools 1989: 8–19 [emphases mine])

In identifying the important characteristics of a social studies curriculum for the twenty-first century, *Charting a Course* stressed the cumulative nature of learning and the correlations between social studies and the arts and humanities. Selective content was recommended over "coverage." In addition to an essay on geography in the report, major changes in grades nine to eleven were encouraged, such as more time for the in-depth study of eras and the inclusion of more geography. Furthermore, in the twelfth grade geography and economics would be closely linked, just as history and political science were. Ultimately, the curriculum will become not what is planned or mandated, but what goes on in the classroom once the door is closed, and that is where the significance of the California Framework and *Charting a Course* will be determined over the next century.

A Gallup poll of 1980, along with a subsequent spate of newspaper articles on what students did not know about geography, brought the subject to public attention. One example was the *New York Times* (1985) survey which found that of the college students only twenty-five percent polled knew where the Amazon River flowed. Such findings were not new, corresponding to those of earlier studies that had gone relatively unnoticed, but they found a new audience. This publicity led to the drawing up of *Guidelines for Geographic Education* by the Joint Committee on Geographic Education (1984) of the National Council for Geographic Education and the Association of American Geographers. The *Guidelines* promulgated five fundamental themes in geography: (1) location, (2) place, (3) relationships within places, (4) movement, and (5) regions. Moreover, a place for geography in the curriculum was recommended, with a specific role and sequence suggested for geography instruction at all grade levels. The guidelines received a great deal of attention and were widely distributed. This led to the formation of the Geographic National Implementation Project (GENIP) and the publication of two subsequent volumes detailing the important knowledge, skills, and attitudes for geographic education, one for grades K–6 and the other for grades 7–12 (GENIP 1987, 1989).

The project has received a great deal of financial support from the National Geographic Society, which offered its first summer institutes for teachers in 1986. When the National Geographic Society celebrated its 100th anniversary in 1987, President and Chairman Gilbert M. Grosvenor announced the formation of the National Geographic Society Education Foundation with an initial funding of twenty million dollars. Through its summer institutes, its network of "Geographic Alliances" in various states as well as a "Kids' Network" linked by telephone and microcomputers, and through its various publications, the society has played a major role in the renaissance of geographic education. The National Geographic Society has also published an interactive laserdisk/computer program, *GTV: A Geographic Perspective in American History.* The program stresses such geographic issues as a population clock, migration, transportation, communication, and urbanization (Fontana 1991). By utilizing the society's resources of maps and photographs, the program includes an immense data base for use in the classroom. Surely, more emphasis will now be placed on geographic issues in the social studies across the nation.

The first National Geographic Awareness Week occurred in the fall of 1987 as a result of a resolution introduced by Senator Bill Bradley (NJ). Subsequent "awareness weeks," along with the National Geography Bee sponsored by National Geographic *World,* have served to heighten student and teacher interest in the subject. In addition, the Rand McNally Geography Teaching Awards and the American Express Geography Competition have demonstrated the interest taken by American businesses in geographic education.

PROJECTIONS

While the outlook for geography in the years ahead appears bright, the difficulties of curricular reform must not be underestimated. The public school system is still a vast bureaucracy, often subject to fads which have a superficial impact, but slow to implement substantive changes. Furthermore, many social studies teachers have had little or no formal training in geography since history and political science tend to dominate their education, with geography and economics swallowed up in the process.

Textbooks continue to be the major factor in determining scope and sequence. While textbook publishers are guided by the established curricula of various state and community school systems, teachers and curriculum committees assess the available textbook materials in defining their scope and sequence. The result for geography instruction is, and will continue to be, a dog-chasing-its-tail situation. The huge investment required for the production of a new geography-based textbook series will make publishers reluctant to gamble on the market for such books. Consequently and subsequently, teachers and curriculum designers are likely to be unwilling or unable to implement more geography instruction.

The middle-school movement appears to offer the most distinct possibility for getting more geography into the curriculum. Geography has traditionally had a spot in the junior high schools, often at the seventh-grade level. In order to develop a sense of place and an associated vocabulary, students must be exposed to peoples and regions beyond their own horizons, and middle-grade students seem to have an innate curiosity about such things. The themes articulated in the *Guidelines for Geographic Education* also lend themselves to the revamped middle school curricula proposed as part of the reform movement in the late 1980s.

The "whole language" movement represents another window of opportunity for furthering geography instruction. Rather than spending an entire year on a single, often bland and superificial textbook, students may be exposed to a stimulating variety of profound, insightful literary works—and not all students have to read the same books. Students exposed to this method may come to appreciate such authors as James Michener, who was recently recognized by the National Council for Geographic Education for his contribution to geographic literature. By developing a *sense of place* through reading and other experiences, students may form rich and many-sided personalities—a worthy educational goal for the twenty-first century.

Operation Desert Storm and other issues related to oil and the Arab World forcefully demonstrated once again the importance of learning geography. The logistics of assembling war materiel and supplies in Saudi Arabia was essentially a problem in geography. The strategies of all wars as well as plans for peace require an intimate knowledge not only of climates and landforms, but also of cultures and demographics. These come together in geography and should therefore be a part of the preparation of teachers. Furthermore, the making of intelligent decisions on such matters requires an informed electorate, a major goal of education.

While the world may appear complex and bewildering, a gestalt can be formed. By studying and experiencing different eras, issues, places, regions, and movements, a student/teacher ultimately forms a mental map, or world view.

A vision of a better future for geography must, of necessity, take into account the realities of the present situation. Street-wise youngsters of the inner city may have a different conception of what knowledge constitutes power in their struggles for daily existence in their non-bullet-proof world. Ultimately, the answer to problems should come from opinions based upon factual knowledge. Even the Drug War cannot be understood without a knowledge of economic geography along with an understanding of personal motivations. Beyond the goals of peace and citizenship, geographic knowledge can lead students into making useful contributions in the world at work while also contributing to the quality of their environments and their personal lives.

REFERENCES

I. General

Bennett, William J. *First Lessons: A Report on Elementary Education in America*. Washington, DC: U.S. Department of Education, 1986.

Buttimer, Anne, and Paul Claval. "IGU Discussion on Geography Today, Yesterday, and Tomorrow." *Professional Geographer* 39 (1987): 221–24.

Flesch, Rudolph. Why Johnny Can't Read—and What You Can Do About It. New York: Harper, 1955; Reprint Harper and Row, 1986.

Fontana, Lynn A. "GTV: A Geographic Perspective in American History." *Social Education* 55 (April/May 1991): 221–22.

GENIP. *K–6 Geography: Themes, Key Ideas, and Learning Opportunities*. Washington, DC: Geographic Education National Implementation Project, 1987.

———. *7–12 Geography: Themes, Key Ideas, and Learning Opportunities*. Washington, DC: Geographic Education National Implementation Project, 1989.

Graves, Norman J. *New UNESCO Source Book for Geography Teaching*. Paris: Longman/UNESCO Press, 1982.

Hass, Mary E. "Becoming Aware of U.S. Geographic Diversity: A Review of *National Inspirer*." *Social Education* 53 (September 1989) 276–77.

Hergesheimer, John H., and Gail L. Hobbs. *Geography in the California Framework: A Guide for Implementing the History-Social Science Curriculum*. Los Angeles: University of California, Los Angeles, 1989.

Hill, A. David. "Geography in American Education." In Gary L. Gaile and Cort J. Willmott, eds., *Geography in America*. Columbus: Merrill, 1989.

James, Preston E. "Continuity and Change in American Geographic Thought." In Saul Cohen, ed., *Problems and Trends in American Geography*. New York: Basic Books, 1967.

———. "The Significance of Geography in American Education." *The Journal of Geography* 68 (1969): 473–83.

Joint Committee on Geographic Education. *Guidelines for Geographic Education: Elementary and Secondary Schools*. Washington, DC: Association of

American Geographers and National Council for Geographic Education, 1984.

National Commission on Excellence in Education. *A Nation at Risk: The Imperative for Educational Reform.* Washington, DC: U.S. Department of Education, 1983.

National Commission on Social Studies in the Schools. *Charting a Course: Social Studies for the 21st Century.* Washington, DC: Joint Project of the American Historical Association, the National Council for the Social Studies, and the Organization of American Historians, 1989.

Natoli, Salvatore J. "The Evolving Nature of Geography." In Stanley P. Wronski and Donald H. Bragaw, eds., *Social Studies and Social Sciences: A Fifty Year Perspective.* Washington, DC: National Council for the Social Studies, 1986.

Shabad, Theodore. "Geography: A Lost Art." *New York Times* (January 15, 1985): C–1–2.

Palmer, J. Jesse, Ben Smith, and John Davis. "Social Studies According to Peter Parley." *The Social Studies* 79 (January/February 1988). 10–13.

Stoltman, Joseph P. "Geographical Education and Society: Changing Perspectives on School Geography in the United States of America." In Agustin Hernando, ed., *Geographical Education and Society: Abstracts and Papers.* Washington, DC: Commission on Geographical Education, International Geographical Union, 1986; also in *Exemplary Practice Series: Geography Education.* Burlington, IN: Phi Delta Kappa Center on Evaluation, Development, Research, 1986.

Superka, Douglas P., Sherryl Hawke, and Irving Morrissett. "The Current and Future Status of the Social Studies." *Social Education* 44 (1980): 577–585.

Vining, James W. *National Council for Geographic Education: The First Seventy-Five Years and Beyond.* Indiana, PA: National Council for Geographic Education, 1990.

Winston, Barbara J. "Teaching and Learning Geography." In Stanley P. Wronski and Donald H. Bragaw, eds., *Social Studies and Social Sciences: A Fifty Year Perspective.* Washington, DC: National Council for the Social Studies, 1986.

II. Geography Textbooks

Atwood, Wallace W., and Helen G. Thomas. *Atwood-Thomas Geographies.* Boston: Ginn, 1932.

Barrows, Harlan H., and Edith Parker. *The Barrows-Parker Geography Series.* New York: Silver Burdett, 1941.

Bradley, John Hodgdon. *World Geography.* 4th ed. Boston: Ginn, 1968.

Colby, Charles C., and Alice Foster. *Economic Geography for Secondary Schools.* Boston: Ginn, 1931.

Davis, William Morse. *Elementary Physical Geography.* Boston: Ginn, 1904.

Maury, Matthew Fontaine. *The World We Live In. Maury's Geographical Series.* New York: University Publishing Company, 1871.

Morse, Jedediah. *Geography Made Easy.* 5th ed. Boston: I. Thomas and E. T. Andrews, 1796.

Rugg, Harold. *America's March Toward Democracy: History of American Life: Political and Social.* revised. Boston: Ginn, 1937.

Smith, J. Russell. *World Folks.* Philadelphia: John C. Winston, 1938.

Woodbridge, William C. *Rudiments of Geography on a New Plan.* 6th ed. Hartford: Oliver D. Cooke, 1826.

8

GOVERNMENT AND POLITICS IN SOCIAL STUDIES

Jack Allen

Democratic government bases its entire value structure on the preservation, enrichment, and enhancement of human freedom. As a societal goal, political freedom is assumed to be essential to the realization of all other types of freedom, social and economic. In democratic societies, the goal of governmental organizations and legal institutions is to redress social inequities and enhance economic opportunities. And so it is that, in American culture, the purpose of political socialization is to cultivate free individuals who will comprise a responsible democratic citizenry.

REFLECTIONS

A close relationship between democratic government and education was much in the minds of the founders of the American republic. Even before ratification of the United States Constitution, the Northwest Ordinance of 1787 gave recognition to the idea of public education: "Religion, morality, and knowledge being necessary to good government and the happiness of mankind, schools and the means of education shall be forever encouraged" (Allen 1969: 10). Founders of the republic expressed similar sentiments.

Such concerns as these for the development of civic competence were mirrored in school textbooks published at that time. Courses in government (mainly devoted to study of the United States Constitution) were offered in secondary schools (Knowlton 1938). But not until the late 1800s did a definite pattern of curricular offerings for the study of government emerge. In 1892 the National Education Association appointed a "Committee of Ten," which had a broad mandate to assess the curriculum of American schools. One of its subcommittees was assigned the task of evaluating curricular offerings related to history, civil government, and political economy. The subcommittee's report recommended a high school program devoted largely to course offerings in history, but also recommended the study of civil government in grade twelve (Tryon 1935: 252–55).

The Committee of Ten's curriculum recommendations for the nation's secondary schools limited focus on the role of political education in the schools can be seen in the Committee's final report which stated that the chief function of the secondary schools is to prepare for the duties of life the small proportion of all the children in the country—a proportion small in number, but very important to the welfare of the nation—who show themselves to profit by an education prolonged to the eighteenth year, and whose parents are able to support them while they remain so long in school. (Committee on Secondary School Studies 1893: 51)

If the goal of a democracy is a responsible democratic citizenry, then the committee's omission of a stronger role for political education represents a serious flaw.

More influential for the high school social studies curriculum than the report of the Committee of Ten, however, were the recommendations of the "Committee of Seven," appointed by the American Historical Association in 1899. Its report, reflecting the judgments and doubtless the biases of the committee membership, was a recommended program, to wit: grade nine, ancient history; grade ten, medieval and modern history; grade eleven, English history; and grade twelve, American history and civil government (Committee of Seven 1909: 48). Begun only six years after that of the Committee of Ten, this report suggested content for each course that mirrored a heavy political emphasis. As for the content of the twelfth-grade course in particular, the committee observed: "Much time will be saved and better results obtained if history and civil government be studied in large measure together, as one subject rather than two distinct subjects" (81). This first official attempt to merge disciplinary contents would lead to future conflicts among professional organizations, many of which still remain unresolved.

The program and assumptions of the Committee of Seven received general, though less than unanimous, approval. One strong challenge came in 1903 from a newly organized professional body, the American Political Science Association. Despite this protest, a subsequent committee of the American Historical Association would reaffirm the view of the Committee of Seven, declaring, "Much that is commonly called government as distinguished from history *can be taught* and should be taught as part of the history course" (Committee of Five 1915: 48). [emphases in original]

Additional recommendations concerning the place of government and politics in the social studies curriculum soon began to appear. In 1915 a special subcommittee of the Committee on Social Studies of the National Education Association's Commission on the Reorganization of Secondary Education published a report entitled *The Teaching of Community Civics.* Among these recommendations was a course in community civics for young adolescents and an advanced course in government which would serve as the capstone of the high school social studies program. The following year the "Committee of Seven" of the American Political Science Association made a similar recommendation.

There also appeared, in 1916, a curriculum report entitled *The Social Studies in Secondary Education,* prepared by the United States Bureau of Education's Committee on Social Studies of the Commission on the Reorganization of Secondary Education. Among its recommendations was a course in civics to be taught in grade nine. Emphasizing good citizenship and social efficacy as the most important functions of social studies instruction, the report also recommended that the civics course include the study of the "world community" as well as stressing citizenship at the local, state, and national levels. A further committee recommendation of long-term curricular significance was a course that would focus on the problems of American democracy. To be offered in the twelfth grade, this year-long or one-semester course would examine economic, social, and political problems for the purpose of conveying "a more definite, comprehensive, and deeper knowledge of some of the vital problems of social life, and thus of securing a more intelligent and active citizenship" (U.S. Bureau of Education 1916: 52).

The 1915 and 1916 committees reports have had a remarkable staying power as influences on the social studies curriculum. Community civics, offered in some form in grade nine, and government, offered either as a separate course or within a "problems" context in grade twelve, remain standard fare, no doubt strongly bolstered by textbooks created to fit the respective levels. A study conducted in the early 1960s by the United States Office of Education, for instance, reported a full-year course in community civics to be clearly the most common social studies offering in grade nine, while the "problems of democracy" course was second only to a course in American government among twelfth grade offerings (Moreland 1962).

Meanwhile, the political content of such courses, influenced by the general interests and concerns of citizenship education and political socialization, was increasingly emphasized in the elementary school social studies program. Woven into the curricular instruction of children were assumptions and values related to the meaning of "good" citizenship and the recognition of out-of-school experiences that contribute to the process of political socialization. In the middle grades, global studies included instruction on the political systems of other nations and, almost invariably, value analyses of the relative efficacy of different societies and cultures.

The prevailing curricular offerings in government and politics during the 1960s were not immune to the educational ferment of the times. One critic reported the civics course to be "universally despised" and denounced the twelfth grade problems course as "hopeless" (Mayer 1963: 77). In more measured language, political scientist Norton Long declared citizenship education to be "perhaps one of the most critical areas, if not the most critical area, of controversy in the field of education in the social studies" (Long 1962: 89). From a different perspective, Evron and Jeane Kirkpatrick questioned the making of good citizens as the main objective of secondary school instruction in political science. Declaring that such an instructional goal was "a distorted conception of how citizens are made" and "a distorted conception of democracy" (Kirkpatrick and Kirkpatrick 1962: 100), they asserted their belief that "one of the most important responsibilities of the secondary school teacher is to inform students about the existence of a field of inquiry into government and politics and to give them some indication of the complexity and difficulty of many public problems" (121). Regardless of the propriety or impropriety of the 1960s critiques, the position of government and politics in the social studies curriculum remained firmly entrenched in grades nine and twelve.

CURRENT ISSUES AND TRENDS

Reminiscent of the turbulent 1960s was another period of national ferment over education that surfaced in the closing years of the 1980s. And while, as earlier, the sciences and mathematics were often at the forefront of national concern, the social studies managed to attract a share of the attention. Early in the 1980s, the social studies profession began to sense the need to examine afresh its educational position and responsibilities. Responding to this concern, the National Council for the Social Studies appointed a Task Force on Scope and Sequence, which issued its first report in 1983, then a revised report in 1989. The 1989 report defined the general purpose of social studies programs as the "responsibility to prepare young people to identify, understand, and work to solve the problems that face our increasingly diverse nation and interdependent world" (National Council 1989: 377). The subject matter deemed essential to fulfilling this general "responsibility" included "government—theories, systems, structures, processes," and "law—civil, criminal, constitutional, international" (ibid.). In the affective realm, "democratic values and beliefs" needed to be emphasized. In the skills area, the goal was the "development of skills and abilities necessary for citizen participation in social, civic, and political processes" (377–78).

Indeed, "participatory citizenship" seemed to have become a watchword of the social studies profession. *Social Education,* the official journal of the National Council for the Social Studies, devoted virtually one entire issue (October 1989) to the subject, and the NCSS annual meeting of 1990 adopted the same theme. One article in the October 1989 issue of *Social Education* appears particularly relevant to this pedagogical trend in government and politics. Entitled "Reflective Civic Participation," the article was by Fred M. Newmann, who observed,

We should constantly be asking about the potential these [participation] experiences have to help us move from the dominant, privatistic view of civic life to public-minded democracy. Unless students are placed in settings and roles that require them to deliberate about the nature of public good and participate in the processes of influence and negotiation to achieve it, they fail to reap the personal benefits of citizenship, and the civic culture will languish. (Newmann 1989: 357)

In today's world of political turmoil, it appears only logical to use the concept of participatory citizenship as a basis for political instruction in the schools.

Contributing to the spate of pronouncements made in 1989 was a social studies curriculum report, national in dimension and broad in sponsorship. The product of the National Commission on Social Studies in the Schools, *Charting a Course: Social Studies for the 21st Century* was a joint project of the American Historical Association, the Organization of American Historians, the National Council for the Social Studies, and the Carnegie Foundation for the Advancement of Teaching. Not surprisingly, the first of five goals for social studies education listed in the report was a curriculum that would enable students to develop "civic responsibility and active participation" (National Commission 1989: 6). Six characteristics of a social studies curriculum for the 21st Century were identified, two of which related to the study of government and politics:

—Because they offer the perspectives of time and place, history and geography should provide the matrix framework for social studies; yet concepts and understandings from political science, economics and other social sciences must be integrated throughout all social studies courses so that by the end of the 12th grade, students will have a firm understanding of their principles and methodologies.

—Selective studies of the history, geography, government and economic systems of the major civilizations and societies should together receive attention at least equal to the study of the history, geography, government, economics and society of the United States. (3)

Adding substance to the statement of goals, the commission offered scope-and-sequence curriculum recommendations. Here, proponents of the study of government and politics might well have felt shortchanges, since only for grade twelve was a course in government recommended— and then only as one of four options. Political scientists might wonder if the heavy emphasis on historical study throughout the recommended curriculum reflected biases of sponsorship by two national historical associations. Indeed, social studies educators with long memories might well taste in *Charting a Course* a flavor reminiscent of the American Historical Association's 1899 "Committee of Seven" report. The specific course requirements recommended by both the NCSS Task Force on Scope and Sequence and the National Commission on Social Studies in the Schools reflect the force of tradition in American education.

However, *Charting a Course* did include a major section entitled "Perspectives of Social Science Associations," in which eight disciplines were discussed in essays by members of the respective associations. One of the essays, "Why Study Politics?" by Richard Brody, is comparable in importance to a 1970 document produced by the Committee on Pre-Collegiate Education of the American Political Science Association (1971) entitled "Political Education in the Public Schools: The Challenge for Political Science." Professor Brody's 1989 essay stated that the study of government and politics in American elementary and secondary schools should:

—Transmit to students a knowledge of the "realities" of political life as well as exposing them to the cultural ideas of American democracy.

—Transmit to students a knowledge of political behavior and processes as well as knowledge about formal governmental institutions and legal structures.

—Transmit to students knowledge about political systems other than the American system, and particularly knowledge about the international system.

—Develop within students a capacity to think about political phenomena in conceptually sophisticated ways.

—Develop within students a capacity to distinguish facts and values and the understanding that both play central roles in political decisions and policies.

—Develop within students an understanding of the capabilities and skills needed to participate effectively and democratically in the life of the society. (National Commission 1989: 60–62)

PROJECTIONS

Having reflected on the American political experience and ways that schools and related agencies have helped to sustain and enhance the American dream, what can be said of education for the future? Can education play a significant role in the development of a citizenry worthy of the democratic tradition? Is the educational goal to pass on information about society and to reinforce what are deemed to be accepted values and modes of behavior? Or should social studies education seek to develop a citizenry of problem solvers capable of using information and ideas? It is axiomatic that there is a measure of relevance in both goals. In the past, however, the problem has been too much devotion to the former goal at the expense of the latter. The future of political education need not be based on some grand new scheme for American education. Indeed, consensus on any new proposed design will be difficult, if not impossible, to attain in the coming century. So, let us consider, for instance, political education within the context of a traditional social studies scope-and-sequence curriculum. The old "expanding-environments" concept of the elementary school curriculum offers a world of opportunities for the development of political understanding, skills, and values along dimensions from the local to the global. Typical history and social sciences content can be useful in the development of citizenship skills and shared values. The courses in more specialized subject areas, such as government, law, and economics, furnish ample opportunities to illuminate and energize the political scene. In fact, given the pace of political events, it seems evident that the students of tomorrow will be bombarded with opportunities to study values and modes of behavior, while also having many chances to help solve the pressing problems of our global society.

With the twenty-first century now at our doorstep, we in the United States can find satisfaction in thinking of the twentieth century as *our* century. We have felt pride in carrying the torch of freedom. We have contributed generously to meet the needs of war-torn peoples and nations. And, we have been the masters of our own economic destiny.

The new political education must deal with issues and problems that will often be global in nature. With the exception of one enduring concern, the quest for peace and security, there is reason to be cautiously optimistic that a new century can mend the ways of this one, the bloodiest years of history. Confronted with a world of monumental change, truly a world in revolution, educational attitudes and actions appear to be decidedly mixed. While there seems to be a strong commitment to democratic ideals, political indifference is apparently the order of the day. Major issues, such as the economy and foreign policy, must evoke greater interest and be coupled with other crucial concerns, such as drugs and abortion, in the education of the youth. But, to be realistic about the problem, it should be noted that political indifference has a long history in American society. A century and a half ago, Alexis de Tocqueville observed that, in America, "political associations are only one small part of the immense number of different associations found there" (Tocqueville 1969[1835]: 500). Americans, then and now, do value their private associations and frequently find them more appealing than the public political arena. It will be the task of the schools in the twenty-first century to attempt to break this tradition and create a truly participatory democratic citizenry.

Here, then, resides the challenge for those in charge of the political education of the nation's youth. Our democratic nation cannot successfully endure an indifferent, disengaged citizenry. Consequently, no greater responsibility confronts social studies educators.

REFERENCES

Allen, Jack. *The American Public School*. New York: McGraw-Hill, 1969.

Allen, Jack, ed. *Education in the 80's: Social Studies*. Washington, DC: National Education Association of the United States, 1980.

Allen, Jack. *Of, By, and For the People: Popular Sovereignty in American History*. Alexandria, VA: The Bicentennial Council of the Thirteen Original States Fund, 1980.

American Political Science Association Committee on Pre-Collegiate Education. "Political Education in the Public Schools: The Challenge for Political Science." *Political Science Quarterly* 31 (1971): 270–75.

Berlin, Carol Ruth. "Virtue and Politics: The Dilemma of the Republic." In Jack Allen. *Of, By, and For the People: Popular Sovereignty in American History*. Alexandria, VA: The Bicentennial Council of the Thirteen Original States Fund, 1980.

Butler, Benjamin R. *Strong Democracy*. Berkeley: University of California Press, 1984.

Butts, R. F. *The Morality of Citizenship: Goals for Civic Education in the Republic's Third Century*. Calabasas, CA: Center for Civic Education, 1988.

Cherryholmes, Cleo H. "Social Studies for Which Century?" *Social Education* 54 (November/December 1990): 438–42.

Committee of Five of the American Historical Association. *The Study of History in Secondary Schools*. New York: Macmillan, 1915.

Committee of Seven of the American Historical Association. *The Study of History in Secondary Schools*. New York: Macmillan, 1909.

Committee on Secondary School Studies. *Report*. Washington, DC: Government Printing Office, 1893.

Engle, Shirley H., and A. S. Ochoa. *Education for Democratic Citizenship: Decision-Making in the Social Studies*. New York: Teachers College Press, 1988.

Gutmann, A. *Democratic Education*. Princeton: Princeton University Press, 1987.

Kirkpatrick, Evron M., and Jeane J. Kirkpatrick. "Political Science." In Erling M. Hunt. ed., *High School Social Studies Perspectives*. Boston: Houghton Mifflin, 1962.

Knowlton, David C. "The United States Constitution in the Schoolbooks of the Past." *The Social Studies* 29 (1938): 7–14.

Long, Norton E. "Political Science." In Bernard Berelson. ed., *The Social Studies and the Social Sciences*. New York: Harcourt, Brace and World, 1962.

Mayer, Martin. *Where, When, and Why: Social Studies in American Schools*. New York: Harper and Row, 1963.

Moreland, Willis D. "Curriculum Trends in the Social Studies." *Social Education.* 26 (February 1962): 73–76, 102.

National Commission on Social Studies in the Schools. *Charting a Course: Social Studies for the 21st Century.* A Report of the Curriculum Task Force of the National Commission of Social Studies in the Schools. Washington, DC: National Commission on Social Studies in the Schools, 1989.

National Council for the Social Studies Task Force on Scope and Sequence. "In Search of a Scope and Sequence." *Social Education* 53 (October 1989): 376–87.

National Education Association. *The Social Studies in Secondary Education.* Bulletin No. 28. Washington, DC: U.S. Government Printing Office, 1916.

Natoli, Salvatore J., ed. "Scope and Sequence-Special Issue." *Social Education* 53 (October 1989).

Newmann, Fred M. *The Assessment of Discourse in the Social Studies.* Madison, WI: National Center on Effective Secondary Schools, 1988.

———. "Reflective Civic Participation." *Social Education* 53 (October 1989): 357–60, 366.

Pratte, R. *The Civic Imperative: Examining the Need for Civic Education.* New York: Teachers College Press, 1988.

Riddle, Donald H., and Robert S. Cleary, eds. *Political Science in the Social Studies.* Washington, DC: National Council for the Social Studies, 1966.

Tocqueville, A. *Democracy in America* (1835), translated by G. Lawrence and edited by J. A. Mayer. New York: Doubleday, 1969.

Tryon, Rolla M. *The Social Sciences as School Subjects.* New York: Scribner's, 1935.

9

ECONOMICS IN ELEMENTARY AND SECONDARY SCHOOLS

June V. Gilliard

Compared to the disciplines of history and geography, economics is a relative newcomer to the social studies curriculum. Rejected as a separate course by the 1892 National Education Association Committee on Secondary School Studies, economics did not gain prominence in the curriculum until the 1920s (Tryon 1935: 334). Despite this inauspicious beginning, today over half of the states mandate the teaching of economics. What factors have contributed to a larger role for economics in elementary and secondary schools? What is the current content of economic instruction and what changes are needed to meet the challenges of the twenty-first century? Hopefully, the following discussion will provide the reader with some insight into how we came to be where we are in terms of economic education and what alternatives may be available to us in the immediate future.

REFLECTIONS

A brief look at the nomenclature of the discipline reveals the source of some of the problems associated with defining the purposes and content of economic education in elementary and secondary schools. The word "economics" comes from the Greek *eco* and *nom,* meaning "house" and "law," respectively. Thus, its earliest meaning was "household management" (Groenewegen 1987: 905). This meaning persisted until the seventeenth century when the French terms *économie* and *politique* were combined to denote public administration, or management of the affairs of state. By the second half of the eighteenth century, usage of the term *économie politique* had expanded to include scholarly discourse on the nature and acquisition of wealth. The latter meaning "became more dominant, the word 'science' was added to it . . . and by the 1770s it almost exclusively referred to the production and distribution of wealth in the context of management of the nation's resources" (ibid.). Nineteenth-century attempts to define the method and scope of political economy more precisely resulted in the introduction of the term "economics," which, by the turn of the century, was frequently used as a synonym for political economy. A new dimension was added in 1921 by John Maynard Keynes, who, in his introduction to the *Cambridge Economics Handbooks,* described economics as "a method rather than a doctrine, an apparatus of the mind, a technique of thinking, which helps its possessor to draw correct conclusions" (quoted in Groenewegen 1987: 906).

Over the years, disagreement about the content of economic education has in large part arisen as a result of conflict between advocates of "pure" economics, or "economics as a science" (also sometimes referred to as "mainstream economics"), on the one hand, and advocates of "practical," or "personal," economics, on the other. This conflict has its roots in the historical uses of the term "economics" and the types of activities to which each usage was applied.

Economics began its career in the high school curriculum during the late nineteenth century as "political economy." The content of these early courses in political economy, according to Rolla Tryon, was the "verbatim content" of the available textbook. Regarding these textbooks, Tryon stated that

their theoretical character, their abstract material and the didactic methods used in presenting it, their involved sentence structure, their technical vocabulary and vague meaning made them books to be avoided rather than used by young people. They were more a detriment than an aid to the emerging subject of political economy and to effective training therein. (Tryon 1935: 348)

By the end of the second decade of the twentieth century, "political economy" had virtually disappeared as a course title, having been replaced by the term "economics." This change marked a shift in both the goals and the subject matter of economic instruction at the precollegiate level.

During the 1920s, economic instruction in secondary schools shifted from the highly theoretical approach employed in previous decades to an emphasis on personal or practical applications of economic theory (ibid.: 359). The economic uncertainties of the Depression era led to increased emphasis on problems related to making a living in an industrialized democracy. "In the schools of the 1930s," observes David Jenness, "the personal economics emphasis seemed to be dominant, with much attention to 'thrift education,' economic competence in the personal (often occupational) sphere, and economic 'skills' for living" (Jenness 1990: 207).

The report of the 1938 Educational Policies Commission recommended expanding the scope of economic education to include not only personal economic efficiency, but also civic competence. The latter was viewed as including "familiarity with broad economic issues, conditions, and procedures, and with important economic concepts such as supply and demand, investment, profit, and scarcity" (Armento 1986: 98).

A workshop held at New York University in the summer of 1948 under the leadership of G. Derwood Baker heralded the birth of an organized national movement to raise the level of economic literacy in the United States. The workshop, which was sponsored by the Committee for Economic Development, involved economists, curriculum experts, school administrators, and representatives from business, labor, government, and private research organizations (Howard 1952: 2). Conflict arose over the question of whether high school economics should focus on "pure" economics, as represented by mainstream economists, or on "practical economics." The purists prevailed, and, as Beverly Armento has noted, "the tone was set for the dominant approach the economic movement was to take in the future" (Armento 1986: 100). The following year the Joint Council on Economic Education was founded, with G. Derwood Baker appointed as its first director. Since then the Joint Council has become the foremost, and perhaps most influential, advocate for K–12 programs based on "pure" or "mainstream" economics.

Advocates of economic education have, over the years, used several different rationales to justify economics' inclusion in elementary and secondary school curricula. Among those most frequently cited are the development of skills essential for civic competence, training in logical or analytic reasoning, the development of appreciation for the free enterprise system, and the development of crucial personal or survival skills. Obviously, such differences in the perceived purpose of economic education lead to differences in curriculum content and emphasis.

Nineteenth-century champions of the political economy course relied heavily on the civic-competence rationale to justify the subject's place in the high school curriculum. They argued that it was "equally as important for the cause of effective citizenship for practitioners of the arts to be well informed on multifarious and complex economic topics upon which a citizen must pass on as a voter" as it was "to be informed relative to the past of his country and the laws governing it" (Tryon 1935: 336). One of the most compelling civic-competence arguments for economic education was set forth by Kenneth Boulding, as follows:

An accurate and workable image of the social system in general, and the economic system in particular is . . . increasingly essential to human survival. If the prevailing images of the social system are unreal and inaccurate, decisions which are based on them are likely to lead to disaster. . . . Economic education, therefore, along with education in other aspects of the social system may well be one of the most important keys for man's survival. (Boulding 1969: 10–11)

Similarly, George Stigler noted that, since much legislation on which citizens have an opinion has a strong economic component, "every American must be his own economist" (Stigler 1970: 81).

More recently, Steven Miller has described the connection between economic education and responsible citizenship. Economic education, Miller contends, should empower students "to understand their world, make reasoned decisions, and act appropriately on personal and social issues of significance" (Miller 1991: 37). Reporting the results of a recent survey conducted to ascertain the state of economic education in high schools, William Baumol and Robert Highsmith note, "Teachers believe overwhelmingly that they are teaching students to understand the American economy in order to help them make more intelligent decisions" (Baumol and Highsmith 1988: 261). Stephen Buckles, Director of the Joint Council on Economic Education, states the case for teaching economics as follows:

The most important justification for economic education is that it is training in logical, careful thinking. To the extent that it can enhance our students' abilities to analyze situations and problems in a rational manner, it contributes to the major goals of elementary and secondary education. (Buckles 1991: 26)

Attempts to achieve consensus on the purpose and specific content of economic education have been less than successful. In 1976, Robert Horton and Dennis Weidenaar conducted "a Delphi-like inquiry," involving economists, economic educators, teacher trainers, curriculum specialists, school administrators, social studies teachers, school board members, business people, and government officials. Respondents from all groups represented in the study overwhelmingly favored economic education's stressing how the economic system works. Teachers and school administrators were the only groups, however, who responded negatively to economic instruction that stressed economic analysis. These two groups were also the only ones who responded positively to the idea that economic education programs should focus on solutions to social problems. While most educators and business people rejected the idea that economic education should advocate free enterprise, school board members and government officials showed a decided preference for this option (Horton and Weidenaar 1976: IID).

The free-enterprise rationale enjoyed its greatest influence during the

Cold War era when many state and local governments required high schools to teach the benefits of capitalism, or free enterprise, vis-à-vis communism. Vestiges of this practice can still be found in some state laws requiring school systems to provide instruction in economics. For example, the Alabama economic education mandate requires schools to provide instruction in communism each year so that students might better appreciate the American system (Highsmith 1989: 4). State mandates for economic education tend to be based largely on the civic-competence rationale. As indicated above, however, some mandates also reflect a view of economic education as advocacy for a system of free enterprise; others emphasize practical or personal economics; a few comprise a blend of all three views. Based on a 1989 survey of the fifty state education agencies, Highsmith reported that twenty-eight states require some teaching of economics (ibid.: 2). Among those states mandating economic instruction, twenty-five require instruction in free enterprise, ten require instruction in consumer education, and three of the latter number specify instruction in consumer education as the only required economic instruction.

It would be erroneous to conclude that all of the states mandating economic instruction require schools to provide a separate course. Only sixteen states require that students successfully complete a minimum of a one-semester course in economics for high school graduation. These states, however, account for approximately half of the nation's school-age population. Mandates that do not specify a separate course in economics generally call for the infusion of economic instruction throughout the K–12 curriculum. It is also worth noting that seven states require both a separate course and infusion to satisfy the economic education mandate (ibid.).

Given the differences among state mandates, the different rationales used to justify a place for economics in the curriculum, and the implications of these differences for curriculum content, what is the nature of economic instruction in elementary and secondary schools? As the foremost advocate of "pure," or "mainstream," economics, the Joint Council on Economic Education had exerted considerable influence on the content of economics curricula. The Joint Council's *Framework for Teaching the Basic Concepts* (Saunders et al. 1984), first published in 1977 and revised in 1984, has been used by textbook publishers and local school districts throughout the United States to structure the teaching of economics in both elementary and secondary schools. The authors of the *Framework* identified twenty-two conceptual clusters to be developed in the K–12 curriculum. These concepts are assumed to reflect the structure of the discipline, proceeding from fundamental concepts to microeconomics, macroeconomics, and finally, to international economics. To the extent that state curriculum guides reflect what is actually being taught, there is evidence that the *Framework* is having an impact on classroom instruction.

Perhaps a more accurate view of what is happening in classrooms may be gained by examining the textbooks that teachers use. Studies of classroom practices in social studies indicate that textbooks to a great extent dictate the content and sequence of instruction. There is little reason to believe that economic instruction deviates from this pattern. An examination of high school economics textbooks published over the past ten years reveals the extent to which their content has been influenced by the *Framework*. Generally, the textbooks begin with a discussion of the nature of economics and of economic systems, followed by an overview of the United States' market economy. Subsequent sections focus first on microeconomics, then on macroeconomics, and lastly, on international economics. Perhaps the single most frequent variation in this pattern is where consumer or personal economics is placed. In approximately one-third of the textbooks, a unit on consumer or personal economics immediately follows the introductory section; in another third, consumer economics is covered at the end of the book; and in the remaining third, consumer economics is omitted entirely.

Despite the considerable space devoted to both macroeconomics and international economics in high school textbooks, there is evidence that teachers place less emphasis on these aspects than on the fundamental concepts and microeconomics. In a study of high school economics courses, William Walstad and John Soper found that such "courses now do their best job in teaching students about fundamental economics and related concepts of scarcity, economic systems, economic institutions and incentives, and money and exchange" (Walstad and Soper 1988: 255). At the same time, students showed an "appalling" ignorance of concepts and basic relationships in macroeconomics and international economics. "Either economic concepts in these areas are not taught," Walstad and Soper conclude, "or if they are taught, economics teachers do a poor job of instruction" (ibid.).

In the elementary grades, economics is generally integrated or "fused" with the teaching of history and other subjects in the social studies curriculum. Less frequently, the study of economics is conducted as a separate two- to eight-week unit. Regardless of the approach used—infusion or a separate unit—economic education in elementary schools tends to concentrate on the fundamental concepts, with some attention paid to a limited number of microeconomic concepts, such as supply and demand (Walstad 1991; Watts 1987: 89).

Despite the current push for mainstream economics, evidence suggests that throughout most of the nation what is taught as economics is, in fact, "personal" or practical economics (Jenness 1990: 215). In 1976, Horton and Weidenaar found that "confusion between economics education and consumer, vocational and investment education seriously interferes with the achievement of economic literacy'' (Horton and Weidenaar 1976: II–A3). The reason for this confusion is that school officials and businessmen simply do not understand the nature and scope of economic education (ibid.). The results of a 1981 national survey of high school and middle school teachers support the latter contention. When asked whether the primary focus of their teaching was "theoretical" economics or "practical," "how-to" economics, forty percent of the teachers said they stressed both, thirty-four percent stressed the "practical," and only sixteen percent reported that they stressed "theoretical" economics (Yankelovich, Skelly, and White 1981: 23).

The tendency of teachers to prefer the "practical" economics approach has been attributed to several factors. Yankelovich, Skelly, and White relate this preference to a general belief among teachers that instruction is most effective when students perceive it as relevant to their own lives (ibid.: 22). However, Miller believes that the prevalence of the "practical" economics approach may also be due to the fact that teachers find this approach easier and "often do not have enough economics background to teach economic principles or to distinguish between economics and consumer life skills." As a result, Miller concludes, "there is much less economics in the curriculum and in classroom instruction than there appears to be" (Miller 1991: 44).

CURRENT ISSUES AND TRENDS

As we approach the twenty-first century, the issue of teaching "mainstream" versus "practical" economics remains a source of conflict in education. In a recent article, Buckles supported the advocates of mainstream economics and distinguished this type of economic education from instructional practices frequently employed in classrooms. "The true goal of economic education," he stated, "should be to teach students how to make choices and decisions" (Buckles 1991: 24). If the purpose of economic instruction is to give students an analytic tool, then the "method" of economics must provide the central focus (25). Learning how to write a check, how to budget, how to comparison shop, or how to invest in the stock market, Buckles contended, is not economic education. Although such activities may reinforce basic economic understanding or result in more sophisticated consumers, they "are not economics in and of themselves" (32).

There is some evidence, however, that given a choice a majority of high school students (like their teachers) would opt for the courses that emphasize practical or personal economics. Speaking before a conference convened to examine the state of economic literacy, W. Lee Hansen observed that the demand for economic instruction among high school students was low, yet the economic education movement heretofore had always been far more attentive to the "supply rather than the demand side of the market for economic knowledge and understanding" (Hansen 1977: 63). He went on to say that

the dominant approach to economics teaching, as exemplified by curriculum materials and the formal economics training of teachers, indicates the root of the low demand problem. The effort and resources devoted to producing economic literacy for effective citizenship are frustrated because students perceive individual benefits as minimal. Although students are likely to be more receptive to personal economics because of the individual benefits, the suppliers' interest in and ability to provide such instruction is limited. (65)

A major issue that economic educators need to address, Hansen concluded, is how to strike a balance between "citizenship" or mainstream economics, on the one hand, and "practical" or personal decision-making economics, on the other.

A second issue has to do with the fit between the goals of economic education and the structure of the curriculum. Armento questioned whether the "structure of the discipline" approach employed in mainstream economics results in the intended learning outcomes:

The general aim of this approach is to help students learn subject matter and the inquiry methods of economists: if the approach is successful, students should develop comprehensive ideas for understanding social affairs and for interpreting human events. Does this, indeed, occur? Are students able to synthesize their conceptual knowledge and analytical skills and apply these to personal and social issues? (Armento 1986: 103)

In the fall of 1986, an invitational conference was held at the Massachusetts Institute of Technology (MIT) to reexamine the scope of pre-collegiate economic education. Many of the nation's best-known and most respected economists were asked to evaluate *A Framework for Teaching the Basic Concepts* (the foundational curriculum document of the Joint Council on Economic Education) to determine what changes were needed in order to (1) reflect the views currently held by mainstream economists more accurately, and (2) provide students with the economic knowledge, skills, and understanding needed for the twenty-first century (Highsmith and Kasper 1987: 101). Several speakers offered alternatives to the "structure of the discipline" approach utilized in the *Framework;* others criticized the document on the basis of what they perceived to be errors of omission or of emphasis. Paul Heilbroner, for example, proposed a program founded on "basic empirical knowledge" rather than "basic economic concepts." He suggested that economic instruction should include an examination of the past as a means for helping students understand the present and its implications for the future (Heilbroner 1987: 119). Lester Thurow proposed the use of historical case studies to provide students with concrete examples of what works and what does not (Thurow 1987: 242–45). Although their two proposals differed considerably, both Heilbroner and Thurow agreed that the high school economics course should place more emphasis on economic history and less on economic theory.

John Culbertson and Myra Strober had little problem with the "structure of the discipline" approach, but were critical of the *Framework* for its relative emphasis on certain economic topics and its tendency to ignore other topics entirely. Culbertson (1987) stated that there should be a greater emphasis on international economics, while Strober appealed for more emphasis on the economics of households, labor markets, and income distribution on the basis of the following rationale:

These three topics [households, labor markets, income distribution] are not only some of the most interesting (if controversial) in current economic work, but are also particularly relevant for adolescents questioning their role in their parents' household(s) and anticipating adult family and work roles. For both young men and young women, figuring out how to combine family and work roles in an era of rapid and relatively uncharted social change represents one of their most important developmental tasks. Economics has a great deal of information to impart to them on this subject. (Strober 1987: 143–44)

Strober was also critical of the *Framework* for its inadequate treatment of the economic impact of discrimination. She observed that the document had only one sentence on discrimination and suggested that the topic deserved considerably more attention. "More than half of the students taking economics (all of the women and the minority men)," she stated, "have a personal interest in understanding why they are unlikely, even if they obtain the same education as their white male counterparts, to enter the same occupations or achieve the same earnings" (144).

Attempts to improve economics teaching must be viewed in the larger context of a national call for reform in nearly every aspect of the educational system. It is unclear what effect the various recommendations for "fixing" the schools will have on economic education over the long run. Many of the recommended reforms have yet to be tried in schools. Others are in the earliest stages of implementation, and the extent of their "staying power" is unknown. Nevertheless, certain proposals and trends, while not directly related to economic education, have the potential to effect significant changes in both the quantity and quality of economics teaching (Gilliard 1991: 292). For example, the push for statewide assessment programs could strengthen the position of economic education in the curriculum *if* these include provisions for assessing students' knowledge of economics. Given that the Joint Council on Economic Education is the primary provider of normed tests in economics, using these as assessment instruments could, in some school systems, cause teachers to shift their emphasis from "practical" or consumer economics to a more "theoretical" approach.

It is important to note that the reverse could happen where economics is omitted as an area for assessment. Economics is not now among those subject areas tested by the National Assessment of Educational Progress, nor is economics one of the subjects targeted for nationwide assessment in the federal government's educational reform plan *America 2000: An Education Strategy* (1991). Past experience suggests that teachers will spend more instructional time and place greater emphasis on those subjects on which their students will be tested nationally or by means of state or local assessments, with relatively less emphasis and time being given to other areas of instruction. Thus, to the extent that assessment programs and educational reform strategies at the national level influence curricula at the local school district level, these could have a negative effect on economic instruction.

Current proposals for reform of the social studies curriculum also have the potential to effect changes in economic instruction in the elementary and high school grades. Of particular interest to economic educators are the K–12 curriculum recommendations made by the Bradley Commission on History in Schools (1988) and by the National Commission on Social Studies in the Schools (1989). Both sets of proposals would, if implemented, greatly expand the role of history and geography in the K–12 curriculum, but neither would specifically require a course in economics at the high school level. Although the National Commission on Social Studies called for the integration, or infusion, of economics throughout the curriculum, research has shown that this approach when used alone does not significantly improve students' understanding of and knowledge about economics.

It has not gone unnoticed, however, that California's new *History-Social Science Framework* (1988), although otherwise influenced by the work of the Bradley Commission, also includes a strongly woven strand of economic instruction throughout the K–11 curriculum and a required course in economics at the twelfth-grade level. Thus, despite the potential that various curriculum proposals may hold for reducing the role of economics in the curriculum, there is also a possibility that the process of rethinking the social studies will result in a strengthening of economics' position in the schools.

The quality of economic instruction largely depends on the knowledge and skills of the teachers who provide it. Unfortunately, research indicates that only a small percentage of teachers have had formal training in the discipline. A 1988 survey conducted by the Joint Council on Economic Education revealed that twenty-five percent of those who taught high school economics had less than six semester or quarter hours of course credit in the subject. Twenty-nine percent of the teachers surveyed had six hours of credit, and only two percent were economics majors. Nearly three-fourths of the teachers, however, reported that they had participated in economic education in-service programs (Baumol and Highsmith 1988: 260).

Although that survey did not address the preparation of elementary school teachers, one may assume that this group has even less formal training in economics than high school teachers. This assumption is supported by the fact that there is little incentive for undergraduates planning to teach in the lower grades to take economics. In a vast majority of states, course credit in economics is not required for certification to teach in primary or middle schools. Thus, competency in economic instruction at this level is largely attained through in-service workshops and other types of staff development programs. It is unlikely that reforms in teacher education will significantly improve the quality of teachers' training in economics unless those reforms include more incentives for prospective teachers to pursue course work in the field.

As indicated previously, it is impossible to predict what the long-term effects of the reform movement will be. The educational system has, in the past, been highly resistant to reforms involving any change in values, goals, or organizational structure. To the extent that current proposals for reform require changes in precisely these aspects of schooling, they will not be easily implemented.

PROJECTIONS

Needless to say, we cannot plan effective economics programs for the schools without considering the students who will use them. Demographers have warned the educational establishment that the "students who will be taught in schools of the future will be drastically different from students today, with a greater variety of backgrounds, languages, values, and abilities than ever before" (Hodgkinson 1988: 11). If current demographic trends continue, it is predicted that by the year 2001 forty-eight percent of the nation's school population will be members of ethnic or racial minorities. In some areas of the United States, minorities are expected to constitute a majority by the end of the first decade of the twenty-first century. The extreme heterogeneity of school-age youth in the decades to come, Hodgkinson contends, "represents a new order of pluralism" (14). Furthermore, he states, it is quite possible that a demographic shift of this magnitude among the students moving through the educational system will effect more rapid and profound changes in schools than any of those envisioned or enacted by reformers.

If traditional approaches to teaching economics have failed to generate enthusiasm for the subject among today's students, they are unlikely to do so in the decades ahead. In order to meet the challenges presented by demographic changes, we need to reexamine both the content and the pedagogy of economic instruction in elementary and secondary schools. As James Banks has pointed out,

All students, including all groups of ethnic minority students, have some generalized intellectual and affective needs that can be satisfied by a sound comprehensive program in economic education. However, some minority students, because of their unique experiences in this society, have some special needs that are not met by universalistic approaches. Their differences often imply the selection of unique concepts, teaching strategies, materials, and examples. (Banks 1977: 121–22)

Banks has also cautioned educators against designing economics programs based on a conceptualization of ethnic minorities as "a homogeneous group with a set of stereotypic needs" (122). Such programs, despite the best of intentions, can be as detrimental to minority children as the educational practices that they would replace.

The "new order of pluralism" will inevitably give rise to questions pertaining to educational equity. John Goodlad has predicted that "increasingly, the issue will be whether students, as a consequence of the schools they happen to attend and the classes to which they are assigned, have equality of access to knowledge" (Goodlad 1984: 131). The controversy over practical, or consumer, economics versus mainstream economics illustrates this point. For example, do students assigned to classes in consumer economics have the same access to economic knowledge as those assigned to classes in mainstream economics? Questions of equity, however, go beyond assuring equal access to knowledge. Equity also requires "setting uniformly high expectations for the learning and achievement of *all* students, paying special attention to at-risk populations, and teaching from a multicultural perspective" (Kourilsky and Quaranta 1987: 277).

If the goal of economic education is economic literacy and if economic literacy is essential for civic competence, then we have a responsibility to provide programs that will enable students—regardless of race, ethnicity, socioeconomic status, or gender—to achieve this goal. A first step in designing programs for the future is to define more clearly what we mean by "economic literacy." What are the essential components of economic literacy? What distinguishes an economically literate person from one who lacks the requisite knowledge and skills? In 1976 Leonard Silk, a columnist for the *New York Times,* observed that "no useful definition of economic literacy appears to exist" (Silk 1977: 81). This statement is equally true today. Yet such a definition is essential to determining the content and design of economic education programs for the future. At a minimum, advocates of economic literacy need to translate that goal into broad guidelines for structuring curricula and for measuring progress toward attaining such literacy.

The selection of economics content, as well as the sequence in which it is taught, has heretofore been influenced by the "structure of the discipline" of economics, by current classroom practices, and, to a lesser extent, by research on cognitive development. Responding effectively to the educational challenge confronting the schools will require curriculum developers to be more attentive to that research as well as to research on teaching and learning styles. Furthermore, an effective response will require the investment of considerably more resources in research on the "what" and the "when" of economic education and in translating research results into curricular and instructional practices.

Certainly, a clear definition of economic literacy is long overdue. Thus, giving concrete meaning to the term is imperative to effecting significant reform in economic education curricula. It is also imperative to use research more effectively in responding to questions about the "what," the "when," and the "how" of economic education. We must also remain ever cognizant of the implications that alternative curricular and instructional practices hold for educational equity. Finally, to meet the challenge of the "new order of pluralism" in the schools, we must be far more attentive to the demand (student) side of the education equation than we have been in the past.

REFERENCES

America 2000: An Education Strategy. Sourcebook. Washington, DC: U.S. Department of Education, 1991.

Armento, Beverly J. "Promoting Economic Literacy." In Stanley P. Wronski and Donald H. Bragaw, eds., *Social Studies and Social Sciences: A Fifty Year Perspective.* Bulletin No. 78. Washington, DC: National Council for the Social Studies, 1986.

Banks, James A. "Economic Education for Ethnic Minorities." In Donald R. Wentworth, W. Lee Hansen, and Sharryl H. Hawke, eds., *Perspectives on Economic Education.* New York: Joint Council on Economic Education, National Council for the Social Studies, and the Social Studies Education Consortium, 1977.

Baumol, William J., and Robert J. Highsmith. "Variables Affecting Success in Economic Education: Preliminary Findings from a New Data Base." *The American Economic Review* 78 (May 1988): 257–61.

Boulding, Kenneth E. "Economic Education: The Stepchild Too Is Father of the Man." *The Journal of Economic Education* 1 (Fall 1969): 7–11.

Bradley Commission on History in Schools. *Building a History Curriculum:*

Guidelines for Teaching History in Schools. Washington, DC: Educational Excellence Network, 1988.

Buckles, Stephen. "Guidelines for Economic Content in School Programs." In William B. Walstad and John C. Soper, eds., *Effective Economic Education in the Schools*. Washington, DC: National Education Association and Joint Council on Economic Education, 1991.

Committee on Secondary School Studies, of the National Education Association. *Report of the Committee on Secondary School Studies*. Washington, DC: U.S. Bureau of Education, Government Printing Office, 1893.

Culbertson, John M. "A Realistic International Economics." *The Journal of Economic Education* 18 (Spring 1987): 161–75.

Gilliard, June V. "Future Requirements for Programs and Materials." In William B. Walstad and John C. Soper, eds., *Effective Economic Education in the Schools*. Washington, DC: Joint Council on Economic Education and the National Education Association, 1991.

Goodlad, John I. *A Place Called School: Prospects for the Future*. New York: McGraw-Hill, 1984.

Groenewegen, Peter. " 'Political Economy' and 'Economics.' " In John Eatwell, Murray Milgate, and Peter Newman, eds., *The New Palgrave: A Dictionary of Economics*. Vol. 2. New York: Stockton Press, 1987.

Hansen, W. Lee. "The State of Economic Literacy." In William B. Walstad and John C. Soper, eds., *Perspectives on Economic Education in the Schools*. New York: Joint Council on Economic Education, National Council for the Social Studies, and the Social Science Education Consortium, 1977.

Heilbroner, Paul A. "How Economics Has Changed." *The Journal of Economic Education* 18 (Spring 1987): 111–20.

Highsmith, Robert J. *A Survey of State Mandates for Economic Education*. New York: Joint Council on Economic Education, 1989.

Highsmith, Robert J., and Hirschel Kasper. "Rethinking the Scope of Economics." *The Journal of Economic Education* 18 (Spring 1987): 101–5.

History-Social Science Framework for California Public Schools. Sacramento: California State Department of Education, 1988.

Hodgkinson, H. "The Right Schools for the Right Kids." *Educational Leadership* 45 (February 1988): 10–15.

Horton, Robert V., and Dennis J. Weidenaar. "Surmounting Obstacles to Economic Literacy: A Delphi-Like Inquiry." Paper No. 557. West Lafayette: Krannert Graduate School of Management, Purdue University, June 1976.

Howard, James T. *Improving Economic Understanding in the Public Schools*. New York: Committee for Economic Development, 1952.

Jenness, David. *Making Sense of Social Studies*. New York: Macmillan, 1990.

Kourilsky, Marilyn, and Lory Quaranta. *Effective Teaching: Principles and Practices*. Glenview, IL: Scott, Foresman and Company, 1987.

Miller, Steven L. "The Case for Economic Education in the School Curriculum." In William B. Walstad and John C. Soper, eds., *Effective Economic Education in the Schools*. Washington, DC: Joint Council on Economic Education and the National Education Association, 1991.

National Commission on Social Studies in the Schools. *Charting a Course: Social Studies for the 21st Century*. A Report of the Curriculum Task Force of the National Commission on Social Studies in the Schools. Washington, DC: National Commission on Social Studies in the Schools, 1989.

Saunders, Phillip, G. L. Bach, James D. Calderwood, and W. Lee Hansen, eds. *A Framework for Teaching the Basic Concepts*. 2d ed. New York: Joint Council on Economic Education, 1984.

Silk, Leonard. "A Response to 'The State of Economic Literacy.' " In Donald R. Wentworth, W. Lee Hansen, and John C. Soper, eds., *Perspectives on Economic Education in the Schools*. New York: Joint Council on Economic Education, the National Council for the Social Studies, and the Social Science Education Consortium, 1977.

Stigler, George J. "The Case, If Any, for Economic Education." *The Journal of Economic Education* 1 (Spring 1970): 77–84.

Strober, Myra H. "The Scope of Microeconomics: Implications for Economic Education." *The Journal of Economic Education* 18 (Spring 1987): 135–49.

Thurow, Lester C. "Evaluating Economic Performance and Policies." *The Journal of Economic Education* 18 (Spring 1987): 237–45.

Tryon, Rolla M. *The Social Sciences as School Subjects*. Report of the Commission on the Social Studies, Part XI. New York: Charles Scribner's Sons, 1935.

Walstad, William B. "A National Study of the Economic Knowledge of Intermediate Elementary Students." Paper presented at the American Educational Research Association meeting, Chicago, April 5, 1991.

Walstad, William B., and John C. Soper. "A Report Card on the Economic Literacy of U.S. High School Students." *The American Economic Review* 78 (May 1988): 251–55.

Watts, Michael. "Survey Data on Precollege Scope-and-Sequence Issues." *The Journal of Economic Education* 18 (Winter 1987): 71–91.

Yankelovich, Skelly, and White. *National Survey of Economic Education*. New York: Playback Associates, 1981.

10

HIGH SCHOOL TEACHING
OF PSYCHOLOGY

Edmund T. Emmer and
Martin L. Tombari

REFLECTIONS

Psychology began to be taught in high schools during the middle of the
nineteenth century, although widespread interest in the subject did not
develop until the 1930s. Even then, courses in psychology were not commonplace and appear to have been offered mainly in fifteen states, according to Robert Noland (1966), with enrollments in psychology
amounting to less than half of one percent of the school population. By
1950, schools in at least thirty-four states offered psychology as a separate
course, and by the mid-1960s it was taught in around twenty percent of
those schools with a student population greater than 100. By the early
1980s, nearly sixty percent of United States high schools offered a psychology course (National Center 1984: 58). This significant increase in
the percentage of high schools offering a psychology course between 1950
and 1980 can be attributed to several factors: (1) an increasing number of
college students choosing psychology as a major or minor field of study;
(2) the growing emphasis in psychology on applied research that addressed
issues and problems of everyday life; and (3) the availability and development of popular-media outlets for psychological knowledge, most notably in television programming and in periodicals (e.g., *Psychology Today*
and articles emphasizing psychological applications in the mass media).
A recent survey of high school graduation requirements in the fifty states
indicates that psychology is typically offered as an elective course, either

as part of the social studies sequence or as a "free" elective (Council 1990: 4–50). In most instances, the content of the course is text-driven, with a limited number of high school psychology texts available. For reference, we present recommendations for high school psychology developed by the American Psychological Association.

The Content of the High School Psychology Course

In 1986 the American Psychological Association (APA) Committee on Psychology in the Secondary Schools recommended content for the high school psychology course. The APA's objectives were to

Set a standard for the high school psychology course;
Help teachers design and implement a well-integrated psychology course;
Provide school administrators and curriculum officers with examples of psychology course content; and
Provide state certification agencies and training colleges with a uniform set of recommendations. (APA 1986: 1)

The committee identified a core curriculum comprising the following six major areas:

1. Scientific methods of psychology;
2. Growth and development;
3. Learning;
4. Personality;
5. Mental health and behavioral disorders;
6. Social psychology. (Ibid.: 4)

The committee also identified other major areas as optional, depending on the time available and the teacher's interests. These areas include the biological bases of behavior, emotion, motivation, sensation, perception, states of consciousness, history of psychology, ethnic minority and gender issues, psychology and the law, and environmental psychology.

In order to determine which areas of psychology are being addressed in high school psychology texts, as well as the sequencing of these areas, we reviewed four high school textbooks and three widely used introductory college texts (see Table 1). The high school texts' contents are displayed in the table's first four columns, while the last three columns display the contents of college texts. (We included these latter texts because many high school teachers use them for personal reference or for planning and, in advanced courses, either as primary texts or as supplements to the high school books.)

Table 1
Content Coverage in Psychology Texts[a]

	Engle & Snellgrove (535 pp.)[b]	Ragland & Saxon (532 pp.)[b]	Kasschau (572 pp.)[b]	McNeil et al. (465 pp.)[b]	Gleitman (860 pp.)[c]	Bernstein et al. (715 pp.)[c]	Atkinson et al. (790 pp.)[c]
MAJOR AREAS:							
Scientific Methods	Ch. 2[d] (4%)		Ch. 1 & 17 (9%)	Ch. 16 (3%)		Ch. 1 (4%)	Ch. 1 (4%)
Growth and Development	3 & 4[d] (8%)	1–3 (16%)	1–3 (12%)	4 (9%)	14–15 (11%)	2 (7%)	3 (5%)
Learning	9–11 (15%)	5–7 (15%)	6–8 (16%)	8–10 (18%)	4, 7–9 (23%)	7–10 (17%)	7–9 (15%)
Personality	6–9 (13%)	11 (5%)	11 & 14 (12%)	1 (8%)	16–18 (15%)	14 (11%)	12–14 (15%)
Mental Health and Behavioral Disorders	15–17 (14%)	12–13 (12%)	12–13 (11%)	13–15 (17%)	19–20 (10%)	13, 15–16 (16%)	15–17 (16%)
Social Psychology	18–20 (15%)	14–16 (18%)	15–16 (10%)	2–3 (10%)	12–13 (10%)	17–18 (10%)	18–19 (10%)

Table 1 (*continued*)

	Engle & Snellgrove (535 pp.)[b]	Ragland & Saxon (532 pp.)[b]	Kasschau (572 pp.)[b]	McNeil et al. (465 pp.)[b]	Gleitman (860 pp.)[c]	Bernstein et al. (715 pp.)[c]	Atkinson et al. (790 pp.)[c]
OTHER AREAS:							
Sensation	12 (3%)	4 (3%)	5 (3%)	6 (3%)	5 (6%)	4 (6%)	4 (5%)
Perception	12 (2%)	4 (2%)	5 (3%)	6 (4%)	6 (5%)	5 (6%)	5 (5%)
Motivation	13 (2%)	9 (2%)	9 (3%)	11 (6%)	3 (5%)	11 (5%)	10 (5%)
Emotion	13 (3%)	9 (2%)	9 (2%)	12 (6%)		12 (4%)	11 (5%)
Consciousness		10 (5%)		7 (5%)	2 & 10 (9%)	6 (5%)	6 (7%)
Biological Bases of Behavior	5 (5%)	8 (4%)	4 (6%)	5 (6%)		3 (5%)	2 (4%)

[a]Number in parentheses represents approximate percentage of text pages for the topic.
[b]High school text.
[c]Introductory-level college text.
[d]Numbers refer to chapters.

The "major areas" and others on the left side of Table 1 are those recommended by the APA. Every text includes substantive coverage of all six major areas except for "scientific methods of psychology," which two texts do not cover. Many of the areas that the APA considers optional are also included. These topics make up nearly all of the chapter headings of the seven books; rarely does a text contain a chapter which covers a topic outside of these general areas; and no text attempts any significant coverage of the optional areas of ethnic minority or gender issues, environmental psychology, or psychology and the law.

The core area dealing with the "scientific methodology of psychology" appears at either the beginning or end of most texts. This area's full range of specific topics (as suggested by APA) is covered, including the logic of science and research design, statistics, and ethics in research, as well as specific data-gathering strategies, such as controlled observations, surveys, interviews, and case histories.

With the exception of the Gleitman text, the area of "growth and development" appears in each textbook at the beginning of the core content sequence. This area includes such topics as life span development, heredity and environment, and cognitive, linguistic, moral, social, and emotional development. Almost all texts include the "biological bases of behavior" in this area. As can be seen in Table 1, the percentage of text pages devoted to developmental issues varies from five percent (Atkinson et al.) to sixteen percent (Ragland and Saxon). The areas of "sensation" and "perception" follow "growth and development" in all but the Engle and Snellgrove text. The proportion of text given to these topics is similar across all books. While the APA guidelines treat these areas as optional, all texts give them substantial coverage. The high school texts cover both areas in a single chapter, while the college texts give each area its own chapter.

"Learning" and "personality" typically follow "sensation" and "perception." "Learning" includes such topics as classical and operant conditioning, memory, language, thinking and problem solving, intelligence, and creativity, while "personality" encompasses discussion of development, theory, and assessment. The college texts place "learning" before "personality," while two of the four high school psychology books reverse this sequence. The learning area is the most heavily emphasized across all texts, ranging from fifteen percent in two high school texts to twenty-three percent in the college text by Gleitman. The percentage of pages covering personality topics ranges from five percent in the Ragland and Saxon text to fifteen percent in the texts by Gleitman and Atkinson et al.

APA guidelines treat "motivation" and "emotion" as optional areas. However, all of these texts devote substantial coverage to them. "Mental health and behavioral disorders" follow "personality" in all books. The former area includes such topics as anxiety, phobias, stress, coping and defense mechanisms, the classifications and causes of disorders, as well as types of counseling and psychotherapy. All texts devote several chapters and from ten to seventeen percent of their total pages to this area.

"Social psychology," which usually concludes the core sequence in such texts, includes interpersonal relations, attitude formation and change, conformity, obedience and social influence, persuasion, group processes and leadership, sex roles, and prejudice and stereotyping. From ten to eighteen percent of each text is devoted to this area, with proportionately more coverage provided by the high school texts.

When we compared high school and college texts we found more similarities than differences in the structure, sequence, and emphasis of the core areas recommended by the APA. One notable difference between the college and high school texts is the relative currency of their references. While all of the texts emphasized basic concepts and broad, long-standing psychological issues, the college texts cited research and theoretical discussions which were current when the book was written or revised. This was not the case with the high school texts. When we examined recent editions of two of these, we found that the authors had added very little to the information contained in earlier editions. In cases where references were updated, the contents of the chapters in which the references were cited remained largely unchanged. For example, in the high school texts, the core area of "mental health and behavior disorders" included very little information about cognitive-behavior therapies. The reader is thus left with the impression that behavior therapies almost exclusively employ operant and classical conditioning techniques to treat behavior disorders and ignore relatively recent advances in the areas of cognitive and social-learning theory.

Our concern with this state of affairs echoes that of a teacher whom we interviewed (in Austin, Texas, May 1991). As is typical of many high school psychology teachers, his primary professional field was not psychology. Consequently, most of his continuing-education efforts, such as journal reading and course attendance, related to his primary certification area. He was particularly concerned about how current a picture of psychology he was able to give his students. (The preparation of psychology teachers will be discussed in more depth in the next section.) Another high school psychology teacher who we interviewed (in Austin, Texas, April 1991) noted that the most recent edition of the psychology textbook adopted in her school district did not use the terminology of the revised *Diagnostic and Statistical Manual of Mental Disorders (DSM-III-R)*, even though it had been available at the time of that edition's publication.

Influences on Content

Most psychologists would describe psychology, first, as a behavioral science and, second, as one of the social studies, although social psychologists and many applied psychologists give more prominence to the "social" features of the discipline. More than most social studies disciplines, psychology borrows, assimilates, and adapts the methods, concepts, and findings of other fields, including biology, physiology, mathematics, medicine, pharmacology, and genetics, in addition to those of other behavioral sciences and the humanities. The life sciences, especially, have played a very important role in recent developments in psychology. Applications of psychology have been widespread, resulting in major specializations in clinical, counseling, health, industrial, and school psychology. Subspecies and hybrid forms of psychology have emerged, making it difficult to represent "psychology" in any simple manner. Finally, among the social studies, psychology focuses to a greater extent on the *individual* than do the other disciplines. Thus, the simple representation of psychology as concerned with the place of the individual in a larger social context is accurate for some areas of psychology, but it distorts the picture of the discipline as a whole.

If we examine the content of the typical high school psychology course and attempt to identify the various influences on that content, we find that one of the primary influences is the representation of psychology as a component of *social studies*. To appreciate the significance of this affiliation, one need only consider what the content of a psychology course would be if psychology were regarded as one of the life sciences. In such a course, the topics of sensation and perception, psychophysics, psychopharmacology, behavior genetics, neuropsychology, the brain and its effects on behavior, along with other aspects of physiological psychology would receive far greater emphasis than is currently the case (see Table 1). We do not mean to imply that such topics would be preferable to those which are currently emphasized, but only to make the easily overlooked point that placing this omnifarious discipline in the social studies has itself had a profound effect on which aspects of psychology are included in the curriculum.

Another influence on the content of the typical high school psychology course is the preparation and commitment of teachers. State and national surveys of teachers (Griggs, Jackson, and Meyer 1989; Rutter 1986; White, Marcuella, and Oresick 1979) have consistently shown that most teachers of high school psychology majored in history, or in composite social studies, rather than in psychology. The typical psychology teacher who was not a psychology major has accumulated fewer credit hours of undergraduate psychology than would be needed to fulfill a major in the field, and often the course work that was completed emphasized educational applications. Rarely is an advanced degree in psychology earned. Thus, the affiliation of the psychology teacher is most likely to be with the broad field of social studies, or with history, rather than psychology. Furthermore, many teachers of psychology teach only one or two sections of the course, especially in smaller high schools, a factor which surely reduces the amount of time and effort that teachers can devote to their psychology course(s). Finally, most schools have only one teacher assigned to psychology, reducing opportunities for professional interaction and collegial collaboration in course development.

Although it has been argued that the relative paucity of psychology majors as teachers has affected the high school course content, a study by R. J. Stahl and J. C. Matiya (1981) in fact revealed few differences among the objectives and topics preferred by psychology teachers whose certification areas were social studies, guidance and counseling, or "other" (this latter category contained psychology majors). All of the groups indicated the greatest preference for objectives to do with self-understanding and personal adjustment, and for such topics as personality, mental health and illness, and emotions.

Thus, relying on social studies teachers to teach psychology probably has mainly indirect effects on content, operating through a commitment to social studies disciplines other than psychology and exacerbated by the limited collegial associations available to the typical high school psychology teacher. The long-term consequences have probably included strengthening the textbook's role in defining course content, emphasizing those aspects of psychology with a social rather than a behavioral science or physiological basis, and reducing the likelihood that recent developments in the field will be integrated into the curriculum.

CURRENT TRENDS AND ISSUES

The National Council for the Social Studies (NCSS) has included the field of psychology as a component in its recent examinations of and recommendations for the social studies curriculum. Chapters in the volume edited by Stanley P. Wronski and Donald H. Bragaw (1986) describe the field of psychology and provide an overview of teaching resources and curriculum development efforts. *Charting a Course: Social Studies for the 21st Century* (National Commission 1989) has a chapter by Cynthia Baum and Ira Cohen that includes recommendations for high school psychology. Although a recent NCSS report identifies psychology as an essential subject "from which knowledge goals for social studies should be selected" (National Council 1989: 377), there is little evidence in the publications just cited to suggest that psychology is regarded as a major contributor to mainstream social studies. Topics and objectives from psychology are virtually nonexistent in the K–11 "21st Century" curriculum, with psychology included only as a possible twelfth grade elective. Curricula for psychology, moreover, have not consistently received attention from the NCSS in its other publications. For example, the 1988 index for *Social Education,* the council's major journal, had twenty-three listings for history, thirty-four for geography, eleven for government, and *none* for psychology. Indeed, during the 1980s, *Social Education* published very few articles about psychology. It should thus come as no surprise that the major force behind curricular definition has been the American Psychological Association rather than the National Council for the Social Studies.

During the past two decades the APA has engaged in a number of activities, in addition to the curriculum statement discussed earlier, that have affected the content of high school psychology courses. Beginning in the 1970s, a curriculum development effort called the "Human Behavior Curriculum Project" was undertaken. Eight instructional units were developed, each representing a significant topic for the psychology curriculum (e.g., Conditioning and Learning, Social Influences on Behavior, Changing Attitudes, and Natural Behavior in Humans and Animals). Units including student readers and teacher handbooks were field-tested and published by Teachers College Press in 1981 (American Psychological Association 1981).

The APA has several publications geared to the high school teacher, including a bimonthly newsletter, *High School Psychology Teacher,* which has been published for over twenty years. The twelve-page newsletter, distributed to the approximately 2,300 teachers who are "high school affiliate" members of the APA, prints book reviews, a calendar of upcoming events in psychology relevant to the high school psychology teacher, information on topics in psychology, and descriptions of demonstrations, experiments, and activities for the classroom. Examples of topics discussed in recent newsletters (*High School Psychology Teacher* Volumes 20–22 [1989–1991]) include the neuropsychology of head injury; conflict, negotiation, and peace; how to conduct experimental research; prejudice and sterotypes; studying personality; teaching adolescents how to understand aging; the neuropsychology of epilepsy; and new research findings on self-esteem. The APA also publishes a resource book of reviews of psychology textbooks, some of which are suitable for high school use, and an activities handbook for classroom use by teachers.

Other high school-related activities of the APA include sponsorship of an annual writing competition for high school students, provision of a national high school teacher-of-the-year award, and participation as a professional organization in the International Science and Engineering Fair competition for secondary school students. The APA also has a standing Committee on Psychology in the Secondary Schools, whose members are chiefly drawn from the current pool of high school psychology teachers, and an ad hoc Task Force on Precollege Psychology, whose members examine ways to generate interest in precollege psychology. The APA organizes workshops and symposia at its annual meetings and during the summer on topics pertinent to secondary school psychology, and high school teachers of psychology are eligible to become affiliate members of the APA for a nominal fee.

State curriculum requirements have had little direct effect on high school psychology, but have had an indirect one through a lack of positive action. According to a recent national survey by the Council of State Social Studies Specialists (1990), psychology is not required for graduation in any state; not surprisingly, therefore, no state that requires statewide social studies testing of secondary students includes questions specifically drawn from psychology in its tests. Psychology is only one of several social studies electives among the graduation requirements of seventeen states; in other states it is either a free elective or not mentioned at all in descriptions of state requirements. The limited role assigned to psychology in the secondary curriculum may contribute to its underemphasis by the NCSS in its curriculum projects and also appears to keep enrollments in psychology courses lower than they might otherwise be. Freedom from mandatory testing programs and from the major responsibility of being a graduation requirement is advantageous to psychology in some respects: curriculum development is not shackled to specifically tested competencies, and teachers can experiment with a variety of activity formats and academic tasks without fear of the accountability bogeyman.

PROJECTIONS

As a discipline that draws its content from very diverse sources and addresses such value-laden topics as mental health, intelligence, human development, and behavior modification, psychology's curriculum development is bound to be affected by many issues and concerns. One critical issue for the high school psychology curriculum is the relative emphasis placed on fundamental disciplinary knowledge versus personal adjustment. Richard Kasschau has argued that the personal-adjustment emphasis is consistent with the intellectual level (i.e., concrete operations) and the moral reasoning of most adolescents who take high school psychology (Kasschau 1985: 14–16). He also believes that the dual curricular objectives reflect psychology's fundamental division between its scientific and humanistic perspectives (ibid.). While some psychologists argue that applications are built on a scientific basis and, therefore, the dichotomy is a false one, others argue that values ultimately determine what questions psychology addresses and how psychological data are interpreted and applied. The 1986 curricular recommendations of the APA sought a middle ground, giving a major place to both basic disciplinary knowledge and its applications in the objectives and topics recommended for the high school psychology course. Unsurprisingly, textbook authors have taken a similar tack, producing texts that are both encyclopedic and uncontroversial.

Research on the classroom practices of teachers, on average, confirms an applications-for-personal-adjustment orientation in their choices of topics and objectives, but they also give some attention to the study of psychology as a discipline (Stahl and Matiya 1981). More research, preferably by means of direct observation and interviews, on the classroom practices of psychology teachers is needed in order to better understand the relationships between the teachers' belief systems and conceptions of the curriculum, on the one hand, and their classroom practices, on the other. At the same time, research on student thinking and how it may be affected by content and method would be very useful to curriculum development.

Another important question for high school psychology is how to incorporate new knowledge into the curriculum. This is especially challenging because of the limited preparation in psychology of many teachers. The field's great array of subspecializations and applications makes it difficult for teachers to keep abreast of current developments in "hot" areas, such as cognitive science, computer applications, and neuropsychology. Yet understanding some of the most exciting recent developments in these areas requires a basic understanding of psychology itself. Although the American Psychological Association provides workshops, newsletters, and publications that discuss recent developments, these efforts reach only a small minority of psychology teachers, and probably those who have the strongest affiliation with the field. One step that might be taken by the APA would be to work with textbook authors to ensure that older material is updated and appropriate new material is covered.

Although hard data on the demographics of high school psychology students are scarce, evidence indicates that more female than male students take these courses and that they are mainly seniors who intend to continue their education beyond high school. Minority students are probably underrepresented (Goldman 1983: 228). Thus, another challenge for high school psychology is to broaden its clientele, especially in the face of its universal elective status. Adolescents regard the study of human behavior as one of the more interesting topics addressed by the social studies (Schug, Todd, and Beery 1984: 385), so the problem seems to be one of *opportunity,* rather than student *motivation.* Those professionals interested in high school psychology need to develop creative ways of encouraging schools to offer more psychology courses in order to allow the adolescent's natural curiosity about behavior to be better satisfied by the curriculum. At the same time, psychology teachers and curriculum designers should consider moving past the "Intro to Psych" format that has dominated curriculum efforts and developing courses with broader appeal and utility for minorities and for students who are not college bound.

It is noteworthy that psychology has recently been added to the advanced-placement testing program, an addition that is likely to have a significant impact on enrollments and curricula. The ability to earn advanced-placement college credit for "Introduction to Psychology" will no doubt encourage college-bound high school seniors to take this course. At the same time, in-service teacher-training workshops sponsored by APA have also been developed to provide more up-to-date preparation for those high school teachers who will be responsible for the AP course. Broader coverage of psychology is also a possibility, assuming that high schools offer more than just the AP class. This is likely to increase the demand for teachers who can teach psychology and may make it possible for more psychology majors to obtain teaching positions in their field. A recent survey indicated that nearly 4,000 psychology majors with teaching certificates graduated in 1986 (National Center 1990: 7–15), yet very few obtained teaching positions in *psychology* during the following year. Assuming that year to have been typical, a substantial pool of teachers may now be available, should the demand for teachers of psychology increase.

Psychology's role as a component of the social studies should be of concern to all social studies educators. Presently, the subject is little more than an appendage to the total social studies curriculum, and very little thought appears to have been given to its role in the program by either psychologists or nonpsychologists. On the one hand, the chapters on psychology in such influential documents as *Charting a Course* and in Wronski and Bragaw (1986) were written by psychologists and from the perspective of that discipline, rather than with a view toward integration into the social studies. On the other hand, the recent scope-and-sequence proposals that have been made in social studies and published in NCSS journals have rarely incorporated any concepts or content from psychology. History, geography, and government dominate the curricular landscape, with a sprinkling of ideas from anthropology and sociology. Social studies educators need to seriously consider the role of psychology (and of other behavioral science disciplines) in the overall conception of the field. It may be true, as some have argued, that social studies in the 1980s was defined more narrowly along the lines of the "cultural literacy" perspective and that the role of the behavioral sciences has been consequently weakened (Evans, Dumas, and Weible 1990). For their part, psychologists need to keep in mind that psychology must contribute to the social science curriculum, a perspective that has been absent from most of the APA publications on high school psychology. For a discipline as eclectic as psychology, such a perspective should not be difficult to accommodate.

REFERENCES

American Psychological Association (APA). *Human Behavior Curriculum Project Pamphlet*. New York: Teachers College Press, 1981.

————. *Statement on the Curriculum for the High School Psychology Course.* Washington, DC: American Psychological Association, 1986.

Atkinson, Rita L., Richard C. Atkinson, Edward E. Smith, and Daryl J. Bem. *Introduction to Psychology.* 10th ed. San Diego: Harcourt Brace Jovanovich, 1990.

Benjamin, Ludy T., and Kathleen D. Lowman, eds. *Activities Handbook for the Teaching of Psychology.* 3d ed. Washington, DC: American Psychological Association, 1990.

Bernstein, Douglas A., Edward J. Roy, Christopher D. Wickens, and Thomas K. Srull. *Psychology.* Boston: Houghton Mifflin, 1988.

Council of State Social Studies Specialists. *National Survey of Course Offerings, Requirements, and Testing in Social Studies.* Washington, DC: Council of State Social Studies Specialists, 1990.

Engle, T. L., and Louis Snellgrove. *Psychology: Its Principles and Applications.* 9th ed. Orlando, FL: Harcourt Brace Jovanovich, 1989.

Evans, Charles S., Wayne Dumas, and Tom Weible. "The Declining Role of Behavioral Sciences in the Preparation of Secondary Social Studies Teachers." *Teaching of Psychology* 17 (1990): 258–59.

Gleitman, Henry H. *Psychology.* 3d ed. New York: Norton, 1991.

Goldman, Jeri J. "Recent Trends in Secondary School Psychology: The Decade from Oberlin to the HBCP." *Teaching of Psychology* 10 (1983): 228–29.

Griggs, R. A., S. L. Jackson, and M. E. Meyer. "High School and College Psychology: Two Different Worlds." *Teaching of Psychology* 16 (1989): 118–20.

Kasschau, Richard A. *Psychology: Exploring Behavior.* Englewood Cliffs, NJ: Prentice-Hall, 1980.

————. "Pressure and Principles: How Shall We Teach Psychology?" *Social Education* 49 (1985): 13–16.

McNeil, Elton B., George D. Fuller, and Jackie J. Estrada. *Psychology Today and Tomorrow.* New York: Harper and Row, 1978.

National Center for Education Statistics. *A Trend Study for High School Offerings and Enrollments: 1981–1982.* Washington, DC: Government Printing Office, 1984.

————. *New Teachers on the Job Market, 1987 Update.* Report No. 90–336. Washington, DC: Government Printing Office, 1990.

National Commission on Social Studies in the Schools. *Charting a Course: Social Studies for the 21st Century.* Washington, DC: National Commission on Social Studies in the Schools, 1989.

National Council for the Social Studies, Task Force on Scope and Sequence. "In Search of a Scope and Sequence for Social Studies." *Social Education* 53 (1989): 376–85.

Noland, Robert L. "A Century of Psychology in American Secondary Schools." *Journal of Secondary Education* 41 (1966): 247–64.

Ragland, Rachel G., and Burt B. Saxon. *Invitation to Psychology.* 2d ed. Glenview, IL: Scott, Foresman, 1989.

Rutter, Robert A. "Profile of the Profession." *Social Education* 50 (1986): 252–55.

Schug, M. C., R. J. Todd, and R. Beery. "Why Kids Don't Like Social Studies."
    Social Education 48 (1984): 382–87.
Stahl, R. J., and J. C. Matiya. "Teaching Psychology in the High School: Does
    Area of Certification Translate into Different Types of Teachers and
    Courses?" *Theory and Research in Social Education* 9 (1981): 55–87.
White, Kathleen M., Henry Marcuella, and Robert Oresick. "Psychology in the
    High Schools." *Teaching of Psychology* 6 (1979): 39–42.
Wronski, Stanley P., and Donald H. Bragaw, eds. *Social Studies and Social
    Sciences: A Fifty Year Perspective*. Bulletin No. 78. Washington, DC:
    National Council for the Social Studies, 1986.

11

SOCIOLOGY IN
THE SCHOOLS

Paul S. Gray

The primary goals of this chapter are to assess the past and present influence of sociology as a discipline in precollegiate education and to contribute to the dialogue concerning its potential influence. Social science educators face a challenge during the 1990s and beyond, namely, to infuse the precollege curriculum with sociological content and ways of knowing. Success in meeting this challenge will have positive implications for improving educational standards generally, both in high school and in college. It is also vital for the future of our democracy. Failure would mean a continuation of the drift and the mutually ambivalent relationship between sociology and the schools which has marked the past 100 years.

There are both formal and informal measures of sociological influence on precollegiate education. In the formal sense, we need to ask how many sociology courses are being taught, who is teaching them, and what they contain. In addition, we need to examine the history of the involvement of professional groups, such as the American Sociological Association (ASA), in precollegiate education. But sociology has also influenced the development of the social studies less formally by contributing to a general cultural milieu which filters down into curriculum development and textbook content in history, civics, and geography. These same cultural patterns also help to determine the public's acceptance of sociology in the schools, as well as the suspicion with which it is occasionally viewed. K. King (1982) has identified two problems that sociologists face when they address the high school setting: "The first is how to increase the presence of sociology in the curriculum . . . and the second is how to improve the quality of instruction" (King 73).

REFLECTIONS

Courses and Instructors

The actual number of courses dealing exclusively with sociology in American schools is unknown. The ASA estimates that there are about 3,000 such offerings at the secondary level. Dean S. Dorn (1986) reported that less than one percent of the social studies classes taught in California during the 1982–83 school year were in sociology, and these were all electives. David Jenness (1990) reported the finding that sociology, when it is taught, is "heavily localized in high schools whose students are 'average blue collar' by family origin" (240). Dorn found that only twenty-three percent of California high schools in one metropolitan area (Sacramento) listed sociology separately. In the primary grades, sociology is even less common. For example, just one course has been taught from time to time in the City of Boston public primary schools, and only three or four more at the middle-school level.

If one uses teachers rather than courses as the measure of sociology's influence, an even more discouraging picture emerges. A California State Department of Education survey conducted in 1985 found that only fifty-nine out of 48,000 teachers taught sociology "almost exclusively." Jenness estimated that high school social studies departments include perhaps only one teacher who has at least minored in sociology (Jenness 1990: 240), which is consistent with Dorn's earlier findings that fifty percent of the teachers in his sample had completed fewer than four college courses in sociology, and over thirty percent had taken no courses at all (Dorn 1986: 13). This pattern is likely to persist because of the increasing demand for economics and history courses, rather than other social studies electives, and because states typically do not encourage credentialing in sociology.

Since less than one percent of college freshmen list sociology as their major, it is clear that not enough high school students are being reached with the existing elective courses. About forty percent of high school sociology courses make use of college-level texts (Howery 1985), but the extent to which they effectively prepare students for college work is open to debate. Perhaps their high school teachers have not sufficiently inspired them or perhaps the precollege courses themselves are poorly structured. The high school sociology elective prominently features social psychology "to the neglect of more structural sociology" (Gray 1989: 72). The most common course titles are "Beginning Sociology" and "Introductory Sociology," but there is a recognizable emphasis on issues of personal and social adjustment in the majority of courses. Dorn (1986) found that the six most frequently covered topics were sociological concepts, culture, socialization, race and ethnicity, the family, and educational institutions. Only one-fifth of the courses which he surveyed taught research methods. Sociology electives typically encourage discussion of the student's own world and personal experience and place less emphasis on the unfamiliar, especially when analyzed systemically.

It will perhaps be useful to contrast the more prevalent course structure summarized above with an unusually well-developed and articulated sociology program offered in Maryland (Montgomery County Public Schools 1990). *Two* sociology electives, beginning and advanced, are available to high school juniors and seniors. The first course

is concerned with human groups and the factors that unite or divide them. Areas of study include culture, values, social groups, social stratification, population, the family, socialization, propaganda, and social institutions. Emphasis is given to the impact of change on mores, norms, and customs. Students engage in modest research projects. (16)

Behavioral objectives for this course are that students should be able to:

describe the point of view of sociological inquiry;

analyze the interrelationship of society and culture;

explain the process and methods of socialization;

describe the components of a social organization;

explain the relationship between social control and deviant behavior;

describe the nature of collective behavior;

identify social stratification in given societies;

analyze the effect of a contemporary social change which has significance for them. (16)

The (optional) second course

offers advanced study of basic concepts.... Emphasis is placed on ... social change (in) American institutions, particularly education and the family. ... Comparisons with institutions of other cultures are made where appropriate. Students are expected to do research papers which focus on community or on-site research. Guest speakers from the community are involved in classroom instruction on a regular basis. Recent research studies in the field are examined as they apply to the coursework. (16)

According to its planners, by the end of this second course, students should be able to

identify various family structures and roles within them;
differentiate the educational roles of administrator, teacher and student and describe the functions of education in American society;
analyze the impact of social change on American institutions;
pose hypotheses and use the scientific method to develop research papers;
identify the use of community resources in the pursuit of scientific investigation. (17)

A 127-page course guide *for the first elective alone* was prepared by eight teachers (Montgomery County Public Schools 1986). This document includes an extensive review of relevant films as well as performance objectives, discussion formats, and lecture outlines in several provocative areas of sociology, such as mass media, gift giving, religious minorities, and social stratification. Data collected by members of the ASA's Task Force on Sociology in the Elementary and Secondary Schools suggest that these courses are unusual in their depth and rigor. They represent a standard toward which many teachers, schools, and school districts might aspire.

Lack of Institutionalization

How did we arrive at a point where we are still hunting for individual models of success more than 100 years after sociology's introduction into American academic life? To use the discipline's own concept, it is apparent that sociology has not become *institutionalized* at the precollege level. This means that it has not become patterned, expected, and accepted as a standard part of the curriculum. The reasons for this state of affairs have been summarized elsewhere (Jenness 1990; Gray 1989). Historically, there have been three pillars of the sociological enterprise: (1) an *ameliorist* approach to society (i.e., identifying social problems and recommending solutions), (2) a *positivistic* emphasis on social facts and the use of the scientific method, and (3) the search for *grand theoretical models* of social behavior. None of these objectives has been especially well adapted to the precollege environment.

Initially, the idea of using knowledge to improve society was extremely influential in American education; indeed, sociological ameliorist thinking exerted considerable influence throughout the educational reform period of 1916 to 1918. However, over the subsequent twenty years, sociology was absorbed into history and civics curricula rather than becoming a distinct high school course offering. In addition, as Jenness notes, "by the 1930s ... the widespread public unease about social reconstruction tended to keep sociological subject matter hidden or contained within other labels" (Jenness 1990: 237). Therefore, when many of today's sociological electives were added to the curriculum during the 1960s and

1970s, they had no firm institutional foundation on which to build. "In spite of young people's undeniable interest in social problems, a thorough and systematic exposition of their causes can strike sensitive nerves at the local level" (Gray 1989: 71).

Positivistic thought in sociology has also encountered ambivalence within American schools. The faith in a thoroughly objective social science, which was derived from Auguste Comte (and which had appeared in modern form by the 1920s in the work of George Lundberg, among others), led to the quest for "unbiased" scientific information that could be used by expert decision makers in business management and government. This "value-free" endeavor received a boost during the 1940s and 1950s, as advances in computer technology and data analysis resulted in the emergence of a technocratic sociology requiring knowledge of statistical tools and data-processing hardware well beyond the grasp of most high school students and instructors. Moreover, "the positivistic emphasis on social engineering and expertise aroused suspicion among some educators, because it appeared contrary to the democratic ethos" (ibid.).

Finally, during the 1940s and 1950s, sociology's theoretical orientation shifted from the community studies and social problems of an earlier era to a search for dominant models (e.g., structural functionalism). As Jenness notes, "Many in the discipline believed this focus of study to be too difficult for precollegiate education" (Jenness 1990: 237). Sociology therefore lost some of its power as a means for describing the worlds familiar to high school and elementary school students. Today, in the 1990s, sociology as a whole is less wedded to extreme positivism (witness the recent emergence of interpretive sociology). The discipline is also more tolerant and theoretically eclectic, having passed through an era that was thoroughly critical of functionalist "grand theories." However, the damage has been done, and the momentum to institutionalize sociology in the schools has faltered.

The Role of the American Sociological Association

In developing and implementing a policy on sociology in the schools, the American Sociological Association, the largest and most influential professional organization of sociologists, has reflected the general historical trends outlined above. Between 1920 and the "New Social Studies" era of the 1960s and 1970s, the ASA did not take an official position on the issue. It was widely believed, however, that sociology in its modern form was technically and theoretically too sophisticated for a high school clientele. There was considerable concern as well that unqualified teachers would be ineffective in transmitting sociology to a young audience, with the result that secondary students would get a watered-down version so dissatisfying as to discourage them from enrolling in sociology courses as college students.

Beginning in 1961, however, the attitude of the ASA membership toward sociology in the schools began to change. A committee on the Social Studies Curriculum of American Secondary Schools was formed.

What lay behind the establishment of this Committee were the beliefs of a number of sociologists that the high school social studies curriculum was outdated and that social scientists were lagging behind physical and biological scientists in their efforts to improve conditions, thus giving sociology as presented in high school a poor image. The "New Math" was sweeping the country; national projects in physics, chemistry, geology, and biology were making rapid progress. The launching of the first Soviet sputnik in 1957 stirred anxieties about the quality of American education. Zeal to improve matters was widespread. (Grahlfs n.d.: 1)

It is interesting to note, however, that in spite of the "zeal" for improving sociology in the schools, ambivalence still remained. Part of the charge given to committee chair Neal Gross was that the group "should avoid accepting as a foregone conclusion the proposition that earlier study of sociology is desirable" (ibid). In 1962 members of the committee prepared a grant application to the National Science Foundation (NSF) for funds to assist the ASA in developing a new course or courses in sociology and in compiling sociology resource materials. By 1964, the proposal had been approved and funded, and the ASA's most significant period of involvement to date in the effort to promote sociology in the schools had commenced. The Sociological Resources for the Social Studies (SRSS) project ran from 1964 through 1971 (Angell 1972).

During this period seventeen sociologists, with a staff of eight to ten assistants, produced a wide variety of materials, much of which was published by the Boston firm of Allyn and Bacon and made available to schools. These publications included seven volumes in the "Readings in Sociology" series on the following topics: urban sociology, the family, race, delinquency, population, complex organizations, and collective behavior. A one-semester course text, *Inquiries in Sociology* (Sociological Resources 1972), was also prepared. This work did not cover the usual array of sociological specialties found in college texts; instead, the major topics included were socialization, institutions, social stratification, and change in the social order. The text was supplemented by engaging photographs and student exercises, and case studies emphasized adolescence, race relations and inequality, and the shift from rural to urban America.

In sponsoring the SRSS project, the ASA was clearly supporting both improvement in and proliferation of separate sociology electives, as well as the diffusion of sociological knowledge into other parts of the curriculum. Among the instructional materials developed by SRSS, and the novel feature for which it is best remembered, were the "Episodes," or units on discrete topics, which could be integrated within history, civics, or other social studies courses. In all, twenty-three SRSS Episodes were produced on topics ranging from "Black Leadership in American Society" to "Social Mobility," from "Small Group Processes" to "Roles of Modern Women," and from "Science and Society" to "Divorce in the United States." Two unusual topics were a comparison between the 1920s and 1960s in American social history ("Two Generation Gaps") and an analysis of values in mass communication ("A Study of the Western").

As Jenness points out, one goal of the SRSS project staff was to develop materials that would encourage students to analyze, reason, and inquire like sociologists:

The overall approach was to divide the content into 30 . . . broad topics or subfields, offer lengthy examples from the sociological literature, and then encourage students to draw generalizations appropriate to, and using terminology of, the field. (Jenness 1990: 239)

The authors adhered to a "no compromise" principle, according to which "the fundamental logic of a discipline (if not a grasp of all the specialized methodology) was accessible to students at any age" (Social Resources 1972: 210). But to the observer in the 1990s the writing seems quite advanced for secondary school students of average ability and would even pose a challenge to the "best and brightest." Members of the ASA's Task Force on Sociology in the Elementary and Secondary Schools, which includes both university and high school teachers, reviewed several SRSS Episodes from 1989 to 1990. They abandoned the idea of revising and updating them primarily because the level of argumentation was, in their judgment, rather too sophisticated for a high school audience. It seemed clear to the reviewers that too much prior background not just in social science, but also in general education, would be needed to fully appreciate the nuances of the writing.

At least by today's standards, the SRSS project authors seemed too determined to convince their young readers that sociology was indeed a science, the insights from which were to be acquired cumulatively and with increasing complexity. While this goal is in itself admirable, it cannot be realistically fulfilled before the basic conceptual building blocks of sociology have been mastered. The Episodes were full of summaries of well-conducted studies and tables showing their results. It is likely that students concentrated on learning these results without fully appreciating the logic underlying the study designs or even the selection of research problems. As Jenness notes such thorough documentation actually inhibited inquiry because it discouraged a genuinely inductive approach to learning. In many cases, students were left to "grope for the right sociological gloss" (Jenness 1990: 239). While generalizations were elicited that took the form of inductively generated ideas, in reality they amounted to more of a "justification" of the text examples than a "discovery" of the students' own ideas. Thus, the text had a "cooked" quality, which could have seemed manipulative to students and which actually conveyed less of the adventurous and creative side to sociology than may be needed in order to fully capture a student's imagination.

Several different evaluation schemes were also implemented as the SRSS materials were being written and pilot-tested. But, as F. Lincoln Grahlfs, Supervisor of Evaluation for most of the project, has noted, there was neither time nor funding to evaluate the effectiveness of SRSS materials after they had reached a maximum saturation point in the schools. There was also little contact between the sociologists working on the SRSS project and professors of education, even on their own campuses. This meant that the SRSS sociologists had no one with whom to discuss the problems of teacher resistance and administrative red tape which they were encountering, among other persistent difficulties in maintaining ties to the classroom. A group of secondary teachers served as consultants to the project, but because most of the sociologists had no background in high school education themselves, they had little appreciation of the problems faced by classroom teachers and sometimes found the implementation phase of the project to be frustrating.

One superintendent of schools with an extensive background in social studies education viewed the ASA project as exemplifying the fact that few, if any, of the attempts to bring the "New Social Studies" into the classroom have worked. "The sociology materials, as well as the other projects have failed completely . . . to alter the teaching and learning of social studies education in our public schools" (Smith 1981: 20). Three reasons were given for the problems of implementation: (1) the reform was not demanded from below; (2) the reform lacked sufficient teacher involvement; and (3) the reform was too narrowly scientific.

With respect to (1), it is important to note that the SRSS project was stimulated by the availability of federal dollars in the form of an NSF grant. Perhaps this stimulation was "artificial," in that there was "little evidence of a grassroots or classroom call for reform" (ibid.). As they have evolved in the history of American education, the worlds of high school and university-based, academic sociology are indeed separate. Even when sociologists make a good-faith attempt to bridge the gap, they have had difficulty in creating a demand for their talents and expertise.

With respect to (2), the project was organized as a "university-based alliance" which lacked significant teacher involvement. According to David Smith,

The SRSS committee claimed that its effort combined the talents of both sociologists and high school social studies teachers. The sociologists provided the scientific information while the teachers provided their expertise on how the subject matter should be applied for purposes of student learning. The purported amalgamation . . . was widely publicized; unfortunately, this publicity was misleading. A genuine coming together of equals from different professions . . . did not occur. (Ibid.)

Smith interviewed several of the teacher-consultants, who told him that "the sociologists called the shots" and that "they didn't put much faith in us" (22). Others noted that, with greater teacher involvement, the materials could have been more useful. "Instead the reform text is too academic and too faddish. It is too difficult to use in a normal large class" (23). Smith also found that the teachers who consulted to the project "were not truly representative of social studies teachers in American high schools" (ibid.); many had taught social studies in the past, but had since moved on to administrative or university positions.

Finally, with respect to (3), the impact of the SRSS project was limited because it tapped into a long-standing disagreement among teachers themselves regarding how courses should be structured. Many social studies educators were unhappy with what they perceived as an "overly scholarly, cognitive . . . approach to social studies education" (Tucker 1972: 560). The SRSS materials were oriented toward sociology as a discipline rather than toward interdisciplinary citizenship education. Thus, they were resisted or misused by some teachers and, ultimately, ignored by most.

In 1977 the National Science Foundation conducted a postmortem evaluation of the ASA project (Weiss 1978) and concluded that the SRSS materials had not achieved the goal of penetrating the precollege curriculum. It was estimated that only two percent of grades 7–9 and eight percent of grades 10–12 were using SRSS materials by 1977. Because the textbook, readings, and episodes were not reissued in subsequent reprints or editions, their influence declined during the 1980s. Many sociologists, including some of those who worked on the SRSS project, now see it as a noble experiment, if not necessarily a model for collaboration between the discipline and the high schools. Many social studies educators, including some who served as consultants to the SRSS design team, see the project as part of "a fad that exemplified [a] longstanding and unthinking subservience to professors in the academic disciplines" (Shaver 1977: 300).

CURRENT TRENDS AND ISSUES

Since 1980 a new era of collaboration has become possible, as an increasing number of younger sociologists identify with the need for improvements in citizenship education. They are perhaps less concerned than past generations of scholars with the purely positivistic impulses and the grand theoretical ambitions which characterized the field for several decades. Reflecting these trends over the past ten years, the ASA has cautiously endorsed a movement to help improve sociology instruction in the schools. This endorsement has taken several forms.

First, the ASA has committed itself to working with other professional organizations in the social sciences, at both the college and precollege levels. For example, the association participated in 1983 in a social science task force that included representatives of six national academic associations and has also conferred frequently with the National Council for the Social Studies (NCSS), the National Commission on Social Studies in the Schools, and other interdisciplinary bodies. The ASA responded to the NCSS "Scope and Sequence" statement, which described the general content of social studies material that should be included at each grade level (Howery 1985).

Second, in 1989 the ASA established a Task Force on Sociology in the Elementary and Secondary Schools, which, in August 1991, was made an ASA standing committee. This body is convened once a year at the ASA annual meetings and otherwise operates as a network for its members and others who wish to be apprised of its work. The committee's membership is drawn from schools and school districts as well as colleges and universities. However, unlike its ASA predecessor during the SRSS era, the emphasis today is more applied than academic. The task force has been as interested in implementation and in maintaining a network with the schools as it has been in developing new curriculum materials. For example, it sponsored a thorough review of SRSS Episodes and developed a model for consultation with local schools which has already been implemented with some success in Maryland, Massachusetts, North Carolina, and Pennsylvania. Essentially, the consultation entails making ASA instructional and academic resources available to classroom teachers for the purpose of developing currently needed materials and exercises. This process involves liaison work between professors and teachers in schools at a variety of locations. The advantage of this model is that it maximizes the connection between the sociologists and the schools, while the disadvantages are that it is time-consuming and that the materials, being designed for specific locations, may not be universally applicable. The goal of this consulting work is to develop a catalog of successful interventions which can be the basis for a renewed national effort to influence the precollege curriculum, with the full participation and collaboration of teachers themselves. These and other complex issues were discussed at a well-attended workshop sponsored by the task force ("Sociology in the Secondary Schools: Needs and Responses") at the 1990 ASA annual meeting.

In its other programming, the ASA is also committed to outreach. Its

Teaching Services section has sponsored several workshops for secondary teachers in conjunction with ASA meetings. In general, the ASA office serves as a facilitator, to put interested parties in touch with each other.

In the years ahead, developing expertise in networking will become increasingly important. Prior experience has shown that success depends upon more than cultivating personal contacts in the schools, although this is obviously important. The fact is that, as organizations, universities and schools are so different that ways must be found to assure that innovations developed by one type of organization can be effectively communicated to, and translated within, the other.

Each year large samples of high school seniors are asked to respond to two statements: (1) "I feel I can do very little to change the world as it is today," and (2) "When I think about all the terrible things that have been happening it is hard for me to hold out much hope for the world." Since 1978 an average of forty-five percent of those polled have answered "mostly agree" or "agree" to the first statement, and about thirty percent have "agreed" or "mostly agreed" with the second (Berman 1990: 75). It is clear that we are facing a crisis of citizenship education, which takes many forms aside from the pessimism reflected in the responses above. Students are not learning enough of the skills of community involvement and social responsibility. They are not being taught a range of potential solutions to social problems or how to think about issues in an analytic way. Perhaps most importantly, they are not being encouraged to make a connection between their personal lives and the domain of public policy. They are therefore easy targets for cynical political campaigns which stress symbolism and imagery over content and substantive debate.

There is a consensus evolving among social studies educators and sociologists on the need to expose precollege students to sociology as a way to help resolve this multifaceted crisis. In the process, the issue of whether sociology should "pander" to a precollege audience will recede in importance. In fact, if appropriately presented, sociology "*may* appeal especially to those who do not go on, at least directly, to liberal-arts programs in universities and colleges" (Jenness 1990: 241).

In 1977, a national task force on citizenship education noted that

the overarching purpose of civic education is to provide youth with the knowledge, values, and skills they require in order to function effectively as responsible adult citizens. A successful ... program must be linked to the kinds of experiences students are likely to encounter upon leaving school. (Watts 1988: 1)

Sociology is uniquely qualified to aid in this mission so long as it heeds the exhortation of C. Wright Mills (1959) to insist on the connection between "private troubles" and "public issues." As I have elsewhere pointed out,

Living in the late 20th century, the individual is confronted with a range of complex choices and unsolved problems unprecedented in human history. People must support themselves, and their families, in a competitive, even predatory environment. They need to work at jobs which are in some measure intrinsically satisfying. They have to stay healthy, feel safe, and learn how to get along with others who may not share their background or beliefs. . . . In trying to make effective choices, "common sense" often fails us. We often feel isolated and confused . . . because we may be unaware that our personal worries and dilemmas are shared by large numbers of our fellow citizens and . . . because the sheer volume of information which must be processed before making decisions is overwhelming. (Gray 1989: 72)

Sociology can reduce the sense of isolation and confusion experienced by young people in a rapidly changing milieu. It can show them, for instance, how international competition and the globalization of the economy have changed the structure of the American labor force, creating an oversupply of workers trained only to perform tasks which are needed less and less as the years go by. Students' families, therefore, may experience the "private troubles" of financial hardship and unemployment as a result of the "public issues" of technological innovation and free trade. Young people pondering which career to choose (a private decision, to be sure) can predicate their decisions on the projected demand for certain types of work.

Other examples of topics addressed by sociology which would be of obvious value for citizenship training at the precollege level are:

Deviance and Social Control—"Why Do People Take Drugs?"

The Family—"Coping with Divorce."

Social Stratification—"The Future of the Middle Class."

Education—"What Are We Taught, and Why?"

Gerontology—"Caring for the Aged among Us."

Each of these topics can be presented in a way that fosters constructive civic roles while at the same time illustrating the sociological perspective and encouraging critical thinking.

PROJECTIONS

As noted in the introduction to this chapter, the overall influence of sociology can be measured both formally and informally. We have already considered a selection of the more formal indicators, namely, acceptability, number of existing courses, teachers' attitudes, and professional association activities. Let us now briefly assess the potential appeal of sociology to the broader public in the years ahead by focusing on three emerging trends in American education: (1) the teacher-accountability movement, (2) a rapidly changing school clientele, and (3) the explosion of knowledge in the social sciences.

Teacher accountability means that more attention will be paid to the instructor's mastery of a particular subject. Already, the College Entrance Examination Board includes sociological questions on its tests for pre-college teachers, while the ASA is beginning to develop recommended standards for state certification in sociology. Clearly, the profession needs to do more to formally codify the sociological knowledge which has become accepted as essential for teachers to have learned. However, accountability also implies renewed scrutiny of *students'* performance. Sociology, if properly taught, motivates young people to master the factual and historical detail with which they may otherwise grow impatient. For this reason, sociology may become more welcome in social studies classrooms.

Unlike other social studies subjects, sociology is not burdened with a rigid legacy of encrusted course content. As we have seen, the number of sociology electives taught in American schools are few, and presently there is no widely recognized or state-mandated curriculum. This means that sociology is ideally suited to address the needs of a new clientele in public education—minorities, immigrant groups, and adult learners. Including sociological "modules," or units, in history, geography, and civics courses would not require a fundamental restructuring of precollege education, but it could be the basis of an appropriate response to those who are calling for more appreciation of cultural diversity and a social-problems emphasis in the schools.

Finally, it is clear that the rapid growth of knowledge in the social sciences is presenting a challenge to educators. They will need to retool and to incorporate new readings, exercises, and media (e.g., videos) into the social studies curriculum in the years ahead. Sociology can provide a framework for this process because it presents students with a basic conceptual vocabulary for looking at emerging issues. There are many teachers who could also benefit from learning this vocabulary. If sociology can determine how best to form collaborative ties with teachers and schools in the years ahead, it is likely to have an increasing impact on American precollegiate education.

REFERENCES

Angell, R. C. "Sociological Resources for the Social Studies Project: A Report by the Director." *The American Sociologist* 7 (May 1972): 16–17.

Berman, Sheldon. "Educating for Social Responsibility." *Educational Leadership* 48 (November 1990): 75–80.

Dorn, Dean S. "High School Sociology: A View from California." *Footnotes* (April 1986): 4.

Grahlfs, F. Lincoln. "Inside SRSS: Lessons from a National Curriculum Project." Manuscript, n.d.

Gray, Paul S. "Sociology." In *Charting a Course: Social Studies for the 21st Century*. A Report of the Curriculum Task Force of the National Commission on Social Studies in the Schools. Washington, DC: National Commission on Social Studies in the Schools, 1989.

Howery, Carla. "Sociology in High School." *Footnotes* (January 1985): 4.

Jenness, David. *Making Sense of Social Studies*. New York: Macmillan, 1990.

King, K. "How Other Academic Disciplines Approach Teaching Concerns and the Consequences for Sociology." *Sociological Spectrum* 2 (1982): 73–95.

Mills, C. Wright. *The Sociological Imagination*. New York: Oxford University Press, 1959.

Montgomery County Public Schools. *Sociology I: A Teacher's Guide* (revised, 12/86). Rockville, MD: Department of Academic Skills, 1986.

————. *Social Studies: Grades 9–12*. Rockville, MD: Office of Instruction and Program Development, 1990.

Shaver, James. "A Critical View of the Social Studies Profession." *Social Education* 41 (April 1977): 300–307.

Smith, David W. "What Went Wrong with the Social Studies Reform Movement." *Indiana Social Studies Quarterly* 15 (April 1981): 19–24.

Sociological Resources for the Social Studies Project Staff. *Inquiries in Sociology*. Boston: Allyn and Bacon, 1972.

Tucker, Jan L. "Teacher Educators and the New Social Studies." *Social Education* 36 (May 1972): 548–60.

Watts, W. David. "Patterns of Social Fragmentation and Cohesion: The Social Context of 21st Century Education for Citizenship." Paper presented at "Citizenship in the 21st Century," a national conference on the future of civic education. Washington, DC, 1988.

Weiss, Iris R. *Report of the National Survey of Science, Mathematics, and Social Studies Education*. Research Triangle Park, NC: Center for Educational Research and Evaluation, 1978.

12

PRECOLLEGE ANTHROPOLOGY/ ARCHAEOLOGY

Marion J. Rice

Anthropology is not a regular school subject, although ideas from anthropology are sometimes used in social studies material. The discipline-oriented decade of the 1960s brought forth three national anthropology projects, and for a short time it appeared that anthropology might achieve a specific identity in school instruction. But before the discipline-based curriculum projects were even in place, the United States moved to new priorities in education with the enactment of the Elementary and Secondary Education Act of 1965. Neither the American Anthropological Association nor its affiliate Council on Anthropology and Education had an infrastructure to support the teaching of precollege anthropology, and the national projects rapidly disappeared from the education scene as federal funding evaporated. Teaching anthropology in the 1990s is very much as it was prior to the 1960s. That is, it is marked by the efforts of a few enthusiasts here and there who make no significant impact since anthropology lacks any endorsement as a requirement in either the training of teachers or the school curriculum. However, the future of school archaeology appears more promising for two reasons: (1) archaeology is nurtured by public education programs associated with state and national archaeological sites, and (2) archaeology may easily find a niche in school instruction through state histories which include Native Americans.

This chapter will offer a brief survey of the past, present, and probable future of precollege anthropology. It will begin with an overview of the

emergence of the study of anthropology, since the formation of a discipline
is often related to its future diffusion.

REFLECTIONS

Anthropology emerged as a separate discipline as part of the flowering
of nineteenth-century science. The Renaissance had stimulated renewed
speculations about man's place in the continuum of nature, and European
voyages of exploration and discovery had brought Europeans into contact
with many new peoples and their cultures, including Indians of the New
World. European images of the American Indian and other preliterate
people were contradictory: fierce, bloodthirsty savages versus noble people existing in a state of nature uncorrupted by the artificialities of civilization. By the middle of the nineteenth century, dilettanti who had the
leisure and resources to pursue independent study had narrowed the speculations of natural and moral philosophy to an area of investigation called
anthropology, the study of man. Increasing emphasis was placed on empirical observation in an effort to answer the four major questions which
today characterize general anthropology:

1. What is the relationship of people in a primitive state to the emergence of
   civilization?
2. How do the works of early man bridge the gap between prehistoric and historic
   cultures?
3. In what ways is the diversity of languages related to the distributions and
   affinities of peoples and their cultures?
4. How did the human species originate and evolve into racial types? (What is
   the relationship of physical to social evolution?)

The first three questions express the emphasis of the three fields of
cultural anthropology—ethnography, archaeology, and linguistics; the last
question(s) reflect the focus of physical anthropology. While the process
of specialization was an early characteristic of anthropology, as with other
sciences, this inclusive, four-field conception of anthropology was established very early in both Europe and the United States, notwithstanding
some differences in terminology. It was reflected in the constitution of
the Anthropological Society of Washington, DC, which was organized in
1879 and was the lineal predecessor of the American Anthropological
Association, founded in 1902 (Hallowell 1960: 101). The organization of
such a professional association reflected the growth and coalescence of
similar interests, anticipated by earlier societies, as did the organization
of a number of natural history museums established subsequent to the
founding of the Smithsonian Institution in 1846. By the beginning of the
twentieth century formal anthropology programs had been initiated at

Columbia, Clark, and Harvard universities, while some universities were offering anthropology courses through other departments. This university movement affirmed the truism that education more often reflects than initiates changes taking place in society.

The maturing of anthropology into a university-based discipline was paralleled by a tremendous expansion in public school enrollments in the United States. There was also the emergence of new modern high schools, with science/mathematics options replacing the traditional emphasis on Latin and Greek. Although there was a recognition by Franz Boas of Columbia University of the value of anthropology in liberal education, both from a substantive and a procedural point of view (Boas 1899, 1911), no attempt was made to adapt anthropology to the curricula of the schools. This was a time when a succession of educational committee reports, including the 1893 report of the "Committee of Ten" and several reports of the Committee on the Economy of Time in Secondary Education, were making recommendations which would establish curricular patterns destined to become dominant in the twentieth century. Anthropologists, however, did not participate in these curricular efforts. E. L. Hewett, who in 1909 established the School of American Archaeology (later the School of American Research) at Santa Fe, had as early as 1904 pointed out the pressing need for a school text in anthropology. He proposed that the National Education Association and the American Anthropological Association collaborate to further the teaching of anthropology, with a focus on Native American studies (Hewett 1904). No effort was made, however, to implement his proposal.

The cooperative involvement of professional associations in implementing the teaching of social sciences in the schools shows the predominant involvement of history, geography, and political science. Geography and history had become a part of the common-school curriculum by the beginning of the 1830s in the better school systems, and thus found secure places in curricula which could be recreated at a higher level in expanded secondary school programs (Cubberly 1934: 297–307; Hertzberg 1981: 20–21). In contrast, the American Anthropological Association did not become involved in the teaching of school anthropology until the National Science Foundation funded the Anthropology Curriculum Study Project in 1963.

Calls for the Teaching of Precollege Anthropology

The annotated bibliography of Susan Dwyer-Schick's (1976) *Study and Teaching of Anthropology within Academic Institutions* includes citations related to the teaching of precollege anthropology. Although not all relevant articles may be cited, it is still a convenient means for noting the progress of interest in the teaching of anthropology in schools.

Table 1
Number of Articles on Precollege Anthropology

Decade/ Year(s)	As a Subject in Schools	In Teacher Training	Articles in *Social Education*
1900	1	1	NA
1910	0	1	NA
1920	0	0	0
1930	8	2	0
1940	3	1	0
1950	11	4	2
1960–62	11	1	2
1963–69	36	4	7[a]
1970–75	38	2	5[b]
1976–79			1
1980			3

[a] Two special issues in 1968: v. 32, 11 articles; v. 32, 5 articles.
[b] One special issue in 1974: v. 38, 5 articles; two appraisal issues; 1970, v. 34, and 1972, v. 36, which included the three national anthropology projects.

Source: Dwyer-Schick (1976).

Dwyer-Schick's bibliography indicates that it was not until the 1930s that the professional literature began to reveal any interest in school anthropology (see Table 1). The first journal articles on the subject were mainly exhortations, extolling the virtues of anthropology, or descriptions of classroom applications. Expansion in the teaching of college anthropology, greater numbers of available or prospective teachers, and continued interest in international/multicultural education all helped to create some interest in the teaching of anthropology. This movement never became strong enough to constitute a trend, although it may have made some teachers more favorably disposed toward trying out new courses in anthropology when they were funded. The expanded conceptualization of social studies and the acceptance of a more active approach to learning were also factors. The increased number of journal publications dealing with anthropology, however, reflects the appearance of funded anthropology curriculum projects in the 1960s. Reporting on these projects in journal articles and at professional meetings became standard ways of diffusing knowledge about the teaching of anthropology. (As is indicated in Table 1, the number of anthropology articles rapidly declined after this period of federal funding ended.) The large number of articles published in the 1970s does not reflect new interest in anthropology, but rather, the impact of MACOS (Man: A Course of Study), diffused by means of NSF funding, which was terminated as a result of a Congressional inquiry in 1975.

The Academically Talented and the Search for Excellence

The funding of anthropology projects (to be discussed in the next section) and other disciplinary projects of the 1960s developed as a result of the conservative reaction of the 1950s. Then, as in the 1990s, a panacea that would revitalize American education was sought. Although found more often in the professional literature than in actual classrooms, progressive education had long been a favorite whipping boy of the popular press. During the late 1940s and early 1950s, there was increasing criticism of the "soft" pedagogy of progressivism, as contrasted to the virtues of learning "hard" subject matter.

One of the most vocal and articulate critics was Arthur Bestor, a historian who founded the Council for Basic Education in 1956. One of the basic themes of his books, such as *Educational Wastelands* and *The Restoration of Learning,* published in 1953 and 1955, respectively, was that while intellectual training was not the only function of schools in a democratic society, it was their major function. The best way to conduct this intellectual training was through the academic disciplines. This theme found wide acceptance among the general public and particularly among university academics, if not among professional educators (Cremin 1964: 344–45). The trauma of Sputnik merely exacerbated the feeling that something must be done. The purpose of the Woods Hole Conference of 1959, reported in Jerome Bruner's *Process of Education,* was not so much to initiate curriculum reform as to marshal financial resources made available by the National Defense Education Act of 1958 (Bruner 1983: 181).

It was not only the academics who saw a need for more substance, even the National Education Association reflected the disciplinary inclination of those years, as did the U.S. Office of Education. Instead of schools providing merely an optimum environment for development, declared the department's Educational Policies Commission (1961), schools should get behind children and actively "push" to ensure that the central goal of American education, the development of intellectual power, was achieved. Thus there was a predisposition to accept Jerome Bruner's (1960) proposition that the young learner should be trained for inquiry. Few curriculum reformers, however, went to such an extreme as Philip A. Phenix (1962) did in asserting that no consideration need be given to the "nature, needs, and interest of the learner" in discipline-based curricula.

Two sources made funds available for school curricular projects in the social sciences—NSF and Project Social Studies. The largest and most generous funding for the major national projects came from the National Science Foundation. While the NSF had been established in 1950, it was not until 1958, with the enactment of the National Defense Education Act, that its mandate was extended to include curriculum development.

The NSF supported two projects in anthropology. The first was the Anthropology Curriculum Study Project, directed by Dr. Malcolm Collier and jointly sponsored by the NSF and the American Anthropological Association. The second project, MACOS (Man: A Course of Study), did not originate as an NSF project, but as the brainchild of Jerome Bruner. Originally, it was conceived as the behavioral science strand of a comprehensive K–12 social studies curriculum that was to be implemented by the Educational Development Center, but was never completed. MACOS actually came to fruition as a one-semester upper-elementary course under the leadership of Peter Dow, head of the history department at Germantown Friends School before he was recruited to join MACOS (Bruner 1983: 188–91).

A third project, "A Sequential Curriculum in Anthropology, Grades 1–7," better known as the Georgia Anthropology Curriculum Project, was funded by United States Office of Education Project Social Studies. Directed by Wilfrid C. Bailey and myself, the project was a collaborative effort by anthropologists and educators. Teachers were involved in various stages of testing and revision in all three anthropology projects. Although each had a different rationale and content, all were conceived as top-down projects separate from the implementing schools. School use was to come in the dissemination phase, when it was hoped that the textbook market would support the publication and sales of project materials through trade channels. Macmillan undertook the commercial publication of materials generated by the Anthropology Curriculum Study Project (all of which are now out of print). NSF funding subsidized the publication of MACOS materials by Curriculum Development Associates, of Washington, DC (those publications are still available). Some Georgia Anthropology Project materials are still in stock, but the project itself ceased to function with the retirement of its remaining personnel in the 1980s.

Notwithstanding the apparent success of the disciplinary approach in the 1960s, there was no mass shift by social studies teachers or professional educators to embrace pure knowledge attainment as the major purpose of social studies instruction. While the National Council for the Social Studies had been flirting with the disciplinary approach (Spindler 1958; Oliver 1962), there was no mass commitment made by this diverse organization to any one approach. In 1962, the same year when it published the papers commissioned by the American Council of Learned Societies for the 1961 NCSS meeting in Chicago, the NCSS reaffirmed its traditional conception of the role of social studies as citizenship education (*National Council* 1962: 315). Citizenship education might be regarded as the lodestar of social studies education, maintaining its guiding role over the competing alternatives of social studies as reflective inquiry and as social science (Barr, Barth, and Shermis 1978).

Furthermore, while the projects of several disciplines appeared to hold center stage in the social studies for a number of years, their importance was an illusion created by their national funding. There was never any national-consensus building in the social sciences for precollege teaching. Most projects reflected the entrepreneurial efforts of individuals or schools, each with its own design and objectives, without any disciplinary sequence. Project Social Studies spawned not only disciplinary projects, but a plethora of other types as well. The Association for Supervision and Curriculum Development (ASCD) index of *Social Studies Education Projects* (Taylor and Groom 1971) listed 111 projects, while twenty-seven national-scope projects were appraised in various issues of *Social Education* in 1970 and 1972.

Before the national discipline projects were even completed, a radical shift in priorities had been signaled by the passage of the Elementary and Secondary Education Act (ESEA) of 1965. Instead of federal funding being directed toward the academically talented, schools in areas with a large population of low-income families were to be given priority for such assistance. With a different definition of the target population and a reduction in federal funding for curriculum diffusion, it was almost preordained that the disciplinary projects would not survive. Anthropology as a subject of study was particularly vulnerable since it was outside the conventional interpretation of social studies as history-geography-civics.

The Three National Anthropology Curriculum Projects

The three national projects to be briefly discussed in this section (and previously mentioned above) are the Anthropology Curriculum Study Project, the Georgia Anthropology Curriculum Project, and MACOS. These projects left important legacies for the future revival of anthropology in the schools, and their salient characteristics will be noted (see References for both project reports and independent appraisals). Thomas L. Dynneson (1975, 1986) is also a good source for descriptions of other anthropology-related curriculum projects of the 1960s.

Anthropology curriculum study project (high school). During its existence, the ASCP developed a variety of experimental materials. Its last major undertaking was a one-semester course, "Patterns in Human History," in four units: Studying [Small] Societies, Origins of Humanness, Emergence of Complex Societies, and Modernization and Traditional Societies. Two case studies of American Indians—*Kiowa Years* by Alice Marriott and *The Great Tree and the Longhouse* by Hazel Hertzberg— were designed to stimulate the study of state history by showing the connection between a particular group and a particular locale.

The ACSP did not attempt to develop a simplified version of introductory college anthropology for high school. The strategy was to assist teachers of history and anthropology who wished to give an overview of changes in different types of world societies.

An examination of world history or American history texts does not indicate that the historical-anthropological approach of ACSP director Malcolm Collier (1975) has made much of an impact. One reason is the emphasis on post–World War II developments in contemporary texts. The space previously devoted to early history has shrunk, making it even more difficult to study emerging civilizations from a comparative anthropological perspective.

The Georgia anthropology curriculum project. This project produced month-long units for K–8 which covered the four major areas of anthropology—ethnography, archaeology, linguistics, and physical anthropology. Of the three anthropology projects, this one was most closely identified with the reductionist model, that is, taking the four main areas of anthropology, selecting their most pertinent concepts, and presenting them in eight units to create an overview of anthropology as a discipline. The practice of sequencing the progressive accumulation of knowledge by grade level was followed by having children repeat certain units in greater depth in subsequent grades. For example, "The Concept of Culture" was introduced in grade 1 and repeated in grade 4; material from "Archaeology" was presented in grade 2 and repeated in grade 5, with additional material on early man and evolution; and "Culture Change and Modernization," introduced in grade 3, was repeated in grade 6. Units on the "Life Cycle" and "Linguistics" were presented in grades 7 and 8. (Although evaluations had shown that young children could learn the content of anthropology when it was taught explicitly as a discipline, it was not possible to evaluate the sequencing approach even within a few grades because of teacher and pupil turnover.)

The project continued after its federal funding ended under the auspices of the University of Georgia and produced a variety of supplementary materials—teaching films, programmed texts, teaching kits—and high school instructional units. In the late 1960s, it collaborated with Committee Three on the Teaching of Anthropology of the Council on Anthropology and Education on the publication of materials about teaching anthropology in schools.

MACOS (Man: A Course of Study). This project evolved from various Educational Development Center ideas and was always behaviorally, rather than culturally, oriented. It sought to answer such specific questions as "What is uniquely human about human beings? How did they get that way? How could they be made more so?" (Bruner 1983: 191). The availability of some unusually fine films supplemented much of the MACOS content, namely, the Netsilik Eskimo films made in Pelly Bay by Asen Baliksi for the Canadian Film Board, and the film footage of baboon troops in the Amoseli Reserve of East Africa made by Irven DeVore.

The main teaching strategy was envisioned by Jerome Bruner as an extended dialogue between pupils and teachers, with the materials forming a stimulus for discussion and exploration. The final product revolved around five units, in a sequence of increasing behavioral-social complexity: Salmon, Herring Gull, Baboon Troop, Netsilik Eskimo. Printed material consisted of twenty-three booklets, largely intended for teacher guidance.

In the 1970s, when other five-year projects in anthropology had been completed, MACOS was heavily funded by NSF for dissemination and implementation. At one time there were as many as eighty-five centers (Dynneson 1975). This dissemination eventually embroiled MACOS in controversy. The comparative approach led creationists and other watchdogs of the elementary schools to raise questions about the appropriateness of the material for public school instruction. At one point, three different investigations were being conducted on MACOS. The National Science Foundation not only cut off support for all project dissemination in 1975, but also reduced the funding level for curriculum development (Wiley 1976). At the heart of the controversy was the difference between social studies perceived as a vehicle for the transmission of accepted beliefs and as a means to promote reflective inquiry. The MACOS controversy is a reminder that when curricular innovation touches public sensitivities, even those of a small but articulate minority, the curriculum can become a source of heated controversy.

In addition to these three anthropology projects, the High School Geography Project (HSGP) developed a very strong unit on cultural geography within the framework of its one-year, six-unit course, "Geography in an Urban Age." Unlike the ethnographic case studies in the anthropology projects, HSGP activities were specifically designed to highlight cultural differences. The first topic, "Ideas about Cattle," forced students to examine the different values placed on cattle in three different societies—as an indicator of wealth, as a source of meat, and as an occasion for sport. Cultural geography has always had a close affinity with anthropology, as exemplified by the work of F. Ratzel in Germany and Vidal de la Blache in France.

Comparing the three anthropology projects. All three projects had common characteristics. First, there was a common tendency to use case studies of preliterate cultures and an emphasis on the ethnographic present, practices which all too often gave the impression that the study groups were frozen in time, whether the subject was the Kalahari Bushmen (ACSP), the Arunta (ACP), or the Netsilik (MACOS). This "museum" approach to the study of peoples obscured the fact that it is rare to find in the modern world a people whose way of life has not in some way been affected by either indirect or direct culture contact. Both the ACSP and the ACP, however, included specific content dealing with culture change.

While the selected societies may have seemed somewhat irrelevant to the modern world, their very difference entailed an examination of cultural values from a different perspective. All three projects confronted the student in various ways with the origins of man's distinctive qualities. No project attempted to consider creationism and evolution as alternative explanations—this controversial issue was imposed on the projects from outside. It only became an issue with MACOS, however, probably because the diffusion of ACSP and ACP material was in decline, while that of MACOS increased with NSF funding.

As to methodology, the three projects all espoused a rationalist, knowledge approach. There was also an implicit assumption that learning general principles from ethnographic comparison was more important than learning ethnographic details. However, none of the projects produced any evidence that nomothetic goals (i.e., principles or generalizations that applied across cultures) were attained instead of the more prosaic idiographic outcomes (i.e., concrete details and characteristics of a particular culture). If anything, elementary grade children in the Georgia project schools appeared to enjoy cultural specifics more than generalizations, an observation which may relate to Piagetian concrete operations or to a greater preference for concrete details about peoples and cultures than for abstract universals.

All of the projects encouraged the development of critical-thinking skills through inquiry. While inquiry was the explicit mode of the ACSP and MACOS, the Georgia project used a combination of approaches—didactic explanation, transfer, and reinforcement through a variety of pupil activities, with inquiry as a supplementary mode. Evaluation reports on all three projects reflected both teacher and pupil approval. Favorable evaluation is common to curricular innovation—the effect of novelty or special attention. These side effects are often overlooked but valuable learning outcomes, irrespective of the content or methods of instruction. Teacher training was more heavily emphasized in the MACOS project because of the use of silent films without narrative explanation.

As measured by their actual usage in the schools, the anthropology projects had a limited impact. A study by Karen Wiley (1976) for the National Science Foundation indicated that NSF high school science projects reached, at the most, less than one percent of the high school population. The disappointing diffusion of the various projects reflected a rather naive view of curriculum development and implementation by both NSF and Project Social Studies. What was needed were experts who would prescribe the new materials, which would stimulate demand by school systems because of the developers' credentials. This demand, in turn, would stimulate commercial and trade publishers to bid for the rights to publish and disseminate the new materials. Such simplistic, linear model of curriculum development and implementation completely overlooked

the fact that there were already established, competing curricular interests—those related to texts that were commercially produced and distributed for profit, affecting publishers, authors, distributors, adopters,
and users; those related to competing ideologies of education and teaching; those related to whoever benefited from established subject matter;
and finally, those related to inertia in the face of change. Just as there is
a pattern in the general culture, there is a pattern in school curricula.

There was no difficulty in finding teachers and schools willing to try
out the experimental materials; volunteers generally saw themselves as
participants in an exciting enterprise. But after the trial period ended,
there was no support mechanism for the teachers, and no psychological
reward for doing anything differently. It was difficult for teachers to continue the use of experimental materials beyond the trial period, even in
the innovative schools. The proposed innovations required a readjustment
in the overall curriculum, an issue which had not been anticipated. It was
much easier for participating teachers to rejoin their colleagues in the use
of the standard materials than to continue as pioneers with new materials.
American educators in particular look for a "quick fix" and are not prepared financially or emotionally for the long haul that curriculum change
requires.

CURRENT TRENDS AND ISSUES

This section reports on the current status of precollege anthropology,
using the 1986 report by Thomas Dynneson and Fred Coleman of a 1985
survey and the more recent 1991 report on precollege anthropology edited
by Paul Erickson for the Committee on Research of the American Anthropological Association Task Force on Teaching Anthropology in
Schools. Other descriptive data will also be presented.

The 1985 Survey of State Departments of Education

Forty states replied to Dynneson and Coleman's (1986) questionnaire.
In terms of teacher training, nineteen states reported that anthropology
played some role in secondary training, but only six reported any role in
elementary training. Twenty-three states reported that encouragement
was given to the teaching of anthropology; fourteen, that no position was
taken; and four, that it was not encouraged. The extent to which anthropology was perceived as a controversial subject was reported in the negative by twenty-five states and in the affirmative by three; no response
was made to this item by fifteen.

The state departments reported that no accurate data were available
on the actual teaching of school anthropology by districts. The most
common materials used were textbooks, films, and filmstrips, but the

Table 2
Anthropology in Education Programs

	Total	Canada	U.S.
Number Responding	75	25	50
Required	28	7	21
Recommended	4	2	2
Elective	28	7	21
Absent	19	8	11

Source: Erickson (1991).

precollege projects were only mentioned by five states. Three reported using MACOS, and two the Anthropology Curriculum Study Project materials (Patterns in Human History), but there was no indication of how extensive or frequent this use was. The conclusion drawn by Dynneson and Coleman, that anthropology was "holding its own as a minor aspect of the curriculum," seems more of an impression than an inference based on data.

The 1991 Erickson Report

Erickson's (1991) report included both American and Canadian schools. It was based on three surveys plus a case study of a precollege classroom in New York City.

Anthropology teacher training. Paul A. Erickson, of Saint Mary's University, Halifax, sent a questionnaire to the forty-seven teacher-training schools in Canada and to a random sample of schools in the United States, four in each state plus Puerto Rico, Guam, and the District of Columbia. Seventy-five responses were received, twenty-five from Canada (fifty-four percent response) and fifty from the United States (twenty-four percent response). Since the data are reported jointly for the two countries, the resulting picture is highly distorted. Nineteen of the schools responding lacked anthropology offerings. The results for the seventy-five schools replying are displayed in Table 2 (because of the overlap of categories, the total exceeds the number of responding schools).

Erickson is careful, in interpreting the significance of this data, to point out that it is based on anthropology courses "on the books" and does not indicate the number of future teachers actually enrolled in these courses. He reports, however, that respondents' comments suggested that the answer is "not many." Erickson's conclusion is substantiated by actual, regular, on-campus registrations at the University of Georgia, Athens, in Spring 1991. Of the 585 students registered in the basic introductory anthropology courses, forty-two, or seven percent, were education majors. Only two education students were among those enrolled

Table 3
Education-Anthropology Enrollments as Percentages of University Enrollment,
Spring 1991, University of Georgia (Preliminary Figures)

	Total	Graduate	Undergraduate
University	24,375	4,678	19,697
Education	3,987	1,887	2,140
% of Univ. Enrollment	(.16)	(.40)	(.11)
Anthropology	773	39	734
Education in Anthropology	53	9	44
% of Anthro. Enrollment	(.07)	(.23)*	(.06)

*All in a course "Anthropology and Education"; none in general anthropology courses.

in sixteen upper-division and graduate anthropology courses (exclusive of nine students in an anthropology and education course taught by an instructor in the College of Education). The insignificant number of education students taking anthropology at the University of Georgia is shown in the preliminary registration figures for Spring 1991 (see Table 3).

The relationship of teacher knowledge of anthropology to pupil achievement in anthropology was indicated by one MACOS research report. Robert Fitch and colleagues (1977) reported that "the higher the teachers' rated accuracy in using anthropological terms, the greater the improvement exhibited by the students in the course" (246). This finding suggests how important training in anthropology is for teachers if their pupils are to develop even a basic familiarity with anthropological concepts.

Teacher certification and anthropology. Sally Plouffe, of the University of New Mexico, sent a questionnaire related to social studies tests and certification to fifty-six certification agencies (Erickson 1991). Responses were received from thirty, of which thirteen indicated that anthropology was required for "any certification." Since "any certification" includes non-teaching certificates, such as those for administrators, curriculum supervisors, and school social workers these vague replies do not mean that one-fourth of the states require anthropology for teacher certification.

The latest NCSS "Standards for the Preparation of Social Studies Teachers," approved September 20, 1987, were published in the January 1988 issue of *Social Education* (National Council 1988). These standards do not specifically endorse anthropology as a subject in teacher preparation, although it may be included: (1) in general studies, as part of "history and the social sciences with specific and separate attention to behavioral science (anthropology, sociology, and psychology) and with inclusion of global/cross/cultural and gender" (11); (2) in Grades 7–12 licensure of comprehensive social studies teachers, as one of "the be-havioral sciences (anthropology, psychology, and sociology)" (11); and (3) in licensure by discipline, "a program of studies in that discipline that is not less demanding than what is required of a B.A. or B.S. degree major" (11). Behavioral science is not mentioned as a subject of prepa-ration for either middle school or departmentalized elementary school, but this preparation should include "world geography and cultures." Li-censure of early childhood teachers (an inclusive term sometimes used as a synonym for "elementary") should require "physical and cultural geography, and other social sciences." The NCSS 1987 standards are no improvement over the 1983 standards, published in the May 1984 issue of *Social Education*. The standards for elementary teachers included "his-tory and the social behavioral sciences," while history and social science teachers should have completed "some course work" in anthropology, sociology, or social psychology, and "course work should include cross cultural and global perspectives and methodology of the disciplines" (Na-tional Council 1984: 360).

With so little emphasis given to anthropology in the standards for the preparation of teachers at any level by the major social studies profes-sional organization, it is likely that the responses to Plouffe's question-naire may have been simply the result of identifying anthropology with behavioral science. An examination of NCSS recommendations indicates that it is possible for high school, middle school, and elementary/early-childhood teachers to be in compliance with NCSS standards with-out having had a single course in anthropology. Yet it is at the middle school level that state history is taught, with its many opportunities for anthropology-archaeology extension, and it is the primary grades that focus on the home, neighborhood, and community. Opportunities for cross-cultural teaching by geographic area come in both the elementary and middle school grades. There is no existing practical preparation in anthropology to support cross-cultural instruction.

Anthropology in high school curricula. Patricia Rice, of West Virginia University, collected data on the teaching of anthropology from state social studies specialists (Erickson 1991). Her report highlights not only the difficulty of obtaining responses, but also the absence of state collec-tions of quantitative data on schools, teachers, and pupil enrollment by subject. She received the usual replies from many states, indicating that anthropology was integrated in the teaching of social studies below the high school grades. At the high school level, anthropology was reported to be an elective by twenty-eight states, but actual enrollment figures were available from only fourteen. Even in states with the highest anthropology course enrollments, Rice found less than one percent of high school stu-dents enrolled.

Data from the CS4 National Survey (Council of State Social Studies

Specialists 1990) show that only twelve states reported the possible inclusion of anthropology as a high school elective, while thirty states mentioned a psychology elective, and twenty-eight a sociology elective in high school. Normally, anthropology is grouped with psychology and sociology as a behavioral-science triad, and in the survey the twelve states that reported an anthropology elective also mentioned psychology and sociology as options. Mention of anthropology as a possible high school elective is thus a token, not a substantive, endorsement. Most students take only the three required units in some kind of world studies or geography course, world history, and American history. A high school elective in anthropology merely serves to legitimize the teaching of such a course should there be a teacher enthusiastic about initiating one.

Anthropology in the elementary school. Pre–high school social studies instruction is ostensibly interdisciplinary, drawing on the various social sciences. This results in state social studies consultants and book publishers assuring inquirers that anthropological concepts are being taught. Patricia Rice, in her excellent review, concluded that "quite a bit of anthropology is being taught in disguise as other topics between the second and tenth grade in most states and provinces" (Council 1990: 10). If this were true, then there would be no need for anthropologists to be concerned about the teaching of precollege anthropology.

The sanguinity that can arise from the assumption that elementary teachers must teach anthropological concepts without realizing it is certainly curious. No discipline has a monopoly on the concepts that constitute the structure of a discipline, for it is the special configuration, or structure of concepts with illustrative material, that permits the perception of phenomena from a particular disciplinary perspective. A careful examination of so-called interdisciplinary, or multidisciplinary, elementary social studies texts, K–3, for six series was made by A. Guy Larkins and Michael Hawkins (1990) and Larkins and Ben Smith (1987). They concluded that these texts were so "trivial and noninformative" that if there were a choice between using these texts or eliminating social studies from the K–3 curriculum, they would prefer to eliminate social studies. Yet it is these grades, where the concepts of family and community are addressed, that should offer some excellent ideas for the development of basic notions of anthropology, yet these ideas have not been developed.

My own examination of elementary texts, K–3, indicates that content is treated with such a high level of generalization and without supporting detail, as to be meaningless from the standpoint of developing any kind of knowledge (Rice 1985). In grades 4–7, social studies instruction uses place (geography) or chronology (history) as organizing principles. As with primary texts, however, there is the same lack of information in depth, with little explicit treatment of anthropological concepts. Therefore, even if a teacher had some background in anthropology, it would be almost impossible to help students gain any anthropological meaning. A comparison with earlier geography texts, such as those of Arnold Guyot (1868) and Matthew F. Maury (1911), shows that, while newer social studies texts have dropped the denigrating language of older texts, they have lost the *ethnographic specificity* of what were formerly treated as distinct physical and cultural differences. Even when ethnographic data is presented in contexts dealing with peoples of other lands, the simplified versions of today seldom match the richness of detail found in the older Atwood-Thomas studies, such as *Visits in Other Lands* by Wallace W. Atwood and Helen Goss Thomas (1943). It would appear that we have become so accustomed to insignificant and meaningless content in social studies texts that even an occasional anthropological word here and there, with reference to indigenous peoples, is accepted as anthropology. Given the concrete evidence that few teachers take anthropology courses, it is not likely that much anthropology is being taught anywhere in the schools.

Materials for the teaching of high school anthropology. Patricia Rice's survey also provided some scanty data on materials used for the teaching of high school anthropology (Erickson 1991). None of her respondents mentioned materials from the Anthropology Curriculum Study Project, although they were of high quality. Unfortunately, the commercial publisher did not keep them in print, so they are no longer available. Most of the anthropology high school texts being used now date from the 1960s; other texts in use are introductory college texts. The length and technicality of college texts in general anthropology have declined over the years, so this author does not see "the lack of a relatively current, high quality, four-field anthropology text written for high school students" to be so much a teaching problem as one of state approval and adoption. The author agrees with Patricia Rice that the lack of demand for high school and elementary texts is a problem. Negotiations with a prospective publisher to publish Georgia ACP materials in the 1970s foundered when the publisher ascertained that there was not a market for a minimum of ten thousand books. It would appear that this is an area which specifically requires external support, of the kind available to archaeology.

ARCHAEOLOGY

The Committee on Research of the American Association for the Advancement of Science (AAA) Task Force on the Teaching of Anthropology in Schools did not seek to separate the teaching of archaeology from that of general anthropology. In recent years, however, state divisions of archaeology have been active in developing materials for education programs. While data is lacking on the extent of pupil contact, either within or outside of school, twenty-five states had eighty materials for teaching archaeology, seventy-one of which were not duplicated (see Table 4).

Table 4

Archaeology Curriculum and Background Materials for Elementary and Secondary Schools by State/by Source of Citation

State/ Country	1 LEAP 1990	2 Workshop 1990	3 FA Report Dec. 1990	4 Soc. Hist. Arch., 1991
Arizona		5		
Arkansas	1	1		—
Colorado		2		1
Dist. Columbia	1	1		
Florida				1
Illinois	1			
Indiana				1
Iowa	3			
Kentucky		4		
Louisiana	1	*		*
Maine	2	1*		
Maryland	1			1
Massachusetts		1	1	1
Minnesota	1			
Missouri		2		
Nevada	1			
New Mexico	1			
New York	1	1		1
Oregon	1			
Pennsylvania				1
Rhode Island	1			
South Carolina	1	*		
Texas		4		2 1—
Utah	1	*	—	
Vermont		3	1	
Virginia		1		3 1—
Wyoming	1			
Canada		5		2
England		1		2
United States	—	—	—	1
	19	36 (4*)	4 (2—)	21 (1*3—)

* Duplicates LEAP

— Duplicates Workshop

1. LEAP: Listing of Education in Archaeological Programs. 1990. Department of the Interior, National Park Service, Archaeological Assistance Division.
2. Everything We Know About Archaeology for You to Use in Your Classroom. 1990. A Workshop for Teachers. Annual Meeting of the National Trust for Historic Preservation. National Park Service, Archaeological Assistance Division.
3. Federal Archaeology Report. December 1990, Vol. 3, No. 4. Archaeological Assistance Division.
4. Exhibit of Educational Resources, 1991. Society for Historical Archaeology, Conference on Historical and Underwater Archaeology, Richmond, Virginia.

Most of the materials were recent (from within the last five years) and thus reflect both new archaeological and related preservation efforts and also modern insights and interpretations about Native Americans, European-Amerindian contact, and the interaction of the two cultures.

Since all states had an indigenous population at the time of white contact, there is a potential for exciting programs which would deepen the scope of state history. However, only half of the states are represented in LEAP (Listing of Education in Archeological Programs). Since reporting is voluntary, it is obvious that many institutions and agencies have failed to report their curriculum materials, either to the Archeological Assistance Division, the Society for American Archaeology, the Society for Historical Archaeology, or other clearinghouses. The characteristic lack of educational investment in southern states is highlighted by the absence of any reported curriculum materials from such states as Georgia, Alabama, Mississippi, North Carolina, and Tennessee, where there was a visible Indian presence until the forced removals occurred in the 1830s. One of the most dynamic fields of anthropological study in the Southeast is that of ethnohistory, of which Dr. Charles M. Hudson is a strong exponent. Unfortunately, there is no evidence that much attention has been given to adapting this knowledge to school use.

Recent School Programs in Anthropology and Archaeology

No attempt has been made to include case studies of recent precollege classes in anthropology or archaeology (descriptions may be found by consulting sources cited in References). While stimulating examples of school anthropology can be found, they tend to be isolated cases, with little replication or diffusion.

The vigor of any subject in school instruction depends largely on the extent to which the subject is mandated and the teachers are required to have specific training for teaching that subject. It is out of the interaction of these two factors that the practical matters of school-text development and efforts at instructional improvement through new materials and teacher upgrading are undertaken. While all of the recent recommendations for social studies sequences allow for the teaching of anthropology, it is not specifically endorsed as a required subject. Prior to the twelfth grade, anthropology exists only as a part of interdisciplinary social studies efforts; in the twelfth grade, it will continue to be one of the many single-subject options. Five recommended curriculum sequences are discussed: *Charting a Course, Project 2061,* the NCSS-approved *Citizens for a Strong and Free Nation,* and two NCSS-approved alternatives, *Principles and Practices in a Democracy* and *Global Education.*

Charting a Course: Social Studies for the 21st Century was issued by the National Commission on Social Studies in the Schools (1989). Part

II, "Perspectives of the Social Science Associations," purports to give the views of a "coalition of social studies educators and university scholars associated with history and the social sciences." *Charting a Course* continues to reflect the past preferences for geography and history and, except for some updating, is closer to recommendations made in 1916 than to those more appropriate for the twenty-first century. Jane J. White, cochair of the American Anthropological Association's Task Force on Teaching Anthropology in the Schools, contributed the section on "Anthropology." She defines the central goal of anthropology as the understanding of diversity among peoples and their cultures. She does an excellent job of suggesting how themes and concepts from anthropology may be integrated into the scope and sequence indicated. However, since academics write subject-oriented texts in their own fields, and social studies textbook writers follow traditional models of social studies texts, it is not likely that much change will be actually generated by her recommendations. Ever since the 1920s, we have heard rhetoric about multidisciplinary texts for social studies, but even where elementary school texts are called "social studies," they typically reflect either a geographical or historical organization of content.

Charting a Course was the object of vitriolic criticism by a number of well-known social studies educators in the December 1990 and January 1991 issues of *Social Education*. Throughout *Charting a Course* there are recommendations to emphasize concepts and systems that cut across time and place, requiring the integration of many disciplines. The most distinctive recommendations, however, are for a three-year sequence of American and world history and geography: to 1750, 1750–1900, and post–1900. In terms of time commitment, these are equivalent to the old pattern of ninth grade geography, tenth grade world history, and eleventh grade American history, with the twelfth grade serving as the happy-hunting ground of electives.

Unless the National Commission undertakes and supports the publication of new materials which reflect its own recommendations, it is unlikely that these will be implemented.

Project 2061: Science for All Americans (American Association for the Advancement of Science 1989) sets forth idealized goals of education for all American students, not for the purpose of prescribing a curriculum, but to endorse scientific literacy. A fundamental premise of the Phase I 1989 reports, which attempt to define scientific literacy in general terms, is that "schools do not need to be asked to teach more and more content, but to teach less in order to teach it better" (20). This idea has been around for years, but there has never been any agreement on "what is essential." If some student is short on a fact or item considered "essential" by an educational critic, this lack of knowledge is taken as another indicator of school failure.

Project 2061 is now in Phase II, a development phase in which teacher panels in various sections of the country are drafting "alternative curriculum models for the use of school districts and the states" (3). This phase is also supposed to consider related aspects, such as teacher education and evaluation and testing. Phase III will be a long-term implementation phase, using the products of Phase II to move the United States toward scientific literacy.

My own evaluation of Project 2061 is that the level of expertise in Phase II does not match the rhetoric of Phase I. Not much support for the teaching of anthropology as a science can be expected because of the lack of anthropological emphasis in Phase I. The probability of finding teachers with adequate backgrounds for Phase II development in the social sciences in general is highly unlikely. The social science aspects of Phase I were highly skewed in the direction of psychology by the representative panel and consultant membership. Of the eight members of the Social and Behavioral Science Panel, three were psychologists; there was only one anthropologist. Among the consultants were six psychologists, three sociologists, two political scientists, one economist, and no anthropologist. The social science concepts emphasized, such as evolution, heredity, nurture, sociocultural systems, communication, conflict/competition, and function/malfunction, are highly generalized (AAA *Project 2061: Social* 1989). While these concepts appear to include ample scope for the development of scientific anthropology, in the absence of teaching materials which reflect the recommended multidisciplinary approach, it is unlikely that these aims will be realized.

Citizens for a Strong and Free Nation: Alternatives

In 1990 the National Council for the Social Studies published three NCSS-approved curriculum scope-and-sequence proposals in *Social Studies Curriculum Planning Resources* (National Council 1990). Shorter versions had appeared in *Social Education* in October 1989. The first of the three alternatives is "Social Studies for Citizens of a Strong and Free Nation," originally developed in 1983 by the NCSS Task Force on Scope and Sequence and published in *Social Education* in April 1984. Revised in July 1989 and approved by the NCSS board of directors, this alternative may be regarded as the official scope-and-sequence recommendation of the NCSS.

The two other approved alternatives are "Themes and Questions to Reflect Principles and Practices in a Democracy" by Michael Hartoonian and Margaret A. Laughlin, and "Social Studies with a Global Education" by Willard M. Kniep, which first appeared in the November/December 1986 issue of *Social Education*. (Three other options, also published in 1986, have not yet received official endorsement.) None of these three

NCSS-approved alternatives gives any special attention to the teaching of anthropology, although there is a reference to "Peoples and Cultures" at several grade levels in the NCSS Task Force option and references to the themes of "cultural heritage" and "culture" in the two other proposals. Anthropology is endorsed as a twelfth grade elective, but so are nine other electives for this grade. The endorsement is just as weak as that made in the "Themes and Questions" alternative. The only major departure by the NCSS Task Force from previous practice is the replacement of the traditional ninth grade world geography course by a year-long course in "Law, Justice, and Economics." World history and American history retain their respective tenth and eleventh grade slots.

The NCSS recommendations seem no more receptive to the teaching of anthropology than *Charting a Course* does. However, the scope-and-sequence recommendations made by Jane J. White in *Charting a Course* can be adapted to those in *Social Studies Curriculum Planning Resources*. But this can also be said of the social studies scope-and-sequence patterns followed for the past thirty years. The fact that so little anthropology of a serious nature is incorporated in either the elementary or the high school curriculum reflects the long tradition of imitation in school texts. It is easy for curriculum committees to imagine multidisciplinary texts, but much more difficult to create the teaching materials and supply the skills training needed to bring a multidisciplinary approach to fruition in the classroom.

Two articles have focused in recent years on the difficulty of getting new text materials into social studies instruction. Tetsko (1979) pointed out that, for a brief time in the 1960s, it appeared that the "new social studies," with their multidisciplinary and inquiry-mode emphases, did have some effect on texts in world history and American history. Tyson-Bernstein and Woodward (1986) agreed with Tetsko's observations on the 1960s, but concluded that whatever ground had been gained was lost, as "edition succeeded edition" and "textbooks reverted to formula" (44). Publishers view texts as not so much a tool of education but a market commodity produced to conform to standardized curricula under the guise of quasi-scholarship. With educational materials depending on publishers who compete for sales, and not on the basis of quality, recommendations for inclusive multidisciplinary curricula, irrespective of the source, are unrealistic.

The NCSS Task Force recommendations will be the most likely ones followed by publishers, supervisors, and teachers in the 1990s. It will permit them to be, in theory, modern and up-to-date, complying with "expert" recommendations. At the same time, they will not have to make any substantial changes in their current practices. Curriculum recommendations thus have a way of validating present practice rather than stimulating curricular change.

None of the scope-and-sequence proposals offers a new role for anthropology instruction in the schools. That will result only from the work of anthropology educators who develop materials which will bring anthropology into the school curriculum. Anthropologists, with their traditional commitment to research rather than to action, may be poorly prepared for the challenge.

PROJECTIONS

As we weigh the future of anthropology in precollege instruction, it is necessary to assay the nature of anthropology in comparison with other school subjects. The popularity of history as a school subject, in the United States as well as in other countries, is largely a product of nineteenth-century nationalism. With the rise of nation-states, some justification for the peculiar existence of national entities had to be developed as a substitute for the older imperial systems which often embraced people of diverse cultures and religions. History in literate cultures serves as the equivalent of the creation myth in preliterate societies, that is, by extolling the virtues of a nation-state and its people while simultaneously glossing over its blemishes. Although geography grew out of early attempts at scientific explanation, school geography has all too often been a braggadocio sidekick for history, emphasizing the happy concurrence of climates and resources which have made a particular people no less fortunate in their place than in their time.

No curriculum developer in anthropology (no anthropologist, for that matter) can be free of a particular cultural heritage, but anthropology has always used a comparative approach, looking at people living in different cultures under different conditions. As a discipline, anthropology is disquieting to school curriculum makers for three main reasons: (1) evolution, (2) culture, and (3) values. Unless these three factors are recognized, they cannot be addressed as problems to be solved.

Evolution continues to be an issue, although most school personnel deny that it is a problem. More than any other discipline, however, anthropology has pursued the discovery of human fossil remains and has accepted evolution as the explanatory mechanism for human physical origins. The issue of culture is a more subtle and insidious one than evolution. Culture is the product of people and is transmitted from one generation to another by living people. While history largely explains itself in terms of the human ego, anthropology emphasizes culture as a creative force which acts on people. An exploration of culture thus inevitably raises questions about the image that people have of themselves (White 1949). One particular aspect of culture which becomes all important in curricular contexts is that of different values. Probably the reason that non-Western cultures are never deeply explored in school study is that they raise questions about the alternative explanations and the different choices that are accepted by people as reasonable. The education of the young tends toward the provision of prescriptive conclusions, or *answers,* while meaningful anthropology raises *questions* about accepted beliefs and practices and exposes the ethnocentrism of various cultures. A striking example of the myopia induced by ethnocentrism appeared in the February 1991 special issue of *Social Education* on "Teaching about Genocide." The implicit definition of genocide here was what bad people do to other people. Since, by implication, Americans are the good guys, it follows that the United States cannot be accused of genocide either in its treatment of American Indians or in its more recent conduct on the "killing fields" of Southeast Asia.

While neither history nor any one of the social sciences has a monopoly on reflection, it is still useful to think of anthropology as a mirror for people and their values, expressed in Clyde Kluckholm's (1949) evocative title *Mirror for Man.* To see other people in their own cultural frames of reference helps us to see ourselves. That reflection is not always flattering. It is to be hoped that the future study of anthropology will not lead to denial, as in the MACOS controversy, but to reappraisal. Anthropology thus has a disciplinary contribution to make to the education of American children and youth, for studying anthropology may enable them to achieve a new sense of identity, with a fuller measure of respect for other people.

REFERENCES

Alder, Douglas D., and Glenn M. Linden, eds. *Teaching World History: Structured Inquiry through a Historical-Anthropological Approach.* Boulder, CO: Social Science Education Consortium, 1977.

American Association for the Advancement of Science. *Project 2061: Science for all Americans.* Washington, DC: American Association for the Advancement of Science, 1989.

———. *Project 2061: Social and Behavioral Sciences.* Washington, DC: American Association for the Advancement of Science, 1989.

Atwood, Wallace W., and Helen Goss Thomas. *Visits in Other Lands.* Boston: Ginn and Company, 1943.

Barr, Robert, James L. Barth, and S. Samuel Shermis. *The Nature of the Social Studies.* Palm Springs, CA: ETC Publications, 1978.

Boas, Franz. "Advances in Methods of Teaching." *Science* 9 (1899): 93–96.

———. "Methods of Teaching." In Paul Munro, ed., *Cyclopaedia of Education,* I, 134, 1911.

———. *Race, Language and Culture.* New York: Macmillan, 1940.

Bruner, Jerome. *In Search of Mind.* New York: Harper and Row, 1983.

———. *The Process of Education.* Cambridge, MA: Harvard University Press, 1960.

Collier, Malcolm. "Anthropology Curriculum Study Project: One Route for Pre-

Collegiate Anthropology." In Thomas L. Dynneson, ed., *Pre-Collegiate Anthropology: Trends and Materials*. Publication No. 75–1. Anthropology Curriculum Project. Athens, GA: University of Georgia, 1975.

Council of State Social Studies Specialists, CS4. *National Survey of Course Offerings, Requirements, and Testing in Social Studies, Kindergarten—Grade 12*. Washington, DC: National Council for the Social Studies, 1990.

Cremin, Lawrence. *The Transformation of the School*. New York: Vintage, 1964.

Cubberly, Ellwood P. *Public Education in the United States*. Boston: Houghton Mifflin, 1934.

Dwyer-Schick, Susan. *The Study and Teaching of Anthropology within Academic Institutions: An Annotated Bibliography*. Publication No. 76–1. Anthropology Curriculum Project. Athens, GA: University of Georgia, 1976.

Dynneson, Thomas L., ed. *Pre-Collegiate Anthropology: Trends and Materials*. Publication No. 75–1. Anthropology Curriculum Project. Athens, GA: University of Georgia, 1975.

Dynneson, Thomas L. "Trends in Pre-collegiate Anthropology." In Stanley P. Wronski and Donald H. Bragaw, eds., *Social Studies and Social Sciences: A Fifty Year Perspective*. Bulletin No. 78. Washington, DC: National Council for the Social Studies, 1986.

Dynneson, Thomas L., and Fred Coleman. "Pre-collegiate Anthropology in the United States." In Ruth O. Selig and Patricia J. Higgins, eds., "Practicing Anthropology in Precollege Education." Special Issue of *Practicing Anthropology* 8 (1986).

Educational Policies Commission. *The Central Purpose of American Education*. Washington, DC: U.S. Department of Education, 1961.

Erickson, Paul A., ed. *Interim Report on Precollege Anthropology Committee on Research to the AAA Task Force on Teaching Anthropology in Schools*. Four reports: Paul A. Erickson, "Anthropology Teacher Training"; Sally Plouffe, "Anthropology Teacher Certification"; Patricia Rice, "Anthropology Curricula"; Serena Nanda, "A Precollege Anthropology Classroom in New York City." Halifax, Nova Scotia: St. Mary's University, 1991.

Fitch, Robert M., John H. Haefner, and Nancie Gonzalez "Differential Teacher Training and the Teaching of Man: A Course of Study." *Social Education* 41 (March 1977): 242–46.

Guyot, Arnold. *The Earth and Its Inhabitants: Common-School Geography*. Guyot's Geographical Series, No. 11. New York: Charles Scribner, 1868.

Hallowell, A. Irving. "The Beginnings of Anthropology in America." In Frederica de Laguna, ed., *Selected Papers from the American Anthropologist*. Evanston, IL: Row, Peterson, 1960.

Hertzberg, Hazel W. *Social Studies Reform, 1880–1890*. Boulder, CO: Social Science Education Consortium, 1981.

Hewett, E. L. "Anthropology and Education." *American Anthropologist* 6 (1904): 574–75.

Higgins, Patricia J., and Ruth O. Selig, eds. *Teaching Anthropology to Students and Teachers: Reaching a Wider Audience*. Publication No. 82–1. Anthropology Curriculum Project. Athens, GA: University of Georgia, 1982.

Holm, Karen Ann, and Patricia J. Higgins, eds. *Archeology and Education: A Successful Combination for Precollegiate Students*. Publication No. 85–

   1. Anthropology Curriculum Project. Athens, GA: University of Georgia,
   1985.
Kluckholm, Clyde. *Mirror for Man.* New York: McGraw-Hill, 1949.
Larkins, A. Guy, and Michael L. Hawkins. "Trivial and Noninformative Content
   in Primary-Grade Social Studies Texts: A Second Look." *Journal of Social
   Studies Research* 14 (Winter 1990): 25–32.
Larkins, A. Guy, and Ben A. Smith. "Social Studies Textbooks Grades 1–4: A
   Review of Literature." *Journal of Social Studies Research* II (Winter 1987):
   22–30.
Maury, Matthew F. *Maury's New Complete Geography.* South Carolina ed. New
   York: American Book, 1911.
Morrissett, Irving, ed. "New In-Depth Evaluations of 26 Social Studies Curricular
   Projects, Programs, and Materials." *Social Education* 34 (November 1972):
   383, 389–90, 409–14.
Moses, Yolanda T., and Patricia J. Higgins, eds. *Anthropology and Multicultural
   Education: Classroom Applications.* Publication No. 83–1. Anthropology
   Curriculum Project. Athens, GA: University of Georgia, 1983.
National Commission on Social Studies in the Schools. *Charting a Course: Social
   Studies for the 21st Century.* Joint Project of the American Historical As-
   sociation, National Council for the Social Studies, and Organization of
   American Historians. Washington, DC: National Commission on Social
   Studies in the Schools, 1989.
National Council for the Social Studies. "The Role of the Social Studies." *Social
   Education* 26 (October 1962): 315–318.
————. "Standards for the Preparation of Social Studies Teachers." *Social Ed-
   ucation* 48 (May 1984): 357–361.
————. "Standards for the Preparation of Social Studies Teachers." *Social Ed-
   ucation* 52 (January 1988): 10–12.
————. *Social Studies Curriculum Planning Resources.* Dubuque, IA: Kendall/
   Hunt, 1990
Nimkoff, Meyer F. "Anthropology, Sociology, and Social Psychology." In Erling
   M. Hunt, ed., *High School Social Studies Perspectives.* Boston: Houghton
   Mifflin, 1962.
Oliver, Douglas. "Cultural Anthropology." In *The Social Studies and the Social
   Sciences.* Sponsored by the American Council of Learned Societies and
   the National Council for the Social Studies. New York: Harcourt, Brace
   and World, 1962.
Owen, Roger C. "Coming of Age in Anthropology." In Stanley P. Wronski and
   Donald H. Bragaw, eds., *Social Studies and Social Sciences: A Fifty Year
   Perspective.* Bulletin No. 78. Washington, DC: National Council for the
   Social Studies, 1986.
Phenix, Philip A. "The Needs of a Curriculum." In A. Harry Pussow, ed., *Cur-
   riculum Crossroads.* New York: Teachers College Press, 1962.
Rice, M. J. "Anthropology: Educational Programs." In Torsten Husen and T.
   Neville Postlethwaite, eds., *International Encyclopedia of Education,* I,
   274–76. Oxford, UK: Pergamon Press, 1985.
Sanders, Norris M., and Marlin L. Tanck. "A Critical Appraisal of Twenty-Six

National Social Studies Projects." *Social Education* 34 (April 1970): 383, 389–90, 409–14.

Selig, Ruth O., and Patricia Higgins, eds. "Practicing Anthropology in Precollege Education." Special Issue. *Practicing Anthropology* 8 (1986).

Spindler, George D. "New Trends and Applications in Anthropology." In Roy A. Price, ed., *Twenty-Eighth Yearbook of the National Council for the Social Studies: New Viewpoints in the Social Sciences*. Washington, DC: National Council for the Social Studies, 1958.

Taylor, Bob L., and Thomas L. Groom. *Social Studies Education Projects: An ASCD Index*. Washington, DC: Association for Supervision and Curriculum Development, 1971.

Tetsko, W. "Textbooks and the New Social Studies." *Social Studies* 70 (March/April 1979): 51–55.

Tyson-Bernstein, Harriet, and Arthur Woodward. "The Great Textbook Machine and Projects for Reform." *Social Education* 50 (January 1986): 41–45.

White, Leslie A. *The Science of Culture*. New York: Farrar, Straus, 1949.

Wiley, Karen B. *The NSF Science Education Controversy: M:ACOS Issues, Events, Decisions*. ERIC Clearinghouse for Social Studies/Social Science Education. Publication No. 191. Boulder, CO: Social Science Education Consortium, 1976.

Wiley, Karen B., and Douglas P. Superka. *Evaluation Studies on New Social Studies Materials*. ERIC Clearinghouse for Social Studies/Social Science Education. Publication No. 193. Boulder, CO: Social Science Education Consortium, 1977.

13

RELIGION IN THE SCHOOLS

Suzanne A. Gulledge

Teaching about religion in social studies courses need no longer be defended as appropriate and desirable. Endorsements for teaching objectively about religion are on record from sources that include the Supreme Court, the National Council for the Social Studies, the Association for Supervision and Curriculum Development, and People for the American Way. Classroom teachers, curriculum specialists, school policymakers and textbook publishers are effecting the institutionalization of what was once a controversial issue. The question that plagued teachers of social studies courses for the last quarter-century, "Should religion be included?" has been answered with a strong and resounding "yes." On the eve of the twenty-first century, the pertinent question has become, "Where, when, and how should religion be taught in social studies courses?"

REFLECTIONS

Studying about religion is justifiable in, if not vital to, all courses included under the umbrella term of "social studies." In courses about history and the development of civilizations, religion ought to be recognized as a determinative element. In courses concerned with civics and human culture, religion should be considered a dynamic and meaningful concept. In fact, religion is such a basic, essential aspect of the subject matter with which social studies is concerned that its place therein ought not to be threatened even by those who insist that the public school curriculum is overcrowded. Religion is a part of the major content of social studies courses, yet what is variable and unpredictable is the specific matter that is actually taught. A retrospective survey of the individual social studies subjects provides a helpful springboard for discussion of trends, issues, and implications for religion's future place in the social studies (see McMillan 1969).

In world history courses, religion, most often "one of the world's great religions," is introduced as a section of a chapter or as a supplementary topic of discussion. Often, religion is included as a peripheral topic, an embellishment, or one of several optional studies, rather than as an aspect of the progressive context of history. Text references to religion tend to be factual and informative rather than interpretive. One is not likely to find in most world history courses a study of religion that explores influence or meaning or that encourages interpretation of religion's relationship to historical events. Generally, less attention is given to Christian beliefs than to those held by members of other religions (Spiro 1989).

In American history courses, religion is most conspicuously included in references to settlement of the New World. These and subsequent references usually provide factual information and basic descriptions from a Eurocentric perspective (Parker 1991). Religious leaders are named, geographic settlements and numbers of followers are identified, with groups outside of the religious "mainstream" being highlighted. Usually, American history courses include only minimal references to religion, and the frequency and depth of those references tend to decrease in studies of recent history.

Civics and government courses may include material about controversial issues involving freedom of religion. Some courses include an examination of the relationship between religion and public education. The problematic area of responsible citizenship in conflict with religious beliefs is less often considered. The topic of conscientious objection to military service is the one most likely to be selected as an example of the problem when it is included in social studies courses. Societal decision making and civic participation have been major areas of focus in the social studies courses called "Civics," "Government," or "Problems of Democracy" (Barr, Barth, and Shermis 1978). With the few exceptions noted above, teaching about religion is barely noticeable in civics and government courses.

Geography relies on its "human geography" aspect as a rationale for being part of social studies. Topics within this subject include languages, settlement patterns, populations, economics, governments, and religions. The latter tends to get minimal attention except for cursory identification and "labelling" purposes. Religion generally is used as an "organizer" for classifying groups of people, rather than as a causal factor in explaining their characteristics and actions.

Economics and political science are sometimes offered as social studies electives. They have in common the idea that individuals and societies make choices and that individual decisions effect changes in societies. Marxian socialism, Smithian capitalism, the formation of governments, and the development of public policy are broad topics of concern. In both subjects, there is some uneasiness about balancing their social science roots with the aims of social studies instruction. Within economics and political science courses in public secondary schools little, if any, study of religion(s) occurs.

Psychology and anthropology may be offered as electives, but certainly not all social studies programs offer them. In spite of the basic differences in these two disciplines, at the precollege level, where social studies subjects are taught as separate courses, both psychology and anthropology tend to emphasize the impact of cultural learning on human behavior. Biological factors that influence human actions get less emphasis in high school courses than do cultural ones. Chemical, biological, and ecological factors receive less attention in anthropology and psychology courses than do those related to family ties, environment, industry, education, and cultural norms. Even with the stress on institutions in these social studies courses, religion is not usually a major topic of study in public secondary school programs.

Sociology courses, often one-semester electives, appear in social studies curricula only slightly more frequently than anthropology, psychology, and economics. Social problems and group behavior are likely to be major areas of concern in precollege courses. Courses may also be organized around the examination of social institutions. The work of Marx, Weber, and Durkheim is often mentioned, and the attention given to religion as a social institution in their writings is significant. Thus, religion is perhaps more likely to be addressed as a major topic of discussion by sociology than by other social studies subjects. Methods of teaching that incorporate inquiry and open-ended discovery are likely to be employed in sociology courses. These methods tend to provide a classroom environment that is somehow more comfortable with discussions about religion(s). Not surprisingly, therefore, it is within sociology courses that teaching about religion is most likely to be found in social studies curricula. But sociology courses are taught less frequently and are almost always electives; course materials are relatively scarce because of their limited sales potential. Consequently, teaching about religion, which might be increased significantly by the inclusion of sociology courses, remains traditionally minimal in social studies curricula (Gulledge 1983).

The courses that are most likely to include studies of religion are invariably senior high school offerings. Yet from the time when kindergartners study about various holidays, the idea of religion(s) is introduced. As elementary students compare and contrast people of different cultures, study famous historical figures, and learn the "Pledge of Allegiance" to the flag, the matter of religion is pertinent. Young children study early exploration and settlement of new worlds and the culture of Native Americans, slaves, and major ethnic groups. As they compare and contrast the nationalities of people, they also consider their cultures and religions.

It is at the junior high or middle school level that the social studies curriculum generally takes on the form of separate courses. At this level, such skills as those needed to distinguish fact from opinion and to identify propaganda and testimony are developed. Specific topics previously introduced, such as religious motivations for exploration and settlement, may be reintroduced in the middle grades. Ethnic and religious groups may be reconsidered with more emphasis on their various contributions to the course of history. Certainly by the tenth grade, studies about religion(s) in public schools occur within the separate subjects discussed above.

Discussions concerning the content of religious subject matter in social studies have been complicated by the challenge of giving due recognition to religion's place in history and culture while at the same time safeguarding the separation of church and state in public schools. Some clarification of the issue has come from the dicta and adjudication of several relevant Supreme Court cases.

In 1946 the *Everson* case demonstrated the difficulty of defining separation of church and state. The appellant in the case charged that public tax money was being used to provide aid and sustenance to some New Jersey parochial schools (*Everson* v. *Board of Education* 1946). The Court handed down a ruling that rested on a distinction between direct benefit to parochial schools and public welfare benefit to the students who attend such schools. In *Everson* the majority opinion indicated that the primary concern ought to be for the welfare of the children involved. The ruling of the Court was that the wall of separation between church and state had not been breached just because free bus transportation had been offered to children attending parochial schools as well as those at public schools since the action benefitted the child rather than the church. It is important to note that *Everson* marked the first of a series of school-and-religion cases. Schools would become a primary arena in which church and state conflicts were thrashed out.

The Court's decision in *Everson* was later questioned in the context of opinions offered in the *Engle* case (*Engle et al.* v. *Vitale et al.* 1962). Mr. Justice Douglas (who voted with the majority in *Everson*) wrote in *Engle* that, in retrospect, he found the ruling in *Everson* to have been out of line with the First Amendment. The First Amendment was applied in *Engle* in 1962 to disallow a mandated prayer recitation in New York public schools. The Court's decision was that prayer is religious and that the practice described in the case was a violation of the First Amendment prohibition against an establishment of religion. The Supreme Court denied that the decision in *Engle* was in any way hostile toward religion.

Because of their similarity, two cases, *School District of Abington Township* v. *Schempp* (1963) and *Murray* v. *Curlett*, were heard together by the Supreme Court in 1963 and are now referred to as one case (*Abington*). The question at the bar concerned Bible reading in the public schools, with a focus on a Pennsylvania statute that required ten verses of the Bible to be read, without comment, in each classroom at the opening of each school day. A child could be excused from this opening exercise if he presented a written request from his parents. In an eight-to-one decision, the Court ruled that this practice of reading the Bible as a devotional exercise violated the First Amendment "establishment clause," as applied to the states by the Fourteenth Amendment. The Court decision in *Abington* made it clear that Bible reading as a religious exercise neither had to be compulsory nor involve expenditure of public funds to be ruled unconstitutional.

Based on the dicta and adjudication of these three Supreme Court cases, several points related to public school curricula may be made. Out of the *Everson* case came the ruling that public-funding aid to religion, preference of one religion over another, or influencing students to believe or not to believe the tenets of any religion is impermissible. The *Engle* and *Abington* cases stipulated that public schools may neither sponsor or mandate devotional Bible readings or prayer, but that neutral instruction about religion could and perhaps should be offered in public schools.

By 1960, the National Council of Churches' Committee on Religion and Public Education had published a lengthy document, the thesis of which was that objective study about religion could be conducted in regular school classes (National Council of Churches 1960). The document detailed, for example, how such studies of religion might be pursued while still adhering to the objectives of whatever subject provided the context for studying religion. Curriculum projects exemplifying that premise soon followed. Most notable were the "Religions of Man" project of the Public Education Religion Studies Center at Wright State University and the Florida State "Religion in Public Schools Project" (see Association for Supervision and Curriculum Development 1987). Departments of education in several states, including North Carolina and Florida, appointed committees to oversee the implementation of study about religion in their public schools. Efforts in Florida were described in detail in a 1969 issue of *Social Education* that included a special section on "Units, Courses, and Projects for Teaching about Religion" (National Council for the Social Studies 1969).

In addition to curriculum projects, organizations devoted to public school religion studies were established in the 1960s and 1970s. At Wright State University, for example, the Public Education Religion Studies Center (PERSC) was formed. The PERSC was primarily concerned with religion studies in secondary and higher education. Assuming the study of religion to be appropriate in public school curricula, the PERSC suggested that competency in teaching religion necessitated a nonsectarian approach (Brancher et al. 1974). From its inception, this organization has promoted the objective study of religion(s) where appropriate in the public school curricula.

Critics then and now express the fear that including religion in school studies necessarily begins with the presumption that religion is intrinsically a good thing (Olafson 1967). They hold that this presumption translates into a form of indoctrination. Others are concerned that studies about religion might be expected to have a moral impact on the education of students in public schools. In response to this concern, much attention has been given to separating and distinguishing among three different matters: (1) teaching about religion, (2) values clarification, and (3) moral education. There is widespread agreement among educators that only the first of these falls within the purview of the social studies.

The academic study of religion, for at least the last forty years, has been recognized as a sensitive but necessary venture for public schools. Over the years, social studies teachers particularly have felt some pressure to acknowledge religious pluralism as well as to maintain neutrality. That pressure at various times, in various places, came from minority religious groups, the courts, and from those whose concern was pedagogical ethics. Morals, values, and religion have, during this period, been scrutinized individually, but often jumbled together, and most often separated out again in public school curriculum projects. A similar fate befell attempts to teach some type of "common core," or "common denominator," religion. Attempts to "steer clear of religion entirely," on the other hand, have been criticized both by the courts and by pedagogues who found the exclusion of religion from public school curricula intolerable (Nolte 1977).

CURRENT ISSUES AND TRENDS

What has endured is the idea that the academic study of religion is appropriate and desirable. The National Council for the Social Studies, the Association for Supervision and Curriculum Development, and the American Association of School Administrators have endorsed this view. A useful annotated bibliography compiled by Nicholas Piediscalzi (1981), of the Public Education Religion Studies Center, includes nineteen sources for material to encourage and facilitate teaching about religion in public schools in ways that are constitutionally acceptable and academically sound. Among the sources cited are numerous organizations and interest groups whose sole purpose is the promotion of public education religion studies.

The matter of specific content and the question of how and where studies about religion(s) should be incorporated into the social studies curriculum are difficult to address. Controversy and uncertainty arise in such discussions, even among those who agree that the study of religion is appropriate in social studies courses. People tend to be cautious about endorsing proposals to teach religion in public schools. Their deepest concerns are usually related specifically to content.

There is a fear on the part of some people that the curriculum followed in government-sponsored schools, especially with a Christian-influenced government, will be one that fails to portray other religions as relevant and vital faiths (Gordis 1962). Although they may acknowledge that the arguments made for objective teaching about religion are incontrovertible, some people nevertheless feel that there is a potential danger of religion studies' becoming a variation on "the camel's head under the tent." That is, they fear that there are those who would use the opportunity to teach about religion as an opening wedge for actual religious instruction. Also, some fear that course materials may be inadequate in terms of objectivity and comprehensiveness (Synagogue Council 1976).

Frequently, questions are raised about the adequacy of training for teachers to teach about religion(s). Another concern related to course content is that some parents might not allow their children to participate in some learning activities, such as visiting various places of worship. Similarly, some parents might be reluctant to have their children learn about religion from members of faiths other than their own. Furthermore, it has sometimes been suggested that, even if teachers could maintain an attitude of objectivity, this might in itself become harmful if a "public school" version of religion came to be misunderstood by students as a composite of all religions.

The issue of objectivity is indeed a legitimate concern with regard to teaching about religions in public schools, yet it has been applied in this matter, perhaps unfairly, more conspicuously than it is in regard to other areas of study. The fact is that the same standards of scholarship and impartiality should be applied to all areas of study. The more important concern, perhaps, should be over motivation. If the suppression or the promotion of any religion were to be the motivation, purpose, or effect of a given course of study, then clearly it would be unacceptable in a public school curriculum.

If motivation is considered a crucial factor in evaluating the integrity of public school religion studies, then not only behavioral but also affective objectives must be considered. The guidelines prepared by the National Council for the Social Studies (1984), "Study about Religions in the Social

Studies Curriculum,'' address both attitudinal and academic rationales. Attitudes, goals, and even the source of a teacher's knowledge about a given subject are valid pedagogical concerns. It is important that instructional materials be scrutinized and that goals and objectives be articulated in teaching about religion or any other subject. The teacher presenting a lesson that includes material about religion in a social studies course, for example, should be sure that the material serves a specific goal of social studies. In short, the mandate for teaching about religion in public schools imposes upon the teacher a responsibility to match the pedagogical purpose of the material on religion with the epistemological structure in which that material is taught.

The influence and thus the responsibility of the teacher encompass things both spoken and unspoken, things both intended and implied. Educators have some responsibility not only for the intellectual content of what they present, but also for whatever they may stimulate students to feel and believe. The social studies teacher, for example, who incorporates some academic study of religion, can potentially enlarge or diminish, attract or repel various religious commitments not only through verbal, concrete instruction, but also through abstract or nonverbal communication. Responsible decision making in the area of content and instruction takes into account the "affective effects" of study about religion(s) in social studies courses.

Contemporary statements about social studies goals and objectives are likely to refer to multicultural understanding, citizenship education, global consciousness, and teaching civic values and responsibility. NCSS President C. Frederick Risinger (1991) has referred to these concerns as dilemmas which "will be on the social studies agenda for some time." Admonitions to teachers both to incorporate material about religion in their social studies courses and to do so objectively certainly make their responsibilities seem heavier, if not unbearable. Charles C. Haynes has effectively pointed out how *not* including studies of religion, plus ignorance about religion, have adversely affected the goals of citizenship education:

The neglect of religion is causing serious problems for the schools. . . . Ironically, the very fear of controversy that kept religion out of textbooks and schools has helped to create the present controversy. . . . It is a matter of some urgency for the health of our constitutional system that we do a better job of educating citizens about our first freedom. (Haynes 1987: 305)

What is scarce in current literature is information on how to teach about religion(s), and do so objectively, while also teaching civic decision making, global responsibility, and citizenship.

Actually, standardized testing of student knowledge and the teacher-accountability movement may serve to reduce some of the tension between advocates of moral and values education and those promoting objective teaching about religion in social studies classes. One predictable outcome of programs to test, measure, and assess teaching is that instruction becomes more "objective" in response. Specific content is more clearly identified and defined. An example of this is found in North Carolina's recent revisions of the state's "Standard Course of Study and Teacher Handbook." Additions and changes made to existing instructional objectives in response to assessment demands have served to "integrate an understanding of the role of religion more fully into the Social Studies curriculum" (North Carolina 1989: 2). Testing and accountability movements that lead to revisions in courses of study may actually simplify and clarify the place of religion content in social studies curricula.

What falls within the realm of moral or values education is to facilitate students' understanding of the process of coping with ethical decision making, faith commitments, and religious affiliations. Moral and values education and religion studies differ also in that it is possible to conceive of the former as instruction in the skills and concepts of moral thought rather than as a separate field of study. The skills of ethical decision making do not conform to traditional disciplinary boundaries. In contrast, study about religion is much more of a field or a part of such a field as social studies. Certainly, as has been pointed out, values education and religion studies in social studies courses need to be clearly distinguished. What should not happen is the reduction of all information about religion in social studies subjects to merely dry facts: numbers of believers, names of leaders, names of religious holidays, and so on. Probing, questioning, challenging, critical thinking, and inquiry should not be considered off-limits when religion is discussed in history or sociology or any other social studies course. The social studies greatly need to be enlivened in all content areas, including studies about religion. This will require much more than a rearranged scope and sequence of the curriculum. Herein lies a major shortcoming of the publication, *Charting a Course* (National Commission 1989). The proposals set forth in this report made no real progress toward breathing life into the social studies, as evinced by the few, lukewarm references to including religion studies. Again, studying about religion would amount to little more than injecting a smattering of dry, inert facts, if the National Commission proposals were to be implemented.

Provoking thought, exploring problems, attempting to make respectful judgments—these approaches need to be a part of an improved social studies curriculum. Shirley Engle's astute assessment of *Charting a Course,* entitled "The Commission Report and Citizenship Education," makes this point very well. According to Engle, "The Social Studies has given students experience in remembering facts but little experience in

using facts to think about any problem past or present" (Engle 1990: 431).
The "moribund curriculum" does need to be ignited. Studies about re-
ligion(s) can be an effective spark in social studies classes. Well-informed,
skilled teachers can handle sensitive and controversial issues in the classroom. Studies about religion do not have to be feared or "handled with
kid gloves." The recommendations of *Charting a Course* were little more
than patronizing and offered nothing new to the matter of teaching about
religion in social studies courses.

Donald Bragaw's introduction to the NCSS bulletin *Social Studies and
Social Sciences: A Fifty Year Perspective,* reminds us that social studies
teachers ought to use the material and methodologies of the humanities
and other disciplines as resources (Wronski and Bragaw 1986). The heavy
reliance on textbook facts alone is clearly insufficient for proper treatment
of religion(s) in social studies classes. The "research, reading and thinking
time" that Bragaw recommends for teachers is desperately needed: social
studies incorporates a massive amount of information, and teaching it
properly requires extensive reading, writing, and discussion. Many social
studies topics are, like religion, either controversial or multifaceted. Opportunities for teachers to be academically and technically brought up to
date and stimulated are vital but sadly lacking, especially in the area of
social studies. Well-prepared, motivated teachers are, without a doubt,
the most important resources for the proper incorporation of studies about
religion in social studies classes.

In summary, the recommendations made to teachers who incorporate
material on religion into their subjects are not unlike the pedagogical
guidelines recommended for incorporation of other topics taught in public
schools. The various concerns expressed about the study of religion (e.g.,
the acknowledgment of pluralism, the preservation of objectivity, the
assurance of accuracy in representing various groups) are appropriate
concerns in other curricular areas as well (Wade 1973). Religion studies
are somewhat different from other academic areas because of the legal
issues in which they have been embroiled. It is imperative that public
school educators know about, understand, and respect those legal aspects.
The concerns and criticisms leveled at public school religion studies
should not be perceived as a formidable, even insurmountable, barrier to
their incorporation into school curricula. Including religion studies in any
curricular area requires the teacher to adhere to the principles of good
instruction in that subject area.

PROJECTIONS

Teaching about religion in the context of an academic subject is an
appropriate place for such study in public schools, and there is reason to
hope that such study will be increasingly found there. All social studies

courses include topics to which religion is relevant. The strength and persistence of some determined interest groups are putting these principles into practice. The study of religion(s) should not be avoided just because the controversial nature of its history makes a teacher uncomfortable. Selection of the content for religion studies should be made on the basis of the same criteria applied to other materials for the given course and in light of its goals and objectives. The methodologies used to teach about religion should be applied consistently as well. If studies about religion(s) are fully integrated into social studies curricula, as they should be, such material about religion will not be "added on" or used as supplementary "fluff."

Increasingly, public school classrooms are populated by students with diverse backgrounds and cultural identities. Pluralism and multiculturalism are phenomena that children more often encounter now in everyday school life. This can be an asset to instructional programs in numerous ways. The mere presence of diversity in increasing numbers of classrooms will serve to remind teachers to acknowledge cultural, ethnic, and religious differences in our society. It will spur teachers to think about incorporating multi-religious and multicultural concepts into their social studies curricula.

Because so many subjects fall within the purview of social studies, the curriculum planner and teacher must constantly refer to the goals, objectives, and structural aspects of the given discipline to guide inquiry. The "knowledge explosion," by making materials more accessible, will prove helpful to social studies teachers, although in other ways it may add confusion and the burden of selection. There is no denying that primary source materials are very important and should be extensively used in teaching about religion(s). Their proper use ought to be coupled with such modes as inquiry, discussion, and reflective thinking, which are also very important to teaching about religion as well as other social studies topics.

The so-called knowledge explosion is coupled with a need for information-processing skills, which integrate active student participation and data manipulation. Also valuable for studies about religion and social studies in general is the related emphasis on developing and putting to use the student's capacity to process information. Ideally, a student is called upon to organize information, identify problems, generate hypotheses, and employ a specific terminology. Such an information-processing model is concerned with social and self-development and with cultural and historical relationships. What should be challenged and developed is the student's capacity to integrate and process information. When this is accomplished, the purposes and goals of social studies and of teaching about religion are well served.

The social studies promote the view that society is a system of interrelated parts. Religion may be considered a part of social living that influences and is influenced by other parts, for in its social manifestations religion is dynamic and functional. The treatment of religion in public schools need not deny that religion may also be something more than a human projection. It is appropriate to allow for the broadest possible definition of religion in this context, that is, one which accommodates animism, totemism, theistic beliefs, and humanistic philosophies. All of these may be defined as religions, depending on the degree to which adherents of the particular "ism" ascribe some transcendental importance to its values. An expansive, functional definition of religion has several advantages that make it especially useful for social studies classes.

A functional definition of religion, in contrast to a theoretical one, could accommodate civil religion, new religions, and cross-cultural, transhistorical, and changing aspects of established religions. Religion would be defined by its social functions; thus the content of religious beliefs and practices would be of less concern than their social consequences. A point of consensus somewhere between a narrow sectarian definition and a catch-all definition, ideally one that accounts for religion's varied functions in history and society, is what the social studies teacher is likely to find most useful.

A definition of religion that might prove useful for social studies in the twenty-first century is one that can be derived from the field of study known as "the sociology of religion." Peter Berger (1967) defined religion as a human enterprise which may include something beyond, and unincorporated by, the limits of social-scientific inquiry. Robert Bellah (1970) elaborated on the "something beyond" as a religious myth or symbol which should be acknowledged and respected on its own terms. Bellah warned that traditions, symbols, and myths should not be subjected to a superimposed reformulation that presumes to substitute for the believer's understanding in a definition of religion. The sociologist of religion Emile Durkheim emphasized the importance of distinguishing the sacred from the profane so that religion might be defined as a unified system of beliefs and practices in the realm of the sacred (Durkheim 1965: 62).

The definitions proposed by Durkheim, Berger, and Bellah can be useful models as we attempt to define religion for the purposes of social studies in the next century. An appropriate definition would include the idea that religion is an institution established on premises of faith and on value systems. Religion reflects those things that people consider to be of ultimate sacred significance in the universe and involves the ritual practices of worship and other behavior or actions that follow from belief. This definition has a distinctly sociological flavor, yet it would need little revision to be employed in other social studies subjects, including history and civics. Broad and functional, rather than theoretical, it supersedes those narrow, sectarian definitions of religion that have been at the heart of the historical and legal controversies vexing the issue of religion and/ in public education.

Teaching about religion in future social studies courses is not likely to be totally unproblematic, given the persistent concerns that have always provoked controversy whenever religion and American public education are juxtaposed. However, in the context of serving the purposes of social studies by considering religion, there should be no need to distinguish study about religion from any other academic topic. It seems improbable that the history classroom would become a battleground for a dispute over constitutional rights if the instruction is pedagogically sound. Furthermore, it is difficult to imagine that anyone, whatever his or her beliefs, could advocate ignoring the impact of religion on history or on human social behavior. Whatever a person might believe about the validity of religious claims, no one can deny the importance of religion as a motivation and explanation for human action (Purpel 1989: 66–68).

The location of religious studies within the context of history and other social studies subjects should remain the same in the twenty-first century. Teacher education courses should include more specific methods for incorporating those studies. Furthermore, teachers and students should continue to reflect on the history of the controversy over religion and public education. This should be a part of social studies curricula for historical, sociological, and pedagogical reasons. The historical investigation of this issue serves as a reminder that no pedagogy lacks an ethical dimension. The act of teaching is in itself an ethically significant transaction between teachers and students. One aspect of the teacher's ethical responsibility is to understand the subject matter as thoroughly as possible. The goals, objectives, and methods of a course ought to be determined before content material is selected. Social studies courses, properly and thoroughly taught, will inevitably include some study of religion(s).

REFERENCES

American Association of School Administrators. *Religion in the Public Schools.* New York: Harper and Row, 1964.

Association for Supervision and Curriculum Development. *Religion in the Curriculum: A Report from the ASCD Panel on Religion in the Curriculum.* Alexandria, VA: Association for Supervision and Curriculum Development, 1987.

Barr, Robert, James Barth, and Samuel Shermis. *The Nature of the Social Studies.* Palm Springs, CA: ETC Publications, 1978.

Bellah, Robert N. "Christianity and Symbolic Realism." *Journal for the Scientific Study of Religion* 9 (Summer 1970): 89–96.

Berger, Peter L. *The Sacred Canopy.* New York: Doubleday, 1967.

Brancher, Peter. *PERSC Guidebook*. Dayton, OH: Wright State University, Public Education Religion Studies Center, 1974.

Durkheim, Emile. *The Elementary Forms of the Religious Life*. New York: Free Press, 1965.

Engle et al. v. *Vitale et al., 370* U.S. 421 (1962).

Engle, Shirley H. "The Commission Report and Citizenship Education." *Social Education* 54 (November/December 1990): 431–33.

Everson v. *Board of Education of the Township of Ewing et al., 330* U.S. 1 (1946).

Gordis, Robert. *The Root and the Branch*. Chicago: University of Chicago Press, 1962.

Gulledge, Suzanne. "Teaching about Religion in Public Secondary School Sociology Courses." Ph.D. diss., Duke University, 1983.

Haynes, Charles C. "Religious Literacy in the Social Studies." *Social Education* 51 (November/December 1987): 488–90.

———. *Religion in American History: What to Teach and How*. Alexandria, VA: Association for Supervision and Curriculum Development, 1990.

Haynes, Charles C., ed., special issue. "Taking Religion Seriously in the Social Studies." *Social Education* 54 (September 1990): 276–310.

McMillan, Richard C. "Religious Content in Selected Social Studies Textbooks." Ph.D. diss., Duke University, 1969.

National Commission on Social Studies in the Schools. *Charting a Course: Social Studies for the 21st Century*. Washington, DC: National Commission on Social Studies in the Schools, 1989.

National Council for the Social Studies. "Units, Courses, and Projects for Teaching about Religions." *Social Education* 33 (December 1969): 917–30.

———. *Study about Religions in the Social Studies Curriculum*. Washington, DC: National Council for the Social Studies, 1984.

National Council of the Churches of Christ of the U.S. *Religion and Public Education*. Washington, DC: National Council of Churches, 1960.

Nolte, M. Chester. "Why the 'Ban' on 'Religion' in the Public Schools is Backfiring on Our Children." *The American Schoolboard Journal* 164 (July 1977): 24, 37.

Nord, Warren A. "Taking Religion Seriously." *Social Education* 54 (September 1990): 287–90.

North Carolina Department of Public Instruction. "Placement of Religion in the Social Studies Curriculum" (January 1989).

Olafson, Frederick A. "Teaching about Religion: Some Reservations." In Theodore Sizer, ed., *Religion and Public Education*. Boston: Houghton Mifflin, 1967.

Panoch, James V., and David L. Barr. "Should We Teach about Religions in Our Public Schools?" *Social Education* 33 (December 1969): 910–13.

Parker, Walter C. *Renewing the Social Studies Curriculum*. Alexandria, VA: Association for Supervision and Curriculum Development, 1991.

People for the American Way. *Looking at History: A Review of Major U.S. History Textbooks*. Washington, DC: People for the American Way, 1986.

Piediscalzi, Nicholas. "An Annotated Bibliography on Public Education Religion Studies for the Beginning Teacher." *Social Education* 45 (January 1981): 32–34.

Purpel, David E. *The Moral and Spiritual Crisis In Education*. New York: Bergin and Garvey, 1989.

"Religious Studies: Appropriate and Essential in Today's Classroom." *A.S.C.D. News Exchange*. Washington DC: Association for Supervision and Curriculum Development, 1979.

Risinger, C. Frederick. "President's Message." *The Social Studies Professional* (May/June 1991): 2.

School District of Abington Township v. *Schempp*, 374 U.S. 203, 225, 300 (1963).

Spiro, Daniel A. "Public Schools and the Road to Religious Neutrality." *Phi Delta Kappan* 70 (June 1989): 761–63.

Synagogue Council of America and National Community Relations Advisory Council. *Religious Studies in Public Schools: The Jewish Response*. New York: Synagogue Council of America, 1976.

Vanausdall, Jeanette. "Religion Studies in the Public Schools." *The Social Studies* 70 (November/December 1979): 251–53.

Wade, Stephen H. "Epistemology and the Matching of Intentions with Models in Religious Teaching." *Religious Education* 70 (May 1973): 9–15.

Wronski, Stanley P., and Donald H. Bragaw, eds. *Social Studies and Social Sciences: A Fifty Year Perspective*. Washington, DC: National Council for the Social Studies, 1986.

14

WRITING IN THE SOCIAL STUDIES

R. Baird Shuman

REFLECTIONS

Throughout the latter two-thirds of this century, the jobs of social studies teachers in American secondary schools have frequently been ill defined. During the progressive movement of the 1930s and 1940s, the teaching of such leftover curricular catastrophes as telephone etiquette and dating deportment frequently fell to social studies teachers, displacing in their classes some of the important topics they were better equipped to teach.

College graduates who had entered teaching with degrees in history, sociology, anthropology, political science, geography, economics, social psychology, and various combinations thereof all fell under the broad rubric that designated the basic minimal substantive requirements for social studies certification in various states. Once certified, such teachers were in many cases called upon to teach a daunting array of subjects, enough to make many of them feel inadequate. Contemporary social studies teachers may be understandably reluctant to have writing added to all of the other things they are expected to teach.

The most commonly used methods books in social studies rarely alluded to having students write, unless it was in their discussion of essay examinations, which were fast being replaced in most curricula by objective tests. Edgar B. Wesley wrote that "the advantage of the essay examination does not rest upon its ability to measure the higher level mental processes; it has no advantages over the term paper in developing the ability to organize and present materials logically'' (Wesley 1950: 542). Wesley contended that essay examinations were not measurement devices because measurement required ''the ascertainment of a rank order of achievement'' (Wesley 1952: 419), which essay examinations could not deliver in as clear-cut a way as objective tests could.

Wesley was not opposed to using writing in the social studies classroom, but he was more concerned with product than with process. He allowed that carefully written work helped provide teachers with information about students' ''legibility, which ones can spell, construct sentences, form paragraphs, maintain a sequence of thought, and organize materials'' (ibid.). He was clearly not yet of the modern frame of mind that promotes writing as a way of knowing and of discovering ideas. When it came to measuring student achievement in the social studies, he cast his lot with objective testing.

From its inception, the National Council for the Social Studies (NCSS) was interested in interdisciplinary approaches to teaching social studies, which are, by their very nature, interdisciplinary. In 1954, the NCSS published *Social Understanding through Literature* by G. Robert Carlsen and Richard S. Alm (1954), both professors of English education who were prominent members and officers of the National Council of Teachers of English (NCTE).

During the 1950s, the core curriculum pervaded many junior high schools and some senior high schools. It was usually organized so that one teacher meeting students in double or triple consecutive periods taught English and social studies, interrelating them as much as possible. Sometimes core arrangements embraced other subjects—mathematics, introductory science, or a foreign language—as well.

Writing was usually implicit in the social studies curriculum, but teachers were not expected to teach it as such nor were they much interested in using it in any organized way as a means of knowing and understanding; instead, they generally viewed it as a product that reflected students' ability to present complex ideas in some coherent, well-organized, and unified form.

The Rush to School-wide Reading Programs

In the mid-1950s, Rudolph Flesch's *Why Johnny Can't Read* (Flesch 1955) revealed to taxpayers already generally cynical about public education one of the darkest blemishes on its pockmarked complexion: many students finish school without having achieved the skills of basic, functional literacy! Administrators, driven certainly by a degree of public pressure that in some quarters approached hysteria, began to focus on problems of basic literacy, particularly reading. Such administrators aimed to make every teacher a teacher of reading and rushed to offer school-wide, interdisciplinary reading programs that predated and, in many instances, provided the models for similar school-wide, interdisciplinary programs in writing.

As the reading-across-the-curriculum movement grew, sociolinguists like William Labov presented research findings that explained some of the social dynamics of modern education, particularly as they affected the learning processes and the desire of minority students to learn (Labov 1970, 1972; Labov, Cohen, Robbins, and Lewis 1968). Superintendents of schools assumed with evangelical ardor the postures of reading zealots—and many of them were indeed wholly sincere in promoting the extensive reading programs for which an aroused public clamored. Educators like Daniel Fader and Elton McNeil demonstrated that students—presumably any and all students—could become "hooked on books" (Fader and McNeil 1968) if only conditions were right.

As school districts revved up to create such conditions, publishers, fully aware of how much profit there could be in promoting basic skills, flooded the schools with all sorts of reading programs, and reading became increasingly a school-wide activity, in some instances involving everyone—including school secretaries and custodial staff—in specified daily or weekly reading periods. A dyspeptic Neil Postman (1970), recognizing the economic and political implications of this snowballing movement, ruminated, with his characteristically penetrating insights, on the implications of this trend in "The Politics of Reading."

As school-wide reading programs spread throughout the country and received favorable press, educators recognized that reading and writing are closely related—although different—activities in that reading is a decoding activity, writing an encoding one. Teachers as well as employers of high school graduates realized that students were plagued by severe deficiencies in their reading and writing, sometimes to the point of being unable to hold the entry-level jobs many of them sought after graduation. Deficits in literacy skills became red ink on the balance sheets of many American industries. Enhancing these skills became a desperate, market-driven educational priority.

Moving toward Writing-Across-the-Curriculum (WAC)

Many colleges and universities—even the most selective institutions—recognized that a large number of their entering students could not read or write well enough to succeed in college-level work. Their voices, too, joined in the chorus of those demanding greater emphasis on teaching the skills of basic literacy at the precollegiate level. A larger number of colleges and universities assumed considerable responsibility for instituting college-level programs that would result in similar ends.

The cover story of the December 8, 1975 issue of *Newsweek* picked up on Flesch's title and called its exposé of the writing situation "Why Johnny Can't Write." Although one may question the article's objectivity, it focused public attention on deficits others had already noticed. This publicity helped to create an atmosphere in which schools could develop programs to alleviate what was generally recognized as a serious problem.

CURRENT TRENDS AND ISSUES

Researchers have worked assiduously to unravel the mysteries of how people communicate effectively, and from their investigations has come a growing recognition through the years of the ineffectiveness of some of the most widely accepted teaching practices in writing. Realizing the fallacies of some common conceptions of the nature of writing, teachers began to inform and reform their classroom practices. It soon became apparent that what English teachers were learning through reading their professional journals, attending workshops (particularly those modeled on the Bay Area Writing Project), and experimenting in their own classrooms had implications for all teachers, not merely those who taught English.

What the Research Revealed

Fundamental research in writing revealed that in schools, although written work was often regarded as a product—a paper to be handed in, marked up, and graded—the product that students hand in represents merely the tip of a large, complex, psycholinguistic perplex that has led up to this final, visible outcome. Lev Vygotsky had drawn the attention of many educators to the connection between language and thinking with his landmark study, *Thought and Language,* in which he wrote, "The relation between thought and word is a living process; thought is born through words. A word devoid of thought is a dead thing" (Vygotsky 1962: 153). This statement proved to be one of the most important postulates of the ensuing WAC programs because it enabled teachers to recognize that writing is a process closely related to thinking and necessary to both discovering and organizing ideas. Writing as a process quickly came to be acknowledged as a significant means of learning and knowing.

Teachers gradually became convinced that process was as important as product in writing, that it in fact decreed an indispensable sequence of steps for everyone who wrote. If teachers require students to submit products (finished papers), but pay little heed to the processes by which those products are achieved, student writing will be predictably be substandard, and some potentially able writers will perform at low levels. More significantly, many students who emerge from product-oriented writing programs may be ill-equipped to meet the writing demands placed upon them in the workplace or in institutions of higher learning because they will not have learned the process through which such writing is successfully generated.

Janet Emig's doctoral dissertation reported on the composing processes of twelfth grade students (Emig 1971), as determined through intensive observation of how four successful high school seniors went about producing pieces of writing. Emig observed her subjects in the physical act of writing. She had them talk into a recording machine to tell what they were thinking and doing as they composed. Emig learned that, as these students wrote, they gave life to ideas, making them visible by simply translating them into the written, syntactic structures they produced.

As imperfect, limited, and artificial as Emig's technique necessarily was, it revealed a great deal about the processes through which writers pass as they move toward producing a desired product, such as an essay or a review. It also revealed that the very act of writing leads people to more writing, to more visualization and elucidation of ideas. In some cases, as writing proceeds, it begins to take on a life of its own, articulating insights that writers did not know they had. Although Emig could not get into her subjects' minds, by doing the next best thing, she gained valuable insights into how people compose and into what the process of writing can do to generate ideas, to order and shape abstract material into realities.

In a later study, Emig identified the protocols by which people write as *enactive* (learning by what one does), *iconic* (learning visually), and *symbolic* (learning through figurative representation) (Emig 1977: 123–24). These techniques occur simultaneously during the writing process and result in outcomes that may exceed teachers' initial expectations of how students can use writing to generate unanticipated insights as they write.

A. D. Van Nostrand, conducting an experiment that required students to take small, specific bits of information and write about them in some analytical way, found that eighty-five percent of the students "incorporated new information beyond the first stated principle of relationship" (Van Nostrand 1979: 179). The implication of this finding is that when they write, writers discover through association information that they sometimes did not realize they possessed and immediately integrate this new information into the information on which they had been focusing.

At about the time when Emig reported on her initial research, a group of researchers in Great Britain headed by James Britton was investigating the kinds of writing students do. Their survey of two thousand samples of student writing produced at four different grade levels revealed that sixty-four percent of that writing was what the group classified as *trans-*

actional—that is, formal writing that people produce to inform, instruct, or persuade others, roughly what colleges and universities call *expository writing*. This group found that among the secondary school seniors in their survey, eighty-four percent, rather than the average sixty-four percent of the writing in the broader group, was transactional—that is, product oriented. The writing that they designated *poetic*—essentially creative writing—accounted for eighteen percent of student writing in the sample, but for only seven percent of the seniors' writing. *Expressive* writing—the kind that people do more for themselves than for external audiences—accounted for six percent of the total papers and four percent of the senior papers (Britton, Burgess, Martin, McLeod, and Rosen 1975).

This study suggests that, although teachers made writing assignments and although students completed the assignments, schools did little to encourage them to explore the writing process and, presumably, offered few students step-by-step instruction in how to write. It also seemed that most of the minimal instruction given by teachers was essentially judgmental and often negative in tone: usually a paper was graded and returned, with the errors noted, as a *fait accompli* and seldom with any opportunity or encouragement to revise. Furthermore, much of the writing for classes other than English was graded solely for content. Generally, the effectiveness of the writing style did not influence the grade, communicating to students that adequate writing did not matter, except in English classes.

The rush to establish WAC programs in the 1980s was stimulated by a combination of the newly publicized research findings about writing as a process and the training programs for teachers that suggested ways to incorporate writing throughout the total curriculum. The focus now shifted to teaching writing within specific curricular contexts, within such subjects as the social studies, mathematics, and the natural sciences.

Research conducted by Arthur Applebee during the early 1980s exploded the myth that secondary school students do most of their writing in English classes. In a study that included close observation in two schools as well as a complementary national study that monitored 13,293 minutes of classroom activity in six subject fields taught by a total of 754 teachers, Applebee found that while forty-one percent of class time in English is spent on writing activities, forty-eight percent of class time in science involves writing. Applebee also discovered that thirty-nine percent of the writing done in English classes involved fill-in-the-blank kinds of exercises, while fifty-three percent of the writing done in science classes was at the sentence level (Applebee 1982a, 1982b). Much of the writing in science classes would probably be classified, by Britton's designation, as *expressive*—notetaking, jottings about experiments, and other writing that was done for the students' own benefit and was not graded. Classes whose teachers require no formal writing from students can, indeed, still be classes in which a great deal of writing is demanded—more by the nature of the subject matter than by the teachers.

The Writing Program at Michigan Tech

The first thoroughgoing WAC program at the college level was established at Michigan Technological University in 1977. Its aim was to make writing an integral part of the learning process in every class on campus. This program became the model for many college and university WAC programs and has provided a major impetus for establishing such programs in secondary schools as well.

Toby Fulwiler, the driving force behind this program, wanted teachers to be guided by three fundamental understandings:

1. that the act of composing a piece of writing is a complex intellectual process;
2. that writing is a mode of learning as well as communicating; and
3. that people have trouble writing for a variety of reasons. (Fulwiler 1986: 21)

The Michigan Tech program, which faculty members—particularly those in the sciences and in engineering—greeted suspiciously at first, was soon able to claim and document significant learning gains among students in various fields of engineering and the sciences. Their performances on national standardized tests improved, and much of this improvement seemed attributable to the deeper understanding that students had developed about subject matter of their writing. Many of the reservations initially felt by the Michigan Tech faculty are still felt by teachers at any level who are suddenly asked to emphasize writing more than they have been accustomed to doing.

Do I Know Enough English to Teach Writing?

Teachers outside English departments, particularly in secondary schools, frequently ask this question or phrase their reservation more directly, declaring "I'm not good enough in English to teach writing." Because many of them do not view themselves as exemplary writers, they feel inadequate to teach writing. Their expressed fears reveal that they view writing strictly as a product and that they are unaware of what WAC programs seek to promote—learning through engaging in a discovery process that involves several kinds of written discourse.

Essentially what is asked of teachers who participate in WAC programs is (1) that they make available new opportunities for students to write regularly in their classes; and (2) that they begin to consider the effectiveness and clarity of expression as a significant element in evaluating the work their students submit. In some cases, teachers routinely offer instruction in research and reporting techniques within their discipline. Many of them, particularly those who require research papers, have been offering this sort of writing instruction all along.

What hesitant teachers must come to realize is that writing regularly is a major step toward learning the substantive material of any discipline. Through writing, students make connections that might otherwise evade them. They begin to see patterns emerging that give them a more comprehensive view of a subject than they would derive from simply listening to lectures and reading textbooks about it. All at once, writers become participants in a process that leads to specific, identifiable learning outcomes.

Creating Opportunities for Students to Write

The learning climate in social studies classrooms—indeed, in all classrooms—can be enhanced by making some writing activity a specific part of every day's routine. Most of the writing that students produce need not and should not be graded. The following techniques have worked well for some teachers:

1. Begin each class hour by having students write a five-minute journal entry that summarizes what they learned in class the preceding day.
2. End each class period by having students write a short journal entry that summarizes what went on in class that day. Do one, not both, of these on a regular basis. Look through the journals occasionally, but do not grade them.
3. Before embarking on classroom discussion, ask students to jot down at least three facts they think are pertinent to what is to be discussed.
4. Teach students how to outline, then have them outline a paragraph, section, or chapter from their textbook.
5. Have students keep a notebook in which they jot down at least one entry a day about some current event that parallels something being covered in class.
6. Have students keep a notebook in which they brainstorm about elements of their world that they would like to change.
7. Occasionally have students rewrite a specific passage in their textbook that they have had difficulty understanding, aiming in their rewrite for greater clarity without loss of essential content. (Shuman 1984: 56–57)

Such tactics create a writing atmosphere in social studies classes.

Introducing Writing into the Social Studies Program

Stephen Tchudi has indicated a number of ways in which writing can be integrated centrally into social studies programs. Focusing on what has already been accomplished in some history courses, he reports that "students have written a range of local histories, involved themselves in letter-writing campaigns on current issues, created fictionalized news broadcasts about historical events, and written reports on the history and impact of science and technology" (Tchudi 1986: 46). Such activities are appropriate in most of the social studies. Keeping courses in touch with the real world is one way of making students value and see meaning in them, particularly in an age when cultural diversity is the hallmark of public education and of society in the United States.

Teachers can devise situations that enable students to engage in various levels of writing with the aim of producing something that will be distributed to readers, possibly a mimeographed or photocopied magazine that will reach an audience within or outside the school. Eliot Wigginton's Foxfire Program (1972) had just such modest beginnings, and it has grown into an enterprise of which a whole, highly worthwhile multidisciplinary curriculum is composed in the public schools of Rabun Gap, Georgia.

The Foxfire program, which has been adapted for use in many school districts, is a systematic project in oral history culminating in a publishable product. Students use a wide variety of communication skills—brainstorming, outlining, interviewing, reporting, consulting, revising, proofreading, and organizing—to gather the information they need to produce a unified work. Although Foxfire had humble, strictly local beginnings and distributed its mimeographed publication only locally, it has since led to the publication and national distribution of a string of Foxfire books. A Broadway play, *Foxfire,* was based on the materials the students in Wigginton's classes uncovered and reported on over the years. In 1989, Wigginton received a MacArthur "genius" grant for his efforts.

Samuel Totten notes that students who, as part of their school work, have collected oral histories can also benefit from reading oral histories. He has complied an extensive bibliography of such works, most of them easily available to teachers. Totten says that "because a person's vital concern about a social issue has its roots in personal beliefs, opinions, and experiences, oral history is one of the most efficacious and fascinating ways to tap into such sources of concern" (Totten 1989: 114). He uses the reading of oral histories as a means of enticing students to continue gathering such histories from the sources that are readily available to them. Such activities create valuable opportunities for students to exercise their writing skills in a variety of ways with specific outcomes and audiences in mind. Writing thus becomes for them both an essential instrument for communicating and a way of learning. A great deal of expressive writing—notetaking, identifying people to be interviewed, formulating interview questions, and outlining—precedes the actual writing up of the information students gather. Preparing the material for publication involves students in a combination of poetic (creative) and transactional writing. Getting the material into its final form forces students to make decisions about the mechanics of expression, usage, organization, logic, and rhetorical style. Involvement in a process of this sort enables students to learn a great deal about responsibility, about coordinating people's efforts, and about the need to meet deadlines.

Interactive Notetaking

The most frequent form of expressive writing is probably notetaking. For many students, this is simply a process of putting on paper comments about what they have read or heard in lectures. Stephen Tchudi suggests that notetaking in all subjects can be more than just a mechanical process. Tchudi urges his students to use their notes in order to "interact constantly with their material—critically, analytically, aesthetically, *personally*" (Tchudi 1986: 22 [Tchudi's emphasis]).

To achieve this end, Tchudi suggests that his students ask themselves: "What do you think of this material? What amazes you? What did you know already? What puzzles you? What makes you angry?" (ibid.). Whereas many notes that students take in class become so copious as to be unusable, notes of the sort that Tchudi suggests engage students in a critical dialogue with their material. The notes need not be referred to again; they have served the necessary learning function merely by having been made. In some cases, the dialogue they engender will also provide a firm basis for future thought, writing, and in-class discussion.

PROJECTIONS

Seers from Nostradamus to Jeanne Dixon have poor track records, being wrong more often than they are right. It is, however, necessary to look ahead and to make some attempt to identify trends if one wishes to plan curricula sensibly. Therefore, a few projections are appropriate at this point.

Every indication is that literacy and "oracy" will be important curriculum-wide concerns in the years immediately ahead; attempts to isolate communication skills from other elements of the curriculum will not be well-received by a public clamoring for the schools to produce young people who can think analytically and communicate the fruits of their thinking in coherent, organized ways.

Research Directions

The most recent comprehensive overview of research in the teaching of social studies, *The Handbook of Research on Social Studies Teaching and Learning,* edited by James P. Shaver (1991) and commissioned by the National Council for the Social Studies, indicates in its fifty-three

chapters where the best minds in the field think social studies education
is heading.

Robert L. Gilstrap's chapter, "Writing for Social Studies," states cat-
egorically that writing in the social studies will receive strong emphasis
in all grades, K–12. Two-thirds of Gilstrap's extended chapter reviews
research that shows how learning outcomes in the social studies are enhanced and made more permanent by having students write regularly in
and outside of class. Gilstrap bemoans the fact that most writing in social
studies classes is still done for purposes of evaluation rather than for the
learning outcomes it can produce, but he is sanguine about the likelihood
that the emphasis will shift and that writing will be used increasingly to
help students master those higher-level skills that they need in order to
speculate, hypothesize, and theorize. He notes that research conducted
over the last half century has shown writing to have an almost magical
power to transform the way that students process information.

Gilstrap's review of research findings considers

1. the kinds of writing students do in social studies;

2. the methods of incorporating writing into social studies that work best;

3. the ways that writing can be used to improve student learning; and

4. the kinds of environments that influence writing activities. (Gilstrap 1991)

Teacher Involvement in Writing Activities

When writing comes to be viewed in the broad terms suggested by this
chapter and by Gilstrap's review of research in the field, social studies
teachers' most significant contribution will be to provide students with
the opportunity and encouragement to write regularly about the subject
matter of their courses. They need to encourage the kinds of prewriting
activities that lead to well-focused transactional writing; they need to
encourage peer evaluation of student writing and extensive revisions by
students in response to such evaluations.

It is, perhaps, even more important that, when students are writing
something to be handed in and graded, the teacher ensures that they have
identified an audience to whom their ideas are directed. Students also
need to define their own roles in the process by asking such questions as
"Am I the expert?" "Am I a novice who has a little special information
to impart?" "Am I writing in a seeking or a giving way relative to the
information with which I am dealing?" Linda Simon (1991) suggests valid
ways for teachers to ensure that students will write at their best possible
levels and produce papers that will be stimulating to read. She particularly
emphasizes the need for writers to identify their audiences.

Teachers can help students to achieve focus by asking them to define what they expect to accomplish through completing a piece of writing. Responses should be direct, specific, and sufficiently narrow that the stated ends can be achieved within the limits of both the assignment and the students' resources. A student whose stated purpose is to "understand the effect Marxist economics had on the American economy of the 1930s and 1940s" is probably going to have to write a three- or four-volume work to fulfill that objective. On the other hand, in a paper that explores the Marxist concept of providing for each person according to need as it is reflected in the plight of one character portrayed in Upton Sinclair's *The Jungle,* the purpose *is* perhaps manageable in a five-or six-page paper.

Some teachers have found it helpful to have students compile lists of terms that are specific to a subject and that they need to know in order to understand the subject. This emphasis, an outgrowth perhaps of E. D. Hirsch's *Cultural Literacy* (Hirsch 1987), apprises students of key terms and requires them to frame definitions. It can also lead to a published product, such as a mimeographed subject-matter dictionary to which every member of the class can contribute and from which that class as well as future classes will benefit.

Certainly, no one expects social studies teachers to become essentially teachers of writing. English teachers in the twenty-first century and beyond will probably continue to provide most of the basic instruction in writing that students need. When teachers in other fields realize the learning benefits that can accrue to students who write regularly about what they are studying, however, they will strive to find ways to incorporate more writing into their own classes, recognizing writing as an effective tool for helping students to focus and clarify their thinking at the most productive, analytical levels.

Some Tactics Teachers Will Use

Social studies teachers in the next millennium—more immediately, in the next half-century—will place increased emphasis on involving students in the kinds of classroom research and synthesis that will teach them not only the facts of the social studies, but also how to use those facts to construct fresh images of the realities with which they are working.

John Marshall Carter, himself a historian with an extensive background in social studies teaching, has been involved with the Bay Area Writing Project's Winston-Salem (North Carolina) satellite. He has suggested several ways to help students move in a new direction, and these ways involve writing: "In addition to performing transactional writing about Benjamin Franklin (such as a biographical sketch), the social studies teacher might ask the student to write a poem depicting Franklin's feelings about his discoveries or an interpretive essay exploring Franklin's conflict between his religious and scientific beliefs" (Carter 1991: 346).

Obviously, following such a procedure would help students to reconstruct a person from historical facts and would also provide individual support for students who are naturally oriented to transactional, interpretive, or creative writing activities. While creative students are encouraged to do some of what they do best, they are also developing the interpretive or transactional skills in which they might be weaker. An assessment of their performance would then be based on a broader range of information than has typically been considered in evaluating student performance.

Carter also proposes a year-long plan for content areas that teachers can use as they go about implementing a WAC program in their schools. He provides as well a set of highly specific guidelines for non-English teachers to use in evaluating their students' writing, not emphasizing the same things that English teachers do, but considering how well students have synthesized (integrated) their material, how well they have organized it, and what signs of creativity they have shown in their writing. Every evaluation would end with positive statements and suggestions for improvement (ibid.: 347).

One history teacher has pretty much done away with having students write formal essays—who, after all, writes essays in real life? Rather than formal writing, Joseph A. Naumann, Jr., assigns his students such letter-writing exercises as "a letter from the Holy Land during the First Crusade" (Naumann 1991: 198) in which they must cover specific details, such as descriptions of the fighting or their feelings about the experience. Naumann contends—and illustrates quite well through a typical student response—that his student "employed all levels of Bloom's taxonomy: knowledge, comprehension, application; analysis, synthesis, and evaluation" (ibid.).

Another history teacher, faced with the prospect of teaching a large class, has employed techniques that will probably characterize many history and social studies classes in the future. He begins his first class by having each student write for three minutes. In a European history class, he might ask students merely to list things that have to do with the Middle Ages. He then "ask[s] students to call out items from their list, and compile[s] a list on the blackboard" (Steffens 1991: 107). He soon has a list of forty or so items from which students select one item and write about it for four minutes (Steffens, too, writes), after which they turn to the person beside them, introduce themselves, and share what they have written. Throughout the term, Steffens keeps his students writing, suggesting that they can learn from a variety of writing activities: "Students respond to the history of courses best when they have the opportunity to write their thoughts about history without concern about immediate evaluation" (ibid.). Steffens represents a new wave of thinking and of pedagogical understanding that is sweeping through all subject areas: writing is a mode of learning; as such, it is pointless to evaluate all of it. An important realization that will hit teachers in the years ahead is that people solve problems and learn information through writing. The day is not far off when students, shown the problem-solving potential of the writing process, will, whenever they have a problem—academic, ethical, personal—reach for pen and paper as a means of dealing with that problem.

In order to move toward this end, those who train teachers will have to involve their students regularly in writing activities and will have to break down some antiquated concepts of the place of writing in the curriculum. Content literacy is a major aim of writing activities. Michael C. McKenna and Richard D. Robinson stress the centrality of reading and writing to content literacy and say that, in writing, it is important "to make clear that the idea of content literacy includes no responsibility for developing mechanical writing skills" (McKenna and Robinson 1990: 185; 1991: 31). They add that "the focus of such follow-up should be meaning, not mechanics." Such an attitude might sound like heresy to many of today's teachers, but the validity of the statement has been quite well proved.

Consistent with newly developed perceptions of how people learn and new attitudes to accommodate this growing body of information in learning theory is the development of the "whole-learning" approach to teaching. This technique has to do with achieving the higher levels of understanding that are an outgrowth of integrating materials from a broad variety of academic fields and synthesizing them into meaningful configurations, which necessarily involves writing or some other method of dissemination.

Whole learning usually entails having an audience other than, but also including, teachers for what one does. Among the principles of whole learning that David and Yvonne Freeman enumerate are the following:

1. Lessons should proceed from whole to part;
2. Lessons should be learner-centered because learning is the active construction of knowledge by students;
3. Lessons should have meaning and purpose for students now;
4. Lessons should engage groups of students in social interaction;
5. Lessons should develop both oral and written language; and
6. Lessons that show faith in the learner expand the student's potential. (Freeman and Freeman 1991: 29)

The direction in which instruction generally is moving seems clear. Most research shows that people must be directly involved in learning activities if those activities are to have any lasting meaning for them. Learning factual information is meaningless if the only purpose for learning is to repeat it on an examination. That old and widespread attitude trivialized learning.

As we move toward an information-dominated society, our nation is making demands upon its citizenry that prior agricultural and industrial societies did not make. For the first time in our history, high-level reasoning skills and effective problem-solving abilities are required of nearly everyone in a work force whose very structure and basic needs have little resemblance to those that were manifested at any other time in history.

REFERENCES

Applebee, Arthur N. "Writing and Learning in School Settings." In Martin Nystrand, ed., *What Writers Know: The Language, Process, and Structure of Written Discourse*. New York: Academic Press, 1982a.

———. *Writing in the Secondary School*. Urbana, IL: National Council of Teachers of English, 1982b.

Britton, James, Tony Burgess, Nancy Martin, Alex McLeod, and Harold Rosen. *The Development of Writing Abilities (11–18)*. London: Macmillan, 1975.

Carlsen, G. Robert, and Richard S. Alm, eds. *Social Understanding through Literature*. Washington: National Council for the Social Studies, 1954.

Carter, John Marshall. "The Social Studies Teacher as Writing Coach." *The Clearing House* 64 (May/June 1991): 346–49.

Emig, Janet. *The Composing Processes of Twelfth Graders*. Champaign, IL: National Council of Teachers of English, 1971.

———. "Writing as a Mode of Learning." *College Composition and Communication* 28 (May 1977): 123–24.

Fader, Daniel, and Elton B. McNeil. *Hooked on Books*. New York: Berkeley, 1968.

Flesch, Rudolph. *Why Johnny Can't Read*. New York: Harper and Row, 1955.

Freeman, David E., and Yvonne S. Freeman. " 'Doing' Social Studies: Whole Language Lessons to Promote Social Action." *Social Education* 55 (January 1991): 29–32, 66.

Fulwiler, Toby. "The Argument for Writing Across the Curriculum." In Art Young and Toby Fulwiler, eds., *Writing Across the Disciplines*. Upper Montclair, NJ: Boynton/Cook, 1986.

Gilstrap, Robert L. "Writing for Social Studies." In James P. Shaver, ed., *Handbook of Research on Social Studies Teaching and Learning*. New York: Macmillan, 1991.

Hirsch, E. D., Jr. *Cultural Literacy: What Every American Needs to Know*. Boston: Houghton Mifflin, 1987.

Labov, William. *The Study of Nonstandard English*. Champaign, IL: National Council of Teachers of English, 1970.

———. "Academic Ignorance and Black Intelligence." *Atlantic Monthly* 229 (June 1972): 59–67.

Labov, William, Paul Cohen, Clarence Robbins, and John Lewis. *A Study of Non-Standard English of Negro and Puerto Rican Speakers in New York City*. New York: Columbia University Press, 1968.

McKenna, Michael C., and Richard D. Robinson. "Content Literacy: Implications for Content Area Teachers." *Journal of Reading* 34 (November 1990): 184–86. Reprinted in *Education Digest* 52 (April 1991): 30–32.

Naumann, Joseph A., Jr. "Letter Writing: Creative Vehicle to Higher-Level Thinking." *Social Education* 55 (March 1991): 198.

Postman, Neil. "The Politics of Reading." *Harvard Education Review* 40 (May 1970): 244–52.

Shaver, James P., ed. *The Handbook of Research on Social Studies Teaching and Learning*. New York: Macmillan, 1991.

Shuman, R. Baird. "School-Wide Writing Instruction." *English Journal* 73 (February 1984): 54–57.

Simon, Linda. "The Papers We Want to Read." *The Social Studies* 81 (January/February 1991): 37–39.

Steffens, Henry. "Using Informal Writing in Large Writing Classes: Helping Students to Find Interest and Meaning in History." *The Social Studies* 82 (May/June 1991): 107–9.

Tchudi, Stephen. *Teaching Writing in the Content Areas: College Level*. Washington, DC: National Education Association, 1986.

Totten, Samuel. "Using Oral Histories to Address Social Issues in the Social Studies Classroom." *Social Education* 58 (February 1989): 114–25.

Van Nostrand, A. D. "Writing and the Generation of Knowledge." *Social Education* 48 (February 1979): 178–80.

Vygotsky, Lev. *Thought and Language*. Cambridge, MA: MIT Press, 1962.

Wesley, Edgar Bruce. *Teaching the Social Studies in High Schools*. 3d ed. Boston: D. C. Heath, 1950.

———. *Teaching Social Studies in Elementary Schools*. Rev. ed. Boston: D. C. Heath, 1952.

"Why Johnny Can't Write." *Newsweek* 92 (December 8, 1975): 58–65.

Wigginton, Eliot. ed., *Foxfire*. Garden City, NY: Doubleday, 1972.

15

THE SOCIAL STUDIES CURRICULUM AND TEACHER PREPARATION

Barbara M. Parramore

In practical terms, the importance and endurance of any area in the school curriculum are related to the extent to which the subject is mandated and the extent to which its teachers are required to have specific preparation. Curriculum guides, textbooks, and instructional materials are part of a wide array of influences on what is taught, but it is the teacher who is most directly involved in shaping the curriculum experienced by pupils. Factors influencing the preparation, selection, and work of teachers are important areas of inquiry with regard to the teaching of history and the social studies. For the purposes of this chapter, questions of what has been, is, and might be teacher education in history and the social studies curriculum are addressed. Among others, both the school curriculum and teacher preparation are subject to such factors as the recommendations of professional organizations, the directives of legal bodies, the intensity of public interest, the pressures of special-interest groups, and the degree of acceptance by teachers.

REFLECTIONS

Teachers for the Schools

During the colonial period and early nationhood, schools were established in local communities without state assistance. Teachers were selected primarily for their knowledge of what was to be taught and their ability to "keep school"; guidelines for licensure rarely existed; appointment to a teaching position was a local matter. There were no schools, as such, for preparing teachers.

Teacher licensure. As ideas about schooling evolved and publicly supported schools were established, teacher training and licensing developed. According to Haberman and Stinnett (1973), in 1800 only seven of the sixteen state constitutions mentioned education. Actual state-certification procedures were initiated in 1825 when the Ohio legislature designated county officers to be teacher examiners for the issuing of teaching certificates. Teacher certification came to be a responsibility shared by state and county authorities, and by 1900 there were about 3,000 licensing agencies in the United States (ibid.: 18). In 1911 only one state made high school graduation a prerequisite for the lowest-grade teacher's certificate, but by 1919 eleven states required it, and by 1928 thirty-three states did so, with others following soon thereafter (Edwards and Richey 1963: 593).

As the nineteenth century ended, the establishment of teachers colleges got under way as normal schools were replaced by state teachers colleges. This change was prompted, in part, by the development of public high schools and the increasing need for teachers who knew the subjects to be taught. During the 1950s, twenty-one states required a college degree of elementary school teachers and forty-two states required a degree of their secondary school teachers; by 1970 secondary school teachers in all states had to meet the degree requirement, and by 1973 a degree was required of all elementary school teachers (Haberman and Stinnett 1973: 13).

Accrediting associations. Standardization in schools became important late in the nineteenth century as regional accrediting associations began their work. These associations, largely an American creation, set standards for colleges and high schools and determine whether or not standards have been met. Haberman and Stinnett report that by 1900 there were four such associations and that competition among normal schools and teachers colleges seemed to have affected accreditation policies as early as 1899, when a report of the Normal School Department of the National Education Association, one of its original departments, distributed information on the policies of normal schools "in regard to practice teaching, professional courses, and academic work" (ibid.: 48).

In 1917, according to Edwards and Richey (1963), the NEA's Normal School Department became the American Association of Teachers Colleges. To provide guidance for colleges and assurances to the employing schools, the association established standards for teachers colleges in the early 1920s. In 1948, this association merged with two others to form the American Association of Colleges for Teacher Education (AACTE), but by 1951 only 246 institutions out of the more than 1,200 that provided teacher preparation were accredited. In 1954, the new and more broadly based National Council for the Accreditation of Teacher Education (NCATE) began issuing standards to be used in evaluating programs and then took over the accrediting function (ibid.: 599–600). Haberman and Stinnett (1973) observed that by the 1970s the shift to a more centralized regulatory process of teacher licensure was firmly in place in the states. State agencies, varying in practices, and the NCATE now set forth standards for preparing teachers and determine that the prescribed standards have been met.

In their work on the changing patterns of teacher education, Edwards and Richey observed that, other than content, the typical teacher's study of the nineteenth century consisted of a little history of educational theory and philosophy plus some practical considerations of methods and classroom management. However, teacher education, in response to such developments as child study, experimental psychology, scientific measurement, and testing soon expanded to include study in these areas. By the 1960s, many colleges and universities were offering five- and six-year programs leading to degrees usually entitled Master of Arts in Teaching (Edwards and Richey 1963: 614–16).

Curriculum for the Schools

Reflection on the school curriculum in the twentieth century really began about 1890 when organizations of national scope began studying and making recommendations on the subjects to be taught in American schools, especially high schools. The National Education Association (NEA) and the American Historical Association (AHA) named committees which exerted influence over history and related subjects in elementary and secondary schools. Other groups, as described in this book, have also exerted influence on the curriculum.

National groups. Committees appointed by the NEA focused on subjects and the sequence of those subjects in the school curriculum, while the AHA established its own committees to make recommendations. In time, history and the social sciences came to be identified as the "social studies." The high school curriculum, largely preparing students for college but also confronting increasing numbers of students who were not bound for college, began including ideas about what students needed to know in life and about their future citizenship.

Officials in states and local communities heeded the advice of those making national reports, which, in many cases, enjoyed widespread acceptance. The AHA "Committee of Eight's" recommendations for the elementary school, for example, set forth a "heroes-holidays-history" curriculum, which has been longlived. The NEA's "Committee of Ten," reporting on the secondary school in 1894, recommended the teaching of

American, English, Greek, Roman, and French history as well as of government. A very influential report prepared by the "Committee of Seven," which was published in 1899 under the sponsorship of the AHA, recommended high school courses beginning with ancient history in grade 9, medieval and modern European history in grade 10, English history in grade 11, and American history and civil government in grade 12.

The National Society for the Study of Education (NSSE) was founded in 1901 and gave history and geography immediate and continuing attention. The society still publishes yearbooks on history and social studies. Its first yearbook was issued in two volumes in 1902: Part I was entitled *Some Principles in the Teaching of History,* and Part II was called *The Progress of Geography in the Schools.* Part I of the second yearbook, of 1903, was entitled *The Course of Study in History in the Common School.* Minimum essentials in elementary school subjects, including social studies, were addressed in the yearbooks of 1915 and 1917. Part II of the twenty-second yearbook, of 1923, focused on the social studies at all levels. A teaching-of-geography yearbook was published in 1933. The fifty-sixth yearbook, Part II, of 1957, was on the social studies in the elementary school, and two decades later the eightieth yearbook, Part II of 1981, was entitled *The Social Studies.*

Debate over the goals and purposes of schools was a part of the dramatic changes taking place in American life in the years before and after the turn of the century. While the two AHA committee reports on school curricula were being considered, the NEA's Committee on the Social Studies was moving toward publishing its own report, which appeared in 1916. It was followed in 1918 by the report of the NEA's Commission on the Reorganization of Secondary Education, of which this Social Studies Committee was a part, describing new objectives for the high school curriculum.

The 1916 and 1918 NEA reports were published, Hertzberg (1981) observes, when two major streams of thought coincided with the rise of progressivism in America. The first was "social efficiency" and the second was social history, or the "new history." In promoting social improvement, the new history was to focus on more modern than ancient history, to address issues of societal progress, and to stress the importance of civic duties (ibid.: 17). The de-emphasis of ancient history allowed time for teachers to focus on community civics in the first year of high school and on government as a separate subject in the last year of high school.

By conforming to the recommendations of the NEA reports, the traditional curriculum gave way to a more practical orientation and the term "social studies" began to be used to describe subject matter of the schools. Dominant elements of the social studies curriculum can be traced to recommendations made by the Committee on Social Studies of the NEA Commission on the Reorganization of Secondary Education. It used the term "social studies" to refer to a curriculum that included history, economics, political science, sociology, and civics, defining the social studies as subject matter relating directly to the organization and development of human society and to an individual as a member of social groups.

A case for upgrading teacher education could be made by the recommendations of the NEA and AHA on curriculum content, but questions remained to be answered about ways to prepare teachers. Should the social studies be organized as a federation of subjects? Should it, or they, be a fusion of subjects organized around a central theme or themes? Teachers were expected to teach the recommended curriculum, which did not parallel college or university study in history and social sciences. With or without formal preparation, teachers began responding to changes in the selection and organization of curriculum content for newly scheduled courses.

Political scientists and historians were important sources of influence on curricular decisions as government and civics courses commanded the attention of school officials and the public at large, but other groups were attending to the high school curriculum also. The anthropologists, as Rice observed in his chapter here, were concerned with their own field and did not seek to affect the school curriculum. The sociologists were interested in schools, but not directly, for they believed their subject to be beyond the capabilities of secondary school students. The adequate preparation of teachers for such a broadly based curriculum tended to focus on a study of history in college, yet some kind of change was needed to help teachers be better prepared for a school curriculum oriented toward more contemporary concerns of the society.

The National Council for the Social Studies. Curricular unrest, among other factors, led in 1921 to the formation of the National Council for the Social Studies. Its founders sought to assert leadership and to impose order on a curricular area not easily defined or understood. In reality, the social studies curriculum was biased toward a collection of separate subjects rather than their fusion into a new entity. In trying to clarify matters, Wesley described the social studies as the disciplines simplified for instructional purposes (Wesley and Wronski 1964: 3). Translating or transforming the social science disciplines into a unified curriculum was a formidable and nearly impossible task. Then, as now, vagueness as to the definition of social studies existed and competition among its proponents occurred both in schools and in the colleges preparing teachers.

Social studies from the 1930s to the 1960s. More study was undertaken by a commission which began working in January 1929 and issued its reports during the early 1930s. Charged with studying the teaching of history and social studies, as Hertzberg has observed, this commission was to be "the most elaborate and comprehensive commission in the history of the social studies, although, as it turned out, not the most influential," due to its timing (Hertzberg 1981: 44). Charles Beard edited the first report and wrote the second, which were followed by a series of volumes by different authors. The resulting "new" content was envisioned as making social studies more useful and relevant to students' daily lives, departing even more from a traditional curriculum relying more on historical study.

Learning citizenship by doing it and a human relations curriculum were favored during the 1940s and 1950s. Efforts aimed at general curriculum reform following World War II were reinforced by the launching of Sputnik and later by the provisions of the National Defense Education Act (NDEA) of 1958. The social studies curriculum was not omitted from reform efforts of the 1960s, although federal support for it was far less than for other areas, such as mathematics and science. However, NDEA institutes on history and projects sponsored by professional organizations and foundations contributed to fleshing out the dimensions of the "new social studies" curriculum, which promoted a renewed and an increased emphasis on history and the social science disciplines. During the 1960s experimental programs, such as those in anthropology and economics, attempted to revamp the scope of curricula in the elementary school, and Jerome Bruner (1960) proposed the "structure of the disciplines" as a way to organize programs.

Teacher preparation. Throughout the century, teacher preparation in history and social studies has not been addressed directly in most reports on the school curriculum. The lack of agreement on a single organizing framework for the curriculum has kept questions of teacher preparation confined to more general concerns. Teacher certification was largely a matter for individual states, school districts, and schools. Teacher preparation, like the school curriculum and in spite of all the rhetoric and recommendations, was dominated by history and supported by general education courses and a few courses in psychology and pedagogy.

Willis D. Moreland's 1956 study of teacher preparation, as reported in Wesley and Wronski (1964: 5), included fifty institutions; social studies majors were offered in thirty-eight. He found that the most common course requirement for future teachers, whatever the major, was history, which was supported by at least one course in each of the social science subjects: geography, economics, sociology, and political science. When not pursuing the practically designed major in social studies education, secondary teachers usually majored in history.

An approved-program approach in teacher education was developed during the 1960s in which institutions had to follow a state's prescribed requirements for certification, but were allowed to plan and offer their own program design. Once approved, the institution then recommended certification for the candidate who had successfully completed the approved program; certification was granted automatically. Adequate scores on standardized tests were also sometimes required.

There are two possible strengths of the program-approval approach. First, the individual institution is theoretically not forced into a narrow prescription of courses for future teachers laid down by certification requirements. Second, an institution can plan its program according to its own philosophy, clientele, faculty, and facilities. Greater flexibility is possible in the planning of institutional programs, but this may not occur when institutions try to meet multiple sets of standards and guidelines issued by several licensing and accrediting bodies. More, not less, regulation of teacher education by the state occurred as competency-based teacher education (CBTE) became the vogue in the 1970s.

In CBTE programs, specific teaching behaviors are developed and evaluated. Lists of competencies are compiled to guide the preparation of future teachers who are expected to demonstrate their ability to perform the aspects of a teacher's role identified by the competencies. Restricting the role of teacher to a mechanistic model, CBTE critics claim, makes observable skills in general pedagogy important, but these are not sufficient to determining how students learn. However, state agencies and accrediting bodies embraced the CBTE model and attempted to shift teacher-education programs previously organized by majors and specified courses to program designs based on sets of competencies.

Competency-based teacher education altered teacher preparation by increasing coverage of social studies content and decreasing emphasis on the disciplines. What teachers needed to know or learn in college was being affected more directly by the scope and sequence of the curriculum to be taught in the schools. No longer as concerned with course titles and college majors as indicators of teacher competence, teacher-education curricula came to be judged on the extent to which competencies were demonstrated by teaching candidates, whether acquired in a course or by experience. As an example, the work of a task force in the state of Minnesota provides information about the CBTE process (Martorella 1976: 436–56).

The Minnesota task force began its work by developing a teacher-competency model that focused on learning outcomes or what might be inferred about the curriculum based on the results of pupil testing. Expectations of student achievement were identified and classified. Pupil expectations were then used in deriving specifications for teachers' competencies, thereby providing a basis for revising regulations in the licensure of social studies teachers. The resulting report of the task force was the "Condensed List of Competencies for Social Studies Teachers." The "Condensed List," as reported in Martorella (1976), describes six teacher behaviors, each with its own detailed set of descriptors and indicators for judging teacher performance. These stipulated that a competent teacher performs as follows:

1. Makes progress toward achieving student outcomes in three areas: cognitive goals, affective goals, and goals specific to community.
2. Demonstrates behaviors in classroom and other teaching situations to facilitate pupils' development toward cognitive and affective goals in the social studies.
3. Demonstrates a knowledge of all of the social sciences as disciplines, including ways of structuring, types of analytical questions asked, methods of explanation used, methods of advancing knowledge, major competing theories, the changing nature of fields, and ways of keeping current with developments in the field, together with the ability to integrate and apply this knowledge to the development and evaluation of curriculum and instructional materials and to the candidate's work in the classroom.
4. Demonstrates the skills and behaviors with which he should be able to help pupils develop, including those in the area of human relations.
5. Demonstrates knowledge of principles of learning, including both cognitive and affective learning, adolescent psychology, individual differences, and social studies methods, curriculum, and materials of instruction, together with the ability to apply this knowledge to the development and evaluation of teaching plans and instructional materials as well as in classroom teaching and other work with pupils.
6. Demonstrates knowledge of ways of using community resources in teaching, of promoting good relationships between the school and the community, and of the professional role of the teacher beyond the classroom situation together with the ability to apply this knowledge to work within the school. (Ibid.)

Theoretically, these six competencies, along with their sets of behavioral indicators, are observable and measurable. Whatever the particular program, the future teachers' behaviors determine success, not the courses he or she has completed successfully. Critics of this approach cite difficulties in agreeing on the validity and degree of importance of some competencies as well as in measuring them reliably. By the 1990s emphasis on the quantitative aspects of teacher preparation fostered by CBTE was giving way to mounting concerns about the quality of future teachers' experiences.

In summary, the twentieth century began with studies conducted by professional organizations and others, with reports issued on the school curriculum but limited commentary on teacher preparation. Very influential were the NEA and AHA reports issued from the 1890s to the 1920s, which affected the kinds of subjects future teachers were expected to study in order to be prepared to teach. The twentieth century has been devoted primarily to a focus on subject matter to be taught and the scope and sequence of the curriculum. For the most part, teacher preparation has been viewed in more general terms as states and accrediting bodies sought to ensure that certain standards were met for teacher licensure. In his review of the history of teaching in social studies, Cuban concluded that instruction in classrooms has been teacher centered and that most planned changes were adapted incrementally or eventually disappeared, resulting in little change (Cuban 1991: 204–5). The legacy of a slowly evolving history and social studies curriculum and mandated standardization of teacher preparation provide a backdrop for considering the status of history and social studies in the closing decades of the twentieth century.

CURRENT TRENDS AND ISSUES

For the first three quarters of the twentieth century, increasingly specific recommendations for the schools' history and social studies curriculum have commanded attention; teacher preparation has been affected indirectly. From the 1920s to the 1960s, and then to the present, school superintendents and their assistants performed their duties by checking on teachers' adherence to the curriculum. They looked for evidence that recommendations for the curriculum were implemented. Whether called "history teachers" or by the more inclusive term "social studies teachers," they were expected to have a solid grounding in history and, because of the citizenship objective, also in political science. Content from geography and the social sciences was included in a teacher's preparation, but not on a systematic basis. The configuration of required courses for teachers varied from one college program to another, but a certain amount of standardization evolved.

In a curricular area, which derives its subject matter from multiple bodies of knowledge, a key question to be addressed by both teachers in the schools and by those designing teacher-preparation programs is: How can knowledge be organized in a coherent and meaningful way? Further, is the knowledge to be studied for its own sake or to produce what are accepted as useful ideas about the social world? Deciding what to teach depends upon what knowledge and which skills are judged to be of greatest worth. But how and by whom is "worth" decided? What knowledge? Factual or conceptual? Is it an "either-or" proposition? Which skills are to be developed? These questions are debated anew as commissions and others study them and issue their reports.

Reform Efforts

Teaching history and social studies in the elementary school has had its share of reform efforts, recommendations by various groups, and continuing controversies. But none is as dramatic or as unresolved as those of the secondary school curriculum. General answers to this problem of deciding what to teach range from focusing on mastery of discipline-oriented subject matter to acquiring knowledge selected for its social usefulness, to developing students' cognitive abilities. Teachers, in choosing a position on this continuum as a guide to their work, are affected by their own preferences and by the rules and regulations of school boards regarding curriculum, among others. They may decide to present each subject as a separate course, create an integrated body of knowledge, or select a core of topics or issues about which students are to discover relevant knowledge. They are likely to be heavily influenced by textbooks and by standardized testing, which favor a curriculum designed primarily for knowledge acquisition.

Teacher educators have responded to new directions in curricula by introducing new methodology into their existing college courses. But their innovations may have been constrained by the need to be sensitive to the preferences of teachers and schools where practice teaching occurs, often untouched by controversy among curriculum developers and teacher educators. Resistance to proposed changes in history and the social sciences curriculum of the 1960s was strong, and later it was found that little had actually changed in the classroom (Weiss 1978; Wiley 1977). Preparing teachers to work in school environments shaped by a wide array of influences tends to result in an inclusive curriculum quite specific in its many elements. Moving from the all-encompassing competency-based approach in teacher education, efforts in the later decades of the century have been directed toward describing "essential" elements to make clearer, and perhaps more realistic, the expectations of both pupils and their future teachers.

Whatever the curriculum, it is believed that teachers who do not have a major in history, or in the discipline on which the curriculum is based, may experience difficulty in deciding what the most important topics of study are. Moreover, they may lack sufficient knowledge in teaching even the agreed-upon topics. Some states and school districts adhere to the notion that a bachelor's degree in the arts and sciences is preferable for teachers and constitutes sufficient preparation. Lateral-entry programs, with little or no professional training required, often seek to recruit college graduates with a strong academic background.

The work of researchers on teacher knowledge and specifically on the teaching of American history, based on Lee Shulman's (1987) concepts, offers a promising base for a better understanding of how to develop a teacher's content-area and pedagogical knowledge (Wilson and Wineburg [n.d.], Wineburg 1987; Wineburg and Wilson 1988). These researchers are exploring ways that teachers integrate content knowledge and teaching skills. They have classified pedagogical skills into at least two sets: general and content-area pedagogy. It is the latter pedagogy which may result in even more attention being given to how a subject area is to be taught and to the requisite knowledge of a teacher.

Departures from the status quo in teaching history and social studies during the 1960s soon faded as schools, as American society, began to cope with a more inclusive school environment for minorities and pupils with special needs. Alarm over perceptions that schooling had departed too much from tradition lent support to proponents of minimum-competency requirements for pupils. During the late 1970s, the rise of competency testing in states provided a glimpse of an accountability movement in education yet to falter. A national testing program, projected for the year 2000, is likely to sustain knowledge objectives of learning as a key goal of the curriculum. Yet, countervailing a focus on such pupil knowledge is a growing concern about pupils' ability to think critically, already leading to expanded ideas about the forms that testing may take in the future. National standards for curricula, proposed to be met on a voluntary basis, may exert a strong influence on the content of the curriculum for the twenty-first century and affect requirements of social studies teachers.

General reports. Just as the NEA and AHA played important roles in the late nineteenth century in focusing attention on the school curriculum, the federal government, private foundations, and other groups have taken on such functions in the late twentieth century. Of note are three reports issued by the president's National Commission on Excellence in Education (1983), *A Nation at Risk;* several education deans known as the Holmes Group (1986), *Tomorrow's Teachers;* and the task force on teaching as a profession of the Carnegie Forum on Education and the Economy (1986), *A Nation Prepared: Teachers for the 21st Century.* Almost uniformly, these reports have called for a "back to the disciplines" orientation in teacher preparation.

In carrying out its charge to "assess the quality of teaching and learning" in the nation's schools, the National Commission on Excellence in Education found teacher-preparation programs lacking in substance and expressed concern that college curricula are "heavy with courses in educational methods at the expense of courses in subjects to be taught" (National Commission 1983: 22). In *A Nation at Risk,* the strengthening of high school curriculum content was recommended and the overriding purpose of social studies was affirmed as preparation of pupils "for an informed and committed exercise of citizenship in a free society." The Commission asserted that the curriculum should be designed to enable pupils to understand (a) the larger social and cultural structure in which they live; (b) ways in which the broad sweep of ancient and contemporary ideas have affected humankind; (c) how our economic system and political system function; and (d) differences between free and repressive societies (ibid.: 25–26). With regard to teaching, the Commission recommended that, in addition to demonstrated aptitude for teaching, teachers meet high educational standards and be competent in an academic discipline and that master teachers be involved in designing preparation programs and in supervising teachers during their probationary years (ibid.: 30–31).

The Holmes Group, composed of education deans from across the nation, issued its report, outlining goals for reform of teacher education, in 1986. Reform recommendations included making the education of teachers more intellectually solid, recognizing career phases of teachers, establishing more demanding entry-level requirements, fostering more collaborative efforts among teacher-educators and teachers, and, ultimately, making schools better places for teachers to work and to learn (Holmes Group 1986: 4). Emphasis was placed on "teachers [who] should know their subjects thoroughly and have the intellectual qualities of educated, thoughtful, and well-informed individuals" (ibid.: 46).

Concerns about the links between economic growth and the educational characteristics of people who contribute to that growth were the basis of a Carnegie Corporation task force report on "teaching as a profession" (Carnegie Forum 1986). In its scenario for staffing schools for the twenty-first century, the task force recommended a new framework to transform the environment for teaching. Its proposals include creating a national board for professional teaching standards, restructuring schools to provide a professional environment, or "teachers' workplace," requiring a bachelor's degree in the arts and sciences as a prerequisite for the professional study of teaching, developing a new professional curriculum in graduate schools of education leading to a Master in Teaching degree, and an array of other objectives to make teaching similar to other professions (ibid.: 55).

Individual critics of schools have added their voices to debate over high school reforms. Mortimer Adler was quoted in the Carnegie report as stating that "the present teacher training programs turn out persons who are not sufficiently equipped with the knowledge, the intellectual skills, or the developed understanding needed to guide and help the young in the course of study we have recommended" (ibid.: 35). In *The Paideia Proposal: An Educational Manifesto,* Adler (1982) called for a single course of studies for all pupils from first grade through high school graduation. A longtime advocate of an education based on great books and ideas, his curriculum would be organized into three, often overlapping approaches. In addition to acquisition of organized learning covering the subject matter of the disciplines and the development of intellectual skills, a third approach focuses on developing a greater understanding of ideas and values. He recommends that teachers rely on the Socratic method of questioning and the discussion of books and other works of art which have been adopted in history and social studies classes.

Focused reports. The NCSS has affirmed its position on the essentials of the history and social studies curriculum and has also adopted guidelines for teacher-preparation programs. Within their broad responsibilities, states, through their certification standards, and the NCATE are taking on expanded roles regarding the preparation of future teachers in specific curricular areas. Two recent reports are among the more visible in relation to the history and social studies curriculum.

Building a History Curriculum: Guidelines for Teaching History in Schools, the report of the Bradley Commission on History in Schools (1988), and *Charting a Course: Social Studies for the 21st Century,* the report of the National Commission on Social Studies in the Schools (1989), affirm the place of history in the school curriculum, yet with differing emphases. Whether or not their influence becomes as widespread as the reports of a hundred years earlier remains to be seen in the new century. Neither group was able, due to time and financial constraints, to devote attention to teacher preparation.

NCSS curriculum essentials. In 1979, the NCSS joined with eleven other professional organizations to declare its support of an "Essentials of Education Statement." The NCSS's own statement of "Essentials of Social Studies" soon followed, affirming citizenship education as an overriding purpose. The knowledge areas of the essentials include history and culture of the nation and world, geography, economics, social institutions, intergroup and interpersonal relationships, and worldwide relationships (National Council [n.d.]: 1). From a knowledge base consisting of these six essentials, NCSS expects pupils to come to understand "the sweep of human affairs" and to develop knowledge of "ways of managing conflict consistent with democratic procedures" (ibid.). Other parts of the "essentials statement" include sections on democratic beliefs, thinking skills, participation skills, and civic action. The NCSS essentials provide a framework for developing school curricula which may affect teacher education.

NCSS standards for teacher preparation. Teacher education programs, although based on college and university campuses and subject to their governing bodies, are heavily influenced by state licensure requirements and the standards set by accrediting agencies. In turn, the preferences of practitioners may be expressed in these adopted guidelines and standards for preparing teachers, such as those of the Minnesota task force described earlier. Having reached some consensus on curriculum essentials, licensing bodies and professional organizations are becoming more active in making recommendations about teacher education, including the NCSS.

During the 1980s, the NCSS board of directors acted twice on a set of standards to guide the development and revision of teacher-education programs. The 1983 and 1987 versions were published in *Social Education* in May 1984 and January 1988, respectively. In the late 1980s, the NCATE began including a "folio" or program review of teacher-education programs by related professional organizations, prompting the NCSS to approve a revision of its 1987 standards (National Council 1991: 1) for use in accreditation. Actually, these standards provide a consolidation of valued teacher-education priorities and practices which have evolved over a century as well as a summary of what are believed to be crucial elements of a teacher's knowledge and skill.

The report on NCSS teacher-preparation standards for the 1990s and beyond, produced by a task force of seven members, sets forth principles of desirable programs for initial certification in social studies. These standards are intended to serve as a guide for professional planning, practice, and program evaluation of state agencies, college and university faculty, and the NCATE (ibid.: 3). They address not only a teacher-education curriculum, but also other aspects of how a program is implemented and governed. They are intended to apply to a range of programs for preparing secondary social studies teachers, secondary teachers specializing in history, economics, geography, or political science, middle school teachers, elementary school teachers, and early childhood teachers.

Colleges and universities that wish to have high-quality programs acceptable to the NCSS should

—have high standards for admission and continuation in programs;

—offer programs of study that include a substantial and challenging foundation in general education;

—provide depth and breadth of preparation in the disciplines that make up the field of social studies (history, geography, economics, political science, sociology, anthropology, and psychology);

—provide for collaboration between education and arts and sciences faculties in program planning and delivery;

—provide a program of research-based professional studies closely integrated with a sequence of systematically planned and well-supervised field experiences;

—create partnerships with schools in providing programs and establishing appropriate mechanisms of accountability for their graduates' teaching performance;

—aggressively recruit and support students representative of diverse populations. (Ibid.: 1–2)

The NCSS standards call for academically oriented programs leading to licensure of teachers (ibid.: 5–11). Further, in designing curricula, program elements need not be organized as specific courses, but should contribute to three categories of teacher preparation: general studies, social studies, and professional education. In apportioning time, well-educated teachers of all levels should spend a minimum of one-third of their total four-year or extended-preparation program in general studies.

Building upon the general-studies component, the remaining two components of a teacher's preparation are the "social studies," that is, subject matter, and "professional education," that is, how to teach. In social studies, the NCSS believes that candidates for initial licensure should have gained "substantial understanding of the information, concepts, theories, analytical approaches, and differing value perspectives, including global and multicultural perspectives," important to teaching social studies (ibid.: 6). In recognizing the need for both breadth and depth in content-area studies, this part of the program should be designed to take into consideration and build upon work completed as part of the general-studies component.

Becoming more specific in its standards for licensure of comprehensive social studies teachers, grades 7–12, the NCSS calls for teacher preparation which includes the study of each of the following: United States history, world history (including Western and non-Western civilization), political science (including United States government), economics, world geography (cultural, physical, economic, with emphasis upon interrelationships), and the behavioral sciences (anthropology, psychology, and sociology). Interdisciplinary social studies courses may be included, but, to assure substantial study beyond introductory survey courses, all programs should require an area of concentration in one of the social studies of not less than eighteen semester hours so that course work in social studies encompasses not less than forty percent of the total four-year or extended-preparation programs. Furthermore, when licensure is by discipline (history, geography, political science, or economics), the program of studies in that discipline should not be less demanding than that required for a B.A. or B.S. degree in that discipline and not less than thirty percent of the program. All single-discipline preparation programs must, according to the NCSS, include study in United States history and government, geography, economics, and non-Western civilization.

For teachers of middle schools or departmentalized elementary schools, programs of preparation may have interdisciplinary social studies courses and should include, at a minimum, the study of United States history and government, geography (cultural, physical, economic, with emphasis upon interrelationships), world history, and economics, all of which should constitute not less than thirty percent of a four-year or extended-preparation program. For self-contained classroom teachers at the elementary school level and for early childhood teachers, course work in social studies should constitute not less than fifteen percent of a four-year or extended-preparation program.

The NCSS standards include a range of recommendations for the professional-education component of a teacher's preparation. These include study of (1) social and philosophical foundations of education, (2) human growth and development and the psychology of learning, (3) students with exceptionalities, (4) multicultural perspectives, (5) technology in instruction, (6) general teaching strategies, including planning and evaluation, and (7) the teaching of communication skills in the content area, including reading, writing, and speaking. Social studies methodology should be appropriate for the level of licensure and teachers should be skillful in teaching a variety of instructional approaches and in different settings and have an array of clinical experiences, including a minimum of fifteen weeks of fulltime teaching experience in the subject(s) and grade level(s) to be licensed. In recognition of initial licensure as a first step in the career path of a teacher, the NCSS expects first-year teachers to be a part of a one- to two-year induction program with the assistance of a mentor teacher and a college specialist in social studies education (ibid.: 7–11). From the NCSS's standards a lengthy array and inclusive set of criteria can be derived for judging how well a program meets those standards and whether or not teacher licensure of a candidate is warranted. The criteria also indicate problems faced by those designing preparation programs, for it is unrealistic to suppose that all expectations will be met. Rather, the expectations are more appropriate descriptions of the experienced, master teacher of history and social studies.

In summary, unlike an earlier period in teacher preparation, much effort is now being exerted on defining standards for teacher preparation and describing a research agenda for learning more about teaching and its resulting effectiveness in relation to a prescribed curriculum. How a teacher's knowledge of subject matter contributes to instructional effectiveness and the extent to which pedagogical training influences aspects of teacher behavior are examples of two research items. Implications for choosing an emphasis in teacher preparation may be derived from Tucker (1977), who defined three different approaches in deciding how curriculum content is selected: (1) social studies as academic disciplines, (2) social studies as personal development, and (3) social studies as social issues. Ochoa (1981), in the eightieth NSSE yearbook, reported on how little is known about the education of social studies teachers.

In the decade following Ochoa's assertion, and her challenge to the profession to attend to understanding itself, Banks and Parker (1990) reviewed teacher education in social studies for the *Handbook on Research in Teacher Education*. Shortly thereafter, in the *Handbook of Research on Social Studies Teaching and Learning* (Shaver 1991), there appeared six chapters (chapters 15–20) devoted to research about social studies teaching and teachers of social studies. The conclusions of Banks and Parker echo those of Ochoa in maintaining that the field of social studies education lacks a cumulative body of coherent research on social studies teaching and teacher education (Banks and Parker 1990: 674). Cuban (1991) reaches a similar conclusion and provides an instructive basis for developing questions to guide future research about teaching and teachers, which he too says is sorely needed. If understanding the past is instructive in making projections about the future, change in the preparation of teachers is likely to be slow and incremental, not dramatic or different from that of the past.

PROJECTIONS

Preparation of a future teacher in history and social studies is affected by expanding sets of directives and recommendations with a specificity far greater than that of the early 1900s or even the 1950s. Bases for developing the school curriculum, which range through a variety of positions expressed in this book, show how varied and often controversial many aspects of the curriculum are and how difficult, if not impossible, it is to adequately prepare teachers for teaching it in initial-certification programs. Also, an examination of recent commission reports, the standards set by accrediting bodies, and the NCSS curriculum essentials and standards for teacher preparation all reveal a broad social agenda to be fulfilled by the school's history and social studies curriculum. History's place in the school curriculum and in teacher preparation appears assured, but differing in content, as the field is enlarged to include topics and issues not usually accepted as a focus of historical inquiry, such as gender and race, among others.

Unresolved issues. Debates about *what* is to be learned and *how* it is to be learned, framed early in this century, continue. Should future teachers of history and social studies be required to focus on content knowledge primarily? Or, should mastering pedagogical skills be a stronger focus? No one advocates all of one or the other, but for social studies, since it embraces many disciplines, the question is: How much study, and in which disciplines, should a teacher have? And, how much of the time spent in a program should be allocated for future teachers to learn to "select, integrate, and translate knowledge and methodology from the social studies disciplines in ways appropriate to the level of certification?" (National Council 1991: 9).

The NCATE provides a means for voluntary accreditation, required by some states, and has consolidated its influence through its 1987 standards, which provide for professional organizations, including the NCSS, to review "program folios." These peer judgments are passed on to the NCATE. Precisely how more detailed regulatory policies will affect the preparation of teachers is not clear, but there may be cause for concern about opportunities for genuine change and improvement when the initial degree programs are required to be so heavily prescriptive. Goodlad (1990), in one of nineteen postulates to guide program development, insists that teacher education must be freed from curricular specifications by licensing agencies and restrained by more professionally driven requirements for accreditation. The joint efforts of the NCATE and the NCSS have the potential to meet Goodlad's postulate.

Current and future program evaluation and accreditation procedures may garner criticisms similar to those directed at the competency-based mode of an earlier time. More than likely, institutions of higher education will be caught in an ever-tightening web spun by competing and sometimes conflicting forces. The work of Goodlad (1990), aimed at restructuring teacher education, may be helpful. His propositions are being used in a series of studies during the 1990s aimed at demonstrating alternative and possibly more effective ways of preparing teachers for the nation's schools. Goodlad is openly critical of the bureaucratization of teacher preparation through centralized organizations.

Restructuring teacher education. Conflicts between those with centralized authority in teacher licensure and proponents of decentralized approaches to designing initial certification programs are likely to increase with the nation's focus on restructuring education for the twenty-first century. Perhaps genuine reform will be undertaken on college campuses. However, those responsible for teacher preparation probably will continue to juggle the myriad sets of expectations which have evolved over time. And they will continue to be criticized by campus colleagues and others for offering programs lacking in academic substance and by practitioners in schools for designing programs too heavily weighted in academics. As each faction competes for dominant authority and control, institutions may need to abandon their efforts to be approved and accredited by regulatory bodies, offering instead, each through its own particular version, genuine choices to future teachers and employing schools. In such an open system, the marketplace, or schools, would select recent graduates and candidates for teaching positions, appoint and supervise them, and make the certification recommendation. In such a deregulated system, schools or school districts could more easily match a teacher's qualifications with the requirements of a particular opening and a school's curriculum. In addressing special needs, schools may seek teachers with strengths in a particular discipline, or with skills in teaching diverse populations, or with an ability to manage controversial issues in the classroom, or with the expertise to establish a global/international curriculum. In restructuring an overregulated system for teacher preparation, colleges and universities could offer more sensible and cohesive programs and, perhaps, avoid problems resulting from deregulation.

Deregulation would mean a restructuring of teacher preparation as choices in program design are made more freely and, probably, more responsibly. In an era when standards and guidelines describing the desired competencies of teachers are fully specified and quite well understood, all participants—the state, the professional organizations, the practitioners in schools—can attend to basic expectations and can allow more flexibility to teacher educators in going beyond them. Legal bodies, of course, are not going to surrender their authority, nor should they, but they could allow for innovative programs. For example, alternatives to teacher certification, referred to as "lateral entry," are already in place in some states, lending support to a differentiated approach in teacher licensure.

Given the heavy and broadly based demands of the school curriculum in history and social sciences, and the existing constraints on teacher preparation, a specialty-within-a-specialty approach to preparing teachers is a possible, but improbable, vision of the future. Reform in the history and social studies curriculum is both a pre- and a co-requisite to reform in teacher preparation and also to a teacher's continuing education as well. As a beginning, while meeting minimum requirements, institutions should be encouraged to plan their own teacher-preparation programs, each according to its own philosophy, clientele, faculty, and facilities. Such a return to the spirit of the approved-program approach in teacher education is one way of restructuring teacher preparation in history and social studies to meet the challenges of the future.

REFERENCES

Adler, Mortimer J. *The Paideia Proposal*. New York: Macmillan, 1982.

Banks, J. A., and W. C. Parker. "Social Studies Teacher Education." In W. R. Houston, ed., *Handbook of Research on Teacher Education*. New York: Macmillan, 1990.

Bradley Commission on History in Schools. *Building a History Curriculum: Guidelines for Teaching History in the Schools*. Westlake, OH: National Council for History Education, 1988.

Bruner, J. S. *The Process of Education*. New York: Vintage, 1960.

Carnegie Forum on Education and the Economy. *A Nation Prepared: Teachers for the 21st Century*. The Report of the Task Force on Teaching as a Profession. New York: Carnegie Corporation of New York, 1986.

Cuban, L. "History of Teaching in Social Studies." In James P. Shaver, ed., *Handbook of Research on Social Studies Teaching and Learning*. New York: Macmillan, 1991.

Edwards, N., and H. G. Richey. *The School in the American Social Order*. 2d ed. Boston: Houghton Mifflin, 1963.

Essentials of Education Statement. A Joint Statement by Twelve Professional Associations. Washington, DC: National Council for the Social Studies, 1980.

Goodlad, J. I. *Teachers for Our Nation's Schools*. San Francisco, CA: Jossey-Bass, 1990.

Haberman, M., and T. M. Stinnett. *Teacher Education and the New Profession of Teaching*. Berkeley, CA: McCutchan, 1973.

Hertzberg, H. W. *Social Studies Reform 1880–1980*. Boulder, CO: Social Science Education Consortium, 1981.

Holmes Group, Inc. *Tomorrow's Teachers: A Report of the Holmes Group*. East
  Lansing, MI: The Holmes Group, 1986.
Martorella, Peter H., ed. *Social Studies Strategies: Theory into Practice*. New
  York: Harper and Row, 1976.
National Commission on Excellence in Education. *A Nation at Risk: The Im-
  perative for Educational Reform*. Washington, DC: Superintendent of Doc-
  uments, U.S. Government Printing Office, 1983.
National Commission on Social Studies in the Schools. *Charting a Course: Social
  Studies for the 21st Century*. Washington, DC: Joint Project of the Amer-
  ican Historical Association, the Carnegie Foundation for the Advancement
  of Teaching, the National Council for the Social Studies, and the Organi-
  zation of American Historians, Washington, DC: National Council for the
  Social Studies, 1989.
National Council for the Social Studies. "Standards for the Preparation of Social
  Studies Teachers." *Social Education* 52 (November/December 1988): 10–
  12.
———. Draft of Revised Standards for the Preparation of Social Studies Teachers.
  Unpublished report of the Task Force for Revision of the Teacher Edu-
  cation Standards. Washington, DC: 1991.
———. *The Essentials Statements: Essentials of Social Studies* (NCSS Tool Kit).
  Washington, DC: National Council for the Social Studies, n.d.
National Education Association. *The Social Studies in Secondary Education*. A
  Report of the Committee on Social Studies on the Reorganization of Sec-
  ondary Education of the National Education Association. No.
  28. Washington, DC: Bureau of Education, 1916.
National Society for the Study of Education. *Yearbooks of the Society*. Chicago,
  IL: University of Chicago Press, 1901–1981.
Ochoa, A. S. "The Education of Social Studies Teachers." In H. D. Mehlinger
  and O. L. Davis, eds., *The Social Studies* (80th Yearbook of the National
  Society for the Study of Education, Part II, 151–69). Chicago: University
  of Chicago Press, 1981.
Shaver, James P., ed. *Handbook of Research on Social Studies Teaching and
  Learning*. New York: Macmillan, 1991.
Shulman, L. "Knowledge and Teaching: Foundations of the New Reform." *Har-
  vard Educational Review* 57 (January 1987): 1–22.
Tucker, J. L. "Research on Social Studies Teaching and Teacher Education."
  In F. P. Hunkins, C. L. Hahn, P. H. Martorella, and J. L. Tucker, eds.,
  Review of Research in Social Studies Education: 1970–1975. Washington,
  DC: National Council for the Social Studies, 1977.
Tucker, J. L., and W. W. Joyce. *Social Studies Teacher Education: Practices,
  Problems, and Recommendations*. Boulder, CO: Social Science Education
  Consortium, 1979.
Weiss, I. R. *National Survey of Science, Mathematics, and Social Studies Ed-
  ucation*. Washington, DC: National Science Foundation, 1978.
Wesley, E. B., and S. P. Wronski. *Teaching Social Studies in High Schools*. 5th
  ed. Boston, MA: D. C. Heath, 1964.
Wiley, K. B. *The Status of Precollege Science, Mathematics, and Social Studies*

Education: 1955–1975. Washington, DC: National Science Foundation, 1977.

Wilson, S. M., and S. S. Wineburg. "Peering at History from Different Lenses: The Role of Disciplinary Perspectives in the Teaching of American History." Unpublished paper, Stanford University, n.d.

Wineburg, S. S. "From Fieldwork to Classwork: Cathy: A Case Study of a Beginning Social Studies Teacher." Unpublished paper, Stanford University, 1987.

Wineburg, S. S., and Suzanne M. Wilson. "Models of Wisdom in the Teaching of History." *Phi Delta Kappan* 70 (September 1988): 50–58.

SELECTED BIBLIOGRAPHY

Allen, Jack, ed. *Education in the 80's: Social Studies*. Washington, DC: National Education Association, 1981.

American Historical Association. *The Study of History in Schools*. New York: Macmillan, 1899.

American Historical Association's Commission on the Social Studies. *Conclusions and Recommendations of the Commission*. New York: Charles Scribner's Sons, 1935.

Atwater, Virginia A., ed. *Elementary School Social Studies: Research as a Guide to Practice*. Washington, DC: National Council for the Social Studies, 1986.

Barr, Robert D., James L. Barth, and S. Samuel Shermis. *Defining the Social Studies*. Washington, DC: National Council for the Social Studies, 1977.

Beard, Charles A. *A Charter for the Social Sciences*. New York: Charles Scribner's Sons, 1932.

Bradley Commission on History in Schools. *Building a History Curriculum: Guidelines for Teaching History in the Schools*. Westlake, OH: National Council for History Education, 1988.

California State Board of Education. *History-Social Science Framework for California Public Schools: Kindergarten through Twelfth Grade*. Sacramento: California State Board of Education, 1988.

Cartwright, William H., and Richard L. Watson, Jr., eds. *The Reinterpretation of American History and Culture*. Washington, DC: National Council for the Social Studies, 1973.

Educational Testing Service. *The U.S. History Report Card*. Washington, DC: Office of Educational Research and Improvement, U.S. Department of Education, 1990.

Goodlad, John I. *Teachers for Our Nation's Schools*. San Francisco, CA: Jossey-Bass, 1990.

Haas, John D. *The Era of the New Social Studies*. Boulder, CO: Social Science Education Consortium, 1977.

Hertzberg, Hazel Whitman. *Social Studies Reform: 1880–1980*. Boulder, CO: Social Science Education Consortium, 1981.

Holmes Group, Inc. *Tomorrow's Teachers: A Report of the Holmes Group*. East Lansing, MI: The Holmes Group, 1986.

Hunkins, F. P., Carol L. Hahn, Peter H. Martorella, and Jan L. Tucker, eds. *Review of Research in Social Studies Education: 1970–1975*. Washington, DC: National Council for the Social Studies, 1977.

Jenness, David. *Making Sense of Social Studies*. New York: Macmillan, 1990.

Johnson, Henry. *An Introduction to the History of the Social Sciences*. Report of the Commission on the Social Studies. New York: Charles Scribner's Sons, 1932.

Kammen, Michael, ed. *The Past before Us: Contemporary Historical Writing in the United States*. Ithaca, NY: Cornell University Press, 1980.

Mehlinger, Howard D., and O. L. Davis, Jr. *The Social Studies*. 80th Yearbook of the National Society for the Study of Education. Chicago, IL: University of Chicago Press, 1981.

National Commission on Excellence in Education. *A Nation at Risk: The Imperative for Educational Reform*. Washington, DC: Superintendent of Documents, U.S. Government Printing Office, 1983.

National Commission on Social Studies in the Schools. *Charting a Course: Social Studies for the 21st Century*. Washington, DC: Joint Project of the American Historical Association, the Carnegie Foundation for the Advancement of Teaching, the National Council for the Social Studies, and the Organization of American Historians, 1989.

National Council for the Social Studies. "Standards for the Preparation of Social Studies Teachers." *Social Education* 52 (November/December 1988): 10–12.

———. Draft of Revised Standards for the Preparation of Social Studies Teachers. Unpublished report of the Task Force for Revision of the Teacher Education Standards. Washington, DC, 1991.

———. *The Essentials Statements: Essentials of Social Studies* (NCSS Tool Kit). Washington, DC: National Council for the Social Studies, n.d.

National Education Association. *Report of the Committee of Ten on Secondary Social Studies*. Washington, DC: Government Printing Office, 1893.

———. *The Social Studies in Secondary Education*. A Report of the Committee on Social Studies on the Reorganization of Secondary Education of the National Education Association. No. 28. Washington, DC: Bureau of Education, 1916.

National Survey of Course Offerings and Testing in Social Studies, Kindergarten—Grade 12. Washington, DC: The Council of State Social Studies Specialists, 1991.

Parker, W. C. *Renewing the Social Studies Curriculum*. Alexandria, VA: Association for Supervision and Curriculum Development, 1991.

Project SPAN Staff and Consultants. *The Current State of Social Studies: A*

Report of Project SPAN. Boulder, CO: Social Science Education Consortium, 1982.

Shaver, James P., ed. *Handbook of Research on Social Studies Teaching and Learning*. New York: Macmillan, 1991.

Shaver, James P., O. L. Davis, Jr., and Suzanne W. Helburn. *An Interpretive Report on the Status of Pre-Collegiate Social Studies Education Based on Three NSF-Funded Studies* (Report to the National Science Foundation). Washington, DC: National Council for the Social Studies, 1978 (ERIC Document Reproduction Service No. ED 164 363).

Social Education. Special Issue. "Scope and Sequence: Alternatives for Social Studies." Vol. 50, no. 7 (November/December 1986).

The Social Studies in General Education: A Report of the Committee on General Education for the Commission on Secondary School Curriculum. New York: Appleton-Century, 1940.

The United States Prepares for Its Future: Global Perspectives in Education. Report of the Study Commission on Global Education. New York: Global Perspectives in Education, 1987.

Wiley, K. B. *The Status of Precollege Science, Mathematics, and Social Studies Education: 1955–1975*. Washington, DC: National Science Foundation, 1977.

Wronski, Stanley P., and Donald H. Bragaw, eds. *Social Studies and the Social Sciences: A Fifty Year Perspective*. Bulletin No. 78. Washington, DC: National Council for the Social Studies, 1986.

INDEX

ABOUT THE CONTRIBUTORS

JACK ALLEN, Professor of History Emeritus, George Peabody College of Vanderbilt, was for many years Chair of Social Sciences at Peabody. His many publications include textbooks and monographs on American history, civics, and government as well as books and articles on social studies education. A past president of the National Council for the Social Studies, he has served on a number of editorial boards and national educational commissions and as an educational consultant.

BEVERLY J. ARMENTO, Professor of Social Studies at Georgia State University, is a former director of the Center for Economic Education at GSU. Her research areas include concept learning, teacher knowledge, and pedagogical skills. She has written the chapters on research on teaching social studies in the *Handbook of Research on Teaching* (1986) and the *Handbook of Research on Social Studies Teaching and Learning* (1991). She is also a contributor to the Houghton Mifflin Social Studies K–8 text series.

BURTON F. BEERS, Professor of History at North Carolina State University, served as consultant to the committee revising North Carolina's social studies curriculum in 1980 and co-chaired the committee developing guidelines for studies about religion in North Carolina's social studies curriculum. He is the senior author of *World History: Patterns of Civilization* (1st–5th eds., 1983–92) and has published numerous articles.

DON BRAGAW, Associate Professor of Education at East Carolina University, was formerly Chief of the Bureau of Social Studies Education, New York Department of Education, and associated with the University of New York at Binghamton. A past president of the National Council for the Social Studies, he co-edited *Social Studies and Social Sciences: A Fifty Year Perspective* (1986) and has published numerous articles.

BETTY M. BULLARD is Associate Professor of Education at the University of South Carolina at Columbia. She also assists schools throughout the United States with internationalizing their curricula, and she has served as a consultant to other nations. For five years she was Education Director of the Asia Society and edited *Opening Doors: Contemporary Japan* (1978) and *Asia in New York City, A Guide for Visiting Students and Teachers* (1981).

EDMUND T. EMMER is Professor of Educational Psychology at the University of Texas at Austin. He has also been a research scientist in the Research and Development Center for Teacher Education and a secondary school teacher. His scholarly interests include teaching and learning in secondary classrooms, with a special interest in classroom management and discipline. He is author of *Classroom Management for Secondary Teachers* (1989).

JUNE V. GILLIARD, formerly Curriculum Director of the Joint Council on Economic Education, was named a JCEE Senior Fellow in January 1992. She began her career in the public schools of North Carolina and was a social studies consultant with the state's Department of Public Instruction. The author of a number of articles, she has also served on the board of directors of the National Council for the Social Studies and as president of the Council of State Social Studies Specialists.

PAUL S. GRAY, Associate Professor and Chair of the Department of Sociology, Boston College, is also chairman of the American Sociological Association's Committee on Sociology in the Elementary and Secondary Schools. He is the author of *Unions and Leaders in Ghana* (1981) and coauthor of *The Research Craft* (1982). His articles have appeared in the *Journal of African Studies, Urban Life, Industrial Relations, Improving College and University Teaching,* and *Charting a Course* (1989).

ROBERT P. GREEN, JR., is Professor of Social Studies Education at Clemson University. Active in both the South Carolina Council for the Social Studies and National Council for the Social Studies, he has written a variety of articles and essays on history and historical pedagogy. He is the senior author of *The American Tradition: A History of the United*

States (1986) and co-author of *American Education: Foundations and Policy* (1989).

SUZANNE A. GULLEDGE is an Assistant Professor of Education at the University of North Carolina at Chapel Hill. Currently, she is part of a UNC faculty team engaged in an experimental approach to teacher preparation. She is the author of *Teaching about Religion in Public Secondary School Sociology Courses* (1983). Her research interests are in clinical aspects of teaching and citizenship education.

BARBARA M. PARRAMORE, Professor of Education and Psychology at North Carolina State University, was the first head of the university's Department of Curriculum and Instruction (1975–1985). She has published numerous articles, including "The Impact of Deregulation on the Partnership in Teacher Certification" in *Action in Teacher Education* (1986). She is currently engaged in a ten-year longitudinal study of the pre- and in-service experiences of an initial group of North Carolina teaching fellows.

MARION J. RICE is Professor Emeritus of Social Science Education, University of Georgia, where he served as department head from 1972 to 1985. He was actively involved in the curriculum reform movement of the 1960s, serving as co-director of the Office of Education-funded Anthropology Curriculum Project, associate director of the Georgia Research and Development Center in Educational Simulation, and director of the Georgia-funded Geography Curriculum Project.

ROBERT N. SAVELAND is Professor Emeritus of Social Science Education at the University of Georgia. A former supervisor of social studies and head of an editorial department for a Boston publisher, Professor Saveland writes frequently for professional journals and boating magazines. His recent work includes co-authorship of the seventh grade textbook *A World View* (1985, 1990).

R. BAIRD SHUMAN is Professor of English, University of Illinois at Urbana-Champaign, where he has served as director of English Education and of Rhetoric and as acting director for Writing Studies. He has taught at Drexel University, the University of Pennsylvania, San Jose State University, and Duke University as well as having written or edited twenty-six books, the most recent of which are *Resources for Writers* (1992) and *American Drama, 1918–1960* (1992).

MARTIN L. TOMBARI is a Senior Lecturer in the Department of Educational Psychology at the University of Texas at Austin, with a primary interest in classroom behavior management. He has held several positions in the field of psychology, including school psychologist for an alternative high school and chief psychologist in a large state institution. He has also taught high school psychology and is the author of "Behavioral Consultation," *School Psychology: Perspective Issues* (1982).

RICHARD L. WATSON, JR., Professor Emeritus of History at Duke University, is a past president of the Southern Historical Association (1976–77). He is the author of *The Development of National Power: The United States, 1900–1919* (1976), co-editor (with William H. Cartwright) of *Interpreting and Teaching American History* (1961) and *The Reinterpretation of American History and Culture* (1973), and has published numerous articles in scholarly journals.

STANLEY P. WRONSKI is Professor Emeritus of Education and Social Science at Michigan State University. He is a past president of the National Council for the Social Studies and co-author (with Edgar B. Wesley) of *Teaching Secondary Social Studies in a World Society* (1973) and co-editor (with Don Bragaw) of *Social Studies and Social Sciences: A Fifty Year Perspective* (1986).

ABOUT THE EDITORS

VIRGINIA S. WILSON is Chair of Humanities at the North Carolina School of Science and Mathematics. She has taught at several public secondary schools and at Duke University. She has published in *The Clearing House, Malaysian Journal of Education, The Social Studies Teacher, AHA Perspectives*, and *Social Education*.

JAMES A. LITLE is Instructor of History and Social Science at the North Carolina School of Science and Mathematics. He has been a social studies teacher and department coordinator in a public high school, and has published in the *International Journal of Social Studies, AHA Perspectives, The Social Studies Teacher*, and *Social Education*.

GERALD LEE WILSON is Senior Associate Dean of Trinity College of Arts and Sciences, Duke University. His publications have appeared in *The South Atlantic Quarterly, The Social Studies Teacher, The North Carolina State Bar Quarterly, The Journal of Southern History, AHA Perspectives*, and *Social Education*. He teaches history at Duke University.